Media in Mind

MEDIA IN MIND

Daniel Reynolds

OXFORD
UNIVERSITY PRESS

Library of Congress Cataloging-in-Publication Data
Names: Reynolds, Daniel, 1978– author.
Title: Media in mind / Daniel Reynolds.
Description: New York, NY : Oxford University Press, 2018. |
Includes bibliographical references.
Identifiers: LCCN 2018049168 | ISBN 9780190872519 (cloth : alk. paper) |
ISBN 9780190872526 (pbk. : alk. paper) | ISBN 9780190872557 (oxford scholarship online)
Subjects: LCSH: Mass media—Philosophy. | Mass media—Psychological aspects.
Classification: LCC P90.R45 2018 | DDC 302.2301/9—dc23
LC record available at https://lccn.loc.gov/2018049168

9 8 7 6 5 4 3 2 1

Paperback printed by WebCom, Inc., Canada
Hardback printed by Bridgeport National Bindery, Inc., United States of America

For Ellen and Robert Reynolds, with thanks

CONTENTS

ACKNOWLEDGMENTS

This book is a product of my relationships with a community of friends, family, and colleagues, all of whose influence is felt throughout these pages.

Those who have read *Media in Mind* in various forms and have offered their generous comments and advice include Tanine Allison, Matthew Bernstein, Edward Branigan, Amanda Evans, Dilek Huseyinzadegan, Zachary Ludington, Karla Oeler, Murray Pomerance, Robert Reynolds, David Rubin, and Michele Schreiber. I am very grateful to my editor, Norm Hirschy, for his enthusiasm and support for this project, and to Lauralee Yeary for guiding me through the process of publishing a first book. Thank you to Suganya Elango for ushering the book through production. Three reviewers offered feedback and suggestions that have benefited the book immensely. Thank you all.

The Department of Film and Media Studies at Emory University has been my academic home during the development of this project, and I cannot imagine a more supportive environment in which to work. Many of my colleagues are named above as readers of the manuscript. I have also benefited from conversations about *Media in Mind* with Amy Aidman, Rob Barracano, Marc Bosquet, Bill Brown, Ryan Cook, Marshall Duke, Jason Francisco, Timothy Holland, David Pratt, Pamela Scully, James Steffen (who also provided invaluable assistance with the images for the book), Nathan Suhr-Systma, Beretta Smith-Shomade, Eddy Von Mueller, and Kate Winskell Enger. I am forever indebted to department staff members Maureen Downs, Gary Fessenden, Annie Hall, and Clare Sterling. Emory's Scholarly Writing and Publishing Fund provided developmental support for this project. The Andrew W. Mellon Foundation supported this work through its grant to establish Emory's Humanistic Inquiry Program. I am grateful to the other Mellon fellows and to Tom Jenkins for his leadership in the program.

Media in Mind germinated from the seed of my doctoral dissertation at the University of California, Santa Barbara, a project overseen by Edward Branigan, Constance Penley, Anna Everett, and Alan Liu. The entire Film and Media Studies faculty at UCSB has left their imprint on this book. Outside of my committee, Janet Walker, Charles Wolfe, Bhaskar Sarkar, Dick Hebdige, and Peter Bloom in particular offered guidance and wisdom as the project was taking shape. In its early stages, this work was supported by a short-stay fellowship at Utrecht University, where I worked under the supervision of Joost Raessens.

Friends and colleagues who have shaped my thinking about the roles of media in mind include (roughly in order of appearance) Roy Grundmann, Charles Warren, J.D. Connor, Despina Kakoudaki, David Rodowick, Joshua Neves, Jeff Scheible, Nicole Starosielski, Regina Longo, Bishnupriya Ghosh, Ethan Tussey, Ryan Bowles, Maria Corrigan, Meredith Bak, Anastasia Hill, Megan Fernandes, Rahul Mukherjee, and Jennifer Barker. This would be a different book, and I would be a different person, had our paths not crossed.

Many thanks to my students, especially those in my Media and the Mind and Platforms and Apparatuses courses.

A version of chapter 6 was originally published as "The Vitruvian Thumb: Embodied Thinking and Lateral Branding with the Nintendo Game Boy," *Game Studies* 16, no. 1 (October 2016). Thanks to Jessica Enevold and the three anonymous reviewers for their comments on that paper, and to Gus Cook for his research assistance. Thank you to the Harvard University Press for permission to reprint two poems by Emily Dickinson. Thank you to HarperCollins, the Wylie Agency, and the Maurice Sendak Foundation for permission to reprint text and an illustration from *A Hole Is to Dig* by Ruth Krauss and Maurice Sendak.

This book is dedicated to my parents, Ellen and Robert Reynolds, whom I thank for, literally, everything. Thank you to Celia Reynolds, Alison Reynolds, Gwain and Richard Evans, Nellie Evans, David Evans, and their families. Thank you to the people with whom I share my life, Amanda Evans and our children, Theo and Louis. Thank you for sharing yours with me.

Media in Mind

Introduction

The Discontinuities

Imagine that you are watching a film or playing a video game. Or (to make this easy) reading a book. In this encounter with media, where do you end, and where does the medium begin?

One answer that suggests itself immediately is "at our edges." You and the film or video game or book are bounded entities in space, coming into close proximity and interaction with one another. A line, both conceptual and physical, could be drawn in three-dimensional space around your body and likewise around this book. Even when you are holding the book in your hands, and these lines come into temporary contact, we can demarcate—at the flesh, at the page—where the one thing ends and the other begins.

For a film, things get a bit more complicated. Does the boundary line around a film simply correspond to the frame line of the screen, or must it account for the film projector or the television or the monitor as well? Ought it encompass the storage medium, such as the filmstrip, disk, or hard drive on which the film is encoded, or the satellite from which it is being streamed? In this last case, must our line then trace the transmission skyward to the satellite itself? Back on earth, for a projected film must we likewise trace the pyramid of light that extends across the room from somewhere above and behind you, or can we ignore the space between the projector and the screen (which is also the space that you occupy)? How might we draw a line around film sound? Habits of seeing, habitual ways of talking about vision, and the tendency to privilege sight in metaphors of comprehension ("I see") all factor into the impression that images on a movie screen are *over there*, while sound comes to us, surrounds us, and even enters our bodies in a way that light seems not to. Sound is an element of the medium of film, but it also takes the air and surfaces of the exhibition venue as *its* medium, creating "a disturbance within the three-dimensional space of the movie theater."[1] Is the movie theater or the living room then an aspect of the media object, much as the interior of a church is the resonating chamber for its pipe organ?[2]

Our task is more complicated still for a video game, in which the "content" of the medium—the images and sounds it produces, the challenges it introduces, the stories it tells—is influenced, moment to moment, by your decisions as a player. In the case of a video game, it seems clear that our medium-tracing line *must* include the media technology, the computational "platform," that makes the game possible. Does our line of demarcation then hew precisely to the microscopic space between your hands and the controller that they hold and manipulate? Does it move with your (and the controller's) every motion, maintaining the essential physical divide between you and the medium that allows you and it to act *upon* one another from without? This last characterization may seem silly, and rightly so. The interactive nature of video games, as well as the physical interaction between video game players and video game technologies, seems to indicate something more intimate, a blurring of the boundary lines among player, game, and technology.

Media in Mind argues that the boundaries we seek between media and their users' minds and bodies are never clear, no matter the medium: for films just as much as for video games, and equally so for books like the one you currently hold in your hands or regard on your screen. The spatiotemporal boundaries of media content, media technology, and media use are always contingent and conceptual. When we talk about them, we do so as a descriptive convenience, and where we draw these lines depends upon how we look at a medium, the theories through which we frame it, and the scales at which we regard it.

The same can be said of us—of you, of me, of anyone—whether we are using media or not. While it may be intuitive to say that the boundaries of your self are at the edges of your body, to do so raises more questions than it answers. How can we account, then, for the changes that you make in the world, such as the marks you produce when you write or draw, the dust you kick up as you hike along a trail, the emotions that you elicit in other people with your actions, or the motion that you elicit onscreen when playing a video game? Beyond these quotidian intimacies with the environment, how might we account for the fact that your physical body never stops changing, absorbing energy and expelling waste, shedding dead cells and regenerating its very substance with every passing moment, not to mention the fact that "your" body is composed in no small part by microorganisms that perform vital functions "for" you, behaving "like a hidden organ, as important as a stomach or an eye but made of trillions of swarming individual cells rather than a single unified mass"?[3] At a more macroscopic scale, what of the ways in which this nominally discrete self is defined, determined, and characterized from "without," via social constraints and identity categorizations, physical abilities, life experiences, environmental contexts, and access to resources? As with the boundaries of a medium, the boundaries of a self depend on where, how, and with what investments you look for them.

The difficult trick is not in suppressing this contingency in one's understanding of media and mind, but rather in acknowledging and honoring it. In attempting to do just this, *Media in Mind* adopts a naturalist perspective on media users, media technologies, and media use. As a philosophical orientation, naturalism conceives of existence as occurring on a single, material plane. It is thus opposed to dualism, or the perspective that existence is split among two or more discrete planes. Dualism is exemplified in René Descartes's conceptual separation of body (res extensa, or corporeal substance) from mind (res cogitans, or mental substance), but this mind-body dualism is not the only kind of dualism; other varieties include, for instance, the conceptual dualism of Plato's theory of eternal "forms" that exist in a "true earth" of which our own is merely an ephemeral shadow.[4] As described by physicist Sean Carroll, naturalism entails three core commitments: that "there is only one world, the natural world," that "the world evolves according to unbroken patterns, the laws of nature," and that "the only reliable way of learning about the world is by observing it."[5] In a naturalist view, the physical world is all that there is, and those things that we might think of as immaterial or as discrete from physical reality, such as ultimate causes, subjectivity, the "spark" of life, the content of fictions, and "the virtual," are more properly ways of characterizing aspects of a continuous material whole. Cognitive science and philosophy of mind have been grappling with the implications of naturalism for decades and millennia, respectively. This tension has been felt in media studies, as well, but it has largely remained hidden in plain sight, not so much a topic of conversation as a structuring influence upon the conversations themselves.

Media in Mind proposes alternatives to conceptual dualisms that have been introduced to media studies over a period of more than a century. The core argument is that, if the mind is an aspect of the physical world, then the mind of a media user must be continuous with and partly constituted by media. The reciprocal is true, as well. Media must be constituted by and continuous with the minds and actions of their users. Media use is not an interaction in which two discrete things, a medium and a mind, come into contact with and act upon one another, but instead a transaction within a continuous field of matter that produces the intertwined phenomena that we (always contingently) may call "media" and "mind."

A number of media theorists, dating at least to the film theory of the 1910s, have approached and nearly articulated antidualist theories of media, though they have generally maintained discontinuities in their frameworks for characterizing the mind. Their theories tend to develop according to a common pattern. Experience of a medium (often a newly emergent medium such as film or, later, video games and other digital media) challenges a theorist's understanding of what the limits of a mind are. The medium seems in some way to externalize aspects of experience—perception, attention, emotion, conceptual thought—that the theorist has previously taken to be internal to the mind. Rather than taking this as a cue to expand that conception of the mind, however, the theorist ultimately posits media use as an exception to how the mind generally works. This preserves the theorist's prior way of understanding the mind and, as a necessary side effect, sets media apart from the continuity of the rest of the world. It also disconnects emerging media from the continuity of media that predate them, overstating both the ontological breaks among media and the disciplinary breaks among branches of media studies.

Resisting such breaks, *Media in Mind* engages with theories and philosophies of media, and with exemplary media objects, that explore the continuity and proximity of media and minds. This is partly an argument about the history of media theory, extending to early film theory and beyond. It is also an argument about the present of media theory, as it extends to phenomenological film theories, to theories of digital media, and to technologically oriented theories of media platforms and interfaces. By adopting a naturalist perspective on media use, *Media in Mind* seeks to preserve the many valuable insights that these approaches have yielded, to illustrate their mutual value for one another, and to nudge them a bit further toward truly nondualist perspectives. This nudge takes cues from contemporary concepts in what have been called "E-approaches" to philosophy of mind, which see the mind as embodied, extended, embedded, ecological, and so on.[6] But its naturalist ethos is rooted in the philosophical naturalism of John Dewey, who developed his antidualist perspective on mind, art, ontology, and education in writings from the late nineteenth to the middle twentieth centuries. This nudge benefits also from the works of artists, poets, filmmakers, video game designers, and media technologists whose work explores the nature of perception, action, and mental representation. These works—theoretical, philosophical, artistic, and technical— exemplify an orientation toward the world, including the self and the mind, as a continuous, intertwined, and entangled whole, and a view of media use as a constituent participant in this whole. Such a commitment to continuity has been the historical exception across the scholarly disciplines, and media theory has been no exception.

DISCONTINUITY IN MEDIA THEORY

The primary domain of media studies has been, naturally, media—film, television, video, digital media, video games, and so on—but the mind has been nearly coequal as an object of fascination for the discipline. Cinema emerged in the late nineteenth century, just as modern psychology was finding its first foothold as a field of study. Among the earliest media theorists were scholars of the mind like the psychologists Hugo Münsterberg and Rudolf Arnheim who, writing in the first decades of the twentieth century, recognized immediately not only that psychology would be crucial for understanding the new medium of film, but that film would have something new to show them about psychology.[7] Münsterberg's approach to psychology changed throughout his lifetime, but he is predominantly associated with the field of applied psychology, while Arnheim was trained as a gestalt psychologist, and each theorist's particular background and theoretical investments in psychology guided his approach to film and other arts. As other ways of understanding the mind emerged, such as Saussurean linguistics, Freudian and Lacanian psychoanalysis, phenomenology, and cognitive science, their own influences were felt, interpreted, and extended in media theory.

Most often, the theories of the mind that have influenced media studies have been dualist (that is, nonnaturalist) theories, in that they have erected essential divisions between the mind and the "outside" world. In particular, they have in one way or another, usually without explicitly stating it, maintained Descartes's distinction between mental and corporeal substance, a distinction that neuroanthropologist Terrence W. Deacon calls "the Cartesian wound that severed mind from body at the birth of modern science."[8] Media theory has largely left this wound open, and it has added some more conceptual cuts of its own for good measure. As we shall see in greater detail throughout *Media in Mind*, media theory has erected conceptual gaps not only between the mind and the world but between media "content" and the world as well. Having established these gaps, media theory has then been obligated to busy itself in positing ways in which media and the mind surmount them, so that media can gain access to the mind and so that the mind can gain access to media. This often leads to equivalencies being drawn between the operation of media and the operation of the mind. Some cognitivist media theory, for example, imagines the mind as a computer that transforms film into mental representations and subsequently reasons by way of the representations and not the film itself, while some psychoanalytic media theories conceive of the mind as an internal theater that exhibits a symbolic picture show influenced by the content and style of film. In either case, the bulk of the "work" of media use occurs in a realm below or separate from consciousness—cognition or the unconscious—inaccessible to conscious thought.

We are left with an understanding of media that is characterized by division rather than by continuity. Bodies reside in the world, and they function as containers or conduits for minds from which they remain essentially separate. Mind-body dualism is deeply entrenched in cognitive science, and it continues to be so in the era of cognitive neuroscience, which often replaces the discrete, internal realm of the mind with the privileged figure of the brain while still treating its operations as if they happen in a vacuum that is connected to, rather than continuous with, the world at large.[9]

Figure I.1 visualizes a general tendency in how media theory has erected gaps that intercede between media, mind, and world. The specifics of how these gaps function, where theory locates them, and how media and mind surmount them vary from one theory to another. In one of many possible examples, the film theorist Christian Metz ascribes the "impression of reality in the cinema" to the work that must be done by spectators *and* by cinema to surmount the discontinuity between them. "The cinematic spectacle," writes Metz, "is completely unreal; it takes place in another world."[10] And yet the images produced by film are partly real. In particular, while its images of objects are representations, film's images of motion

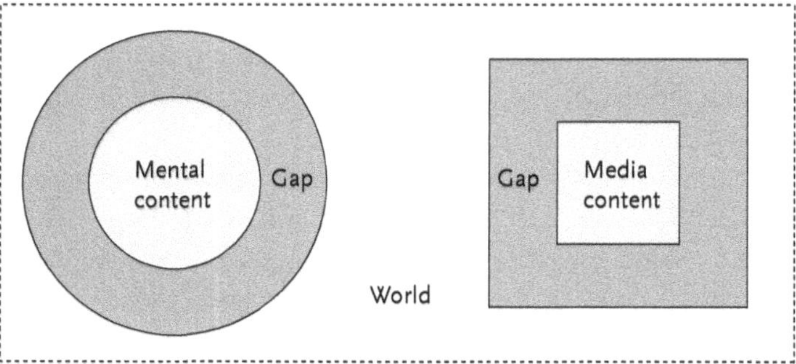

Figure I.1 Gaps among mind, media, and world erected by media theory

are themselves real motion. Through a balance that it achieves in this partial reality, cinema facilitates what Metz calls "the spectator's participation in the film," in which the spectator "is indeed 'disconnected' from the real world, but he must then connect to something else and accomplish a *'transference' of reality* . . . which can be sparked only by a spectacle resembling at least slightly a spectacle of reality."[11] For Metz, film reaches out from its other world to appeal to reality in such a way that spectators then reciprocally reach out across the gap and actively complete film's illusions, an investment that effectively overcomes the unreality of cinematic spectacle.

Although it has largely gone unrecognized, such discontinuity among media, mind, and world has historically been a central assumption of media studies. By no means has *every* theory of media maintained these precise gaps, but antidualism has been a minority perspective, an exception to dominant frameworks both in media theory and in theories of the mind.

COUNTERCURRENTS OF CONTINUITY

In recent decades, a growing number of cognitive scientists and philosophers of mind have expanded the notion of what a mind is, both in space, to encompass aspects of the body and its motion,[12] the immediate and more remote physical environment,[13] and other people and social structures;[14] and in time, recognizing the temporal continuity of mental and brain states,[15] the role of prior experience in how one perceives and navigates the world,[16] and the ways that evolutionary and cultural history function in life and mind.[17] Resisting dualisms inherent to mainstream cognitive science, philosophy of mind, and neuroscience, these frameworks favor spatiotemporal continuity among mind, body, and world. While they position themselves as progressive, they also harken back, sometimes explicitly, to a commitment to naturalist continuity that characterized positions adopted by American pragmatist philosophers of the late nineteenth and early twentieth centuries, such as Charles Sanders Peirce, William James, and especially Dewey. Contemporary E-approaches are radical in multiple senses. They are both connected to their historical roots in pragmatism and invested in the ecological rootedness of the mind in the body and the environment. Pragmatism's influence waned in the mid-twentieth century, overtaken by more computational approaches to philosophy of mind. This shift may have been motivated in part by the urgently analytic political and intellectual tenor of the Cold War era.[18] It was surely influenced also by the concurrent emergence of the computer, both as a research tool and as a fresh metaphor for the functioning of the mind.

Since around 1990, continuity of mind, body, and world has re-emerged as a major (if still minority) framework for understanding the mind. In media studies, this growing trend has been felt mostly in an increased interest in embodiment and affect, or in the ways that media influence sensation, perception, and emotion, *as well as* the conceptual mind. When cognitivist or psychoanalytic media theories incorporate embodiment, they introduce bodily sensation as an animating topic within already-existing theoretical frameworks. As Eugenie Brinkema points out, the ubiquity and vagueness of the term "affect" has "allowed the humanities to *constantly possibly* introject any seemingly absent or forgotten dimension of inquiry, to insist that play, the unexpected, the unthought can always be brought back into the field."[19] "The body" and "embodiment" have seen similar strategic usage, in that they have been employed to *add* consideration of physical sensation to theoretical frameworks that maintain the conceptual separation of body and mind. The Cartesian wound remains unhealed.

This is not to say that media theory has always adopted uniformly dualist frameworks. On the contrary, antidualist approaches to media have appeared throughout the history of the discipline, though always as minority countercurrents. As theorists and as art practitioners, the Surrealists around the 1920s were invested in the reconciliation of conventional dualisms, especially those between mind and world, and they were attracted to film in particular for what they saw as its participation in the processes of material reality. In his *Surrealist Manifestoes*, André Breton defines *surreality* as "the future resolution of . . . two states, dream and reality, which are seemingly contradictory, into a kind of absolute reality."[20] Surrealist playwright and screenwriter Antonin Artaud writes that "we find at the bottom of every emotion, even an intellectual one, an affective sensation of a nervous order," and that "the meaning of pure cinema would lie in the re-creation of a certain number of forms of this kind, it would lie in a movement and follow a rhythm which is the specific contribution of this art."[21]

For French impressionist filmmaker and theorist Germaine Dulac, who collaborated with Artaud on the landmark surrealist film *The Seashell and the Clergyman* (Dulac, 1928), cinema represents a new and invaluable opportunity to discover a previously undisclosed relationship of continuity between mind and world. "It was the slow disclosure by cinema," Dulac writes, "of a new emotive faculty present in our unconscious that led us to the perceptual comprehension of visual rhythms and not our rational longings that made us greet it (cinema) as an art we had been waiting for."[22] In Dulac's film *The Smiling Madame Beudet* (1922), the titular protagonist fantasizes about escaping her emotionally abusive marriage. In figure I.2, Madame Beudet imagines that a tennis champion, a picture of whom she has seen in a magazine, steps out of his mediated confines and materializes in a ghostly form to drag a struggling Monsieur Beudet away and out of her life. As Dulac writes, the cinema finds its way toward rhythmic visualization of emotions, and, as in this double-exposed shot, can depict fantasy and reality as simultaneous and equally worldly. In revealing (and inflecting) the relationship of continuity between mind and world, film participates in the ceaseless motion of material reality, Dulac writes: "To prolong (the life) of what will die is good. But the very essence of cinema is different and it brings Eternity with it since it springs from the very essence of the universe: movement."[23] Preemptively countering André Bazin's later idealist argument that photography and cinema are technologies of preservation and prolongation,[24] Dulac sees cinema not as reflecting or representing reality so much as springing forth from (and within) it, participating in the production of the reality that is also its basis.

Jean Epstein, another French impressionist director and theorist, writes rhapsodically in his 1946 book *The Intelligence of a Machine* about film's ability to explore relationships between continuity and discontinuity, whether in sensation,

Figure I.2 In *The Smiling Madame Beudet* (Germaine Dulac, 1922), the imaginary figure of the tennis champion approaches the abusive Monsieur Beudet, who is seated at his desk.

mathematics, the physical sciences, or film form. "The cinematograph," Epstein writes, "instructs us that continuity and discontinuity, rest and movement, far from being two incompatible modes of reality, are two interchangeable modes of unreality. . . . They are no more mutually exclusive than the colors of a disk and the whiteness that results when it spins."[25] For Epstein, the tension (the intractable contradiction, really) between discontinuity and continuity is what produces the "function" of reality. Because film does not perceive in the same way that people perceive, it can provide its viewers with perspectives of which they would otherwise be incapable, dispelling illusions of discontinuity in the material world.

Philosopher Maurice Merleau-Ponty sees in cinema an analogue and complement to what he calls "the new psychology" or "phenomenological or existential psychology," which

> does not . . . present mind *and* world, each particular consciousness *and* the others . . . [but is] largely an expression of surprise at this inherence of the self in the world and in others, a description of this paradox and permeation, and an attempt to make us *see* the bond between subject and world, between subject and others, rather than to *explain* it as the classical philosophies did by resorting to absolute spirit.[26]

For Merleau-Ponty, film is, like perception itself, "not a sum total of images but a temporal *gestalt*."[27] The relationship between the new psychology and film is furthermore entirely reciprocal and intertwined. Merleau-Ponty cautions against claiming either that cinema grew out of this philosophy of mind or that the ideas of the new psychology grew out of cinema. Rather, he writes, "If philosophy is in harmony with cinema . . . it is because the philosopher and moviemaker share a certain way of being. . . . It offers us yet another chance to confirm that modes of thought correspond to technical methods and that, to use Goethe's phrase, 'What is inside is also outside.' "[28]

Like Merleau-Ponty, philosopher Gilles Deleuze sees cinema and philosophy as comparable modes of thought. Deleuze, more specifically, sees cinema and philosophy as comparable *as* modes of thought: not Merleau-Ponty's shared mode of being so much as parallel, potentially complementary ways of what Deleuze calls "having an idea." As Deleuze writes, "One does not have an idea in general. An idea . . . is already dedicated to this or that domain. It is sometimes an idea in painting, sometimes an idea in fiction, sometimes an idea in philosophy, sometimes an idea in science."[29] To have an idea in cinema is for Deleuze first an act of resistance, and "only the act of resistance resists death."[30] To do so is to participate in an ongoing process of material becoming that brings new forms into contingent being, a process Deleuze characterizes as folding and unfolding, "a continuous variation of matter."[31] Despite this emphasis on the spatiotemporal continuity of matter, Deleuze has been criticized for introducing conceptual gaps between films and the bodies of their spectators. For instance, Mark B. N. Hansen writes that, in his emphasis on the "universal variation of images," Deleuze "effectively imposes a purely formal understanding of cinematic framing and thus suspends the crucial function of the living body."[32]

In her books *The Address of the Eye* and *Carnal Thoughts*, Vivian Sobchack seeks rather to emphasize the reciprocal embodiment of film and spectator. Film spectators are embodied, Sobchack argues, and films are equally so. "Understood as a viewing subject that—by virtue of the particular nature of its embodied existence—can also be viewed, the film no longer merely contains sense, significance, meaning. Rather, it possesses sense by means of its senses, and it makes sense as a 'living cohesion,' as a *signifying subject*."[33] By locating films as *in* reality and coequally corporeal with their spectators, Sobchack's film phenomenology both builds upon Merleau-Ponty's critique of the inside-outside distinction and recalls Epstein's emphasis on film's own perspective, established by the particularities of its physical constitution, processes, and positioning in the world.

Sobchack's insistence on the corporeality of media use, and of media itself, is reflected and extended in the work of scholars including Jennifer Barker and Laura U. Marks.[34] Barker characterizes filmic experience as "tactile," arguing that touch is not (only) a surface sensation but something that pervades the body. Touch, Barker writes, "is not just skin-deep but is experienced at the body's surface, in its depths, and everywhere in between." It is an experience undertaken by spectator and film alike, so that "the forms of tactility that filmgoers experience are shared—in complex, not always comfortable ways—by both spectator and film."[35] For Barker, film and viewer thus have a "mutual investment in shared projects."[36] Breaking down distinctions between bodily surface and depth, and between the action of the film and that of the viewer, Barker articulates a phenomenology of film that reflects the physical continuity of media, user, and world. Marks proposes what she calls "haptic visuality," characterized by "respect for otherness, and a concomitant loss of self in the presence of the other" and a relationship in which a visual object is offered "on the condition that its unknowability remain intact, and that the viewer, in coming closer, give up his or her own mastery."[37] As for Barker and Sobchack, media use, even in the case of nominally visual media, is for Marks always a mutualism between media forms and the *whole* feeling body.

Pursuing the ecological basis of bodily continuity with media, Scott Richmond writes of what he calls "cinematic perceptual and proprioceptive resonance," in service of establishing "an ecological phenomenology as an antiskeptical and nonrepresentational approach to theorizing about the cinema."[38] Tracing a line of connection between Merleau-Ponty's phenomenology and James J. Gibson's theory of ecological perception, Richmond makes a case that "cinema is not a medium for representation but rather a technology that literally modulates our perceptual resonance."[39]

In what are currently considered "new media"—media that are interactive, digital, or networked in varying degrees—the discipline of media studies has found an opportunity to reconsider its commitments to the bounded figures of the body and the medium. In recent decades, issues of continuity and discontinuity have become a more explicitly central focus in media theory—both in theories of "new media" and, by virtue of retrospection, in newer theories of film. These changes of orientation are cued by changes in the technological substrates of established media and by the development of new modes of control of media devices. The advent of "the digital" has been greeted as a prompt to revisit and revise the philosophical underpinnings of film and media theory. Digital technologies are epochal not only for media but for philosophy, requiring "new philosophy for new media," or a reconsideration of "philosophy after the new media."[40] Antidualist thinking about media (both old and new) has more recently coalesced around three key philosophers: Merleau-Ponty, Deleuze, and Alfred North Whitehead. As will be discussed in more detail in chapter 1, the work of these philosophers has provided digital media theorists with tools for exploring the intimate connections among media, their users, and the world in ways that neither flatten nor trivialize the experiential, expressive, and transformative capabilities of media. While this infusion of antidualist thought has invigorated media theory, however, it has brought along various conceptual gaps of its own, such as those between discrete "affects" and "percepts," between the "virtual" and the "actual," between consciousness and its objects, and among the essences of discrete objects.

Media in Mind proposes a naturalist approach to media use as a complement, and sometimes a corrective, to this history of antidualist media theory. Contemporary theories of how "we think though, with, and alongside media," as N. Katherine Hayles puts it, emphasize the mutual relationship between "we" and "media."[41] But I would argue that in the process, they tend, in a variety of ways, to elide not just the underlying continuity of "we" and "media," but also the continuity of both, and of the wider world, with thinking itself. In the terms of contemporary philosophy of mind, the approach of *Media in Mind* is nonrepresentational in that it resists the concept of internal mental images contained by the mind. It conceives of perception as active rather than passive or automatic. And it is embodied and extended in the radical sense, in that it sees the mind not as a fundamentally internal quality (say, of the brain) that reaches "out" to the body and the world to use them, but instead sees the mind as extensional, in that it is by nature always distributed across body and world, in space and in time. From this perspective, the qualities "we," "media," and "thinking" are alternative and overlapping ways of describing an ongoing dynamic that includes and goes beyond them. They can never be definitively distinguished from one another or from the spatiotemporal contexts, whether local, global, or cosmic, with which they are continuous and of which they are constituent parts.

Thus far, reference to the work of John Dewey is largely absent from the story of mind-world-media continuity in media theory. When Dewey's name does appear in media studies, he is often used as a point of comparison to elucidate the perspective of another scholar or of a media maker. For instance, Ray Carney points out resonances between pragmatism's philosophical commitments and attitudes embodied in the filmmaking practices of the director John Cassavetes, whose work, Carney writes, "attempts to bring us to our senses and return us to the world in many of the same ways Emerson, James, and Dewey theorize about."[42] Hansen engages with Dewey's critiques of Whitehead in constructing his own "modified account" of Whitehead's theory of the potentiality of objects.[43] Dewey's relative absence from media theory is curious in that Dewey's 1934 book *Art as Experience* is one of the more provocative and influential works written on the continuity of art with the world "outside" artworks, and the continuity of experience in general with experience of art. In writing about the arts, for Dewey, the "task is to restore continuity between the refined and intensified forms of experience that are works of art and the everyday events, doings, and sufferings that are universally recognized to constitute experience."[44] Media like film and video games, which so often become parts of the practice of their users' everyday lives, would seem to be natural studies in such continuity. However, in terms of media consumption, Dewey seemingly preferred to restrict himself to the "fine" arts (always, of course, a domain bounded by the norms of a particular time and place), as opposed to the popular arts, a tendency that Phillip Seng tentatively attributes to a "guarded, perhaps tradition-laden, attitude towards an increasingly popular form of entertainment."[45] Indeed, because of the conceptual separation of the nominally fine arts from popular arts such as "the movie, jazzed music, the comic strip," and so on, Dewey writes that "the objects acknowledged by the cultivated to be works of fine art seem anemic to the mass of people," so that the "esthetic hunger" of that mass "is likely to seek the cheap and the vulgar."[46]

Reference to Dewey has appeared occasionally in the younger subfield of video game studies, in which scholars have suggested that Dewey's emphasis on the experiential nature of art is particularly suited to interactive media.[47] If Dewey felt disdain for film as a popular medium, I shudder to think what he might have thought of video games. Although who knows—perhaps the whimsy of *Super Mario Bros.* (Nintendo, 1985) would have won the heart of a 126-year-old philosopher who thought he had seen it all. In any event, I would argue that Dewey's insistence on the continuity of art with the world, and of artistic experience with everyday experience, is powerful precisely because it does *not* rely on art being "interactive" in any conventional way for it to participate fully in the lived experience of its users.

Dewey's insistence on continuity is instructive for conceiving of media's relationship to the mind, the relationship of old media to new, and the disciplinary divisions that are so often erected between, for instance "film theory" and "media theory." Putting this principle into practice, *Media in Mind* sees film theory as a part of media theory and film history as an aspect of media history. Media and theory coevolve, and in theory's gravitation over the last few decades toward points of reference like Deleuze, Merleau-Ponty, and Whitehead, all of whom emphasize proximity over distance in their models of mind, body, self, and world, we can see a mirroring of what seem to be increasingly proximate and intimate relationships between media and the bodies of their users. Dewey's perspective is especially useful at this moment, as his commitment to continuity reveals all such user-media continuities to be fundamentally prior. We were never discontinuous with media, in other words. If anything, digital media merely do less to disavow their enactive continuity with their users than do older media.

Dewey's philosophy is a transdisciplinary project by necessity. In a universe characterized by spatiotemporal continuity, no hard and fast boundary between things and concepts holds up to scrutiny. Categories such as "media" and "mind" must be contingent, adaptable, and permeable. The contingency inherent in this way of seeing the world is not a weakness but a strength. The categories used to describe things are, after all, things themselves.

TRANSACTIONS WITH MEDIA

In the book *Knowing and the Known*, Dewey and coauthor Arthur F. Bentley make a distinction among ways of knowing that they term "self-action," "interaction," and "transaction." Self-action sees every *thing* as unitary, discrete, and self-motivated. Things behave as they do because they are internally compelled to do so. Interactional thinking treats relationships between things in the world as interactions between fundamentally separate entities in the context of shared environmental laws and constraints. Self-action and interaction allow for knowledge *of a thing* as discrete from oneself and from the other things around it. Interactionism is a way of describing the world that also describes itself: to understand the world in interactionist terms is also to understand understanding in interactionist terms.

As a naturalist alternative to self-action and interaction, Dewey and Bentley propose what they call "transactional" ways of knowing, which conceive of objects as continuous with one another, entangled and ultimately never discrete.[48] Ways of knowing are also fundamentally entangled with that which is known. In what I will call a *transactionist* perspective, we cannot conceive of knowledge as separate from the world, as it is a phenomenon *of* the world. Nor can we conceive of the subjective character of the mind as discrete, or internal, as it is a phenomenon that comes into being via transactions among bodies, objects, and environments.

Forms of embodiment in cognitive science, philosophy, and media studies that proceed by introducing "the body" into existing interactionist theoretical models of the mind attempt to bridge the gaps between mind, body, world, and media by reaching across them with appeals to embodied interaction, cognition, and affect, while still maintaining that such gaps do exist. These theories are interactionist in that they imagine discrete things encountering one another across a divide that separates them. Even many strains of media theory that are nominally antidualist still conceive of media or mind or both along interactionist paradigms. Antidualism, in other words, is not necessarily nondualism. A transactional perspective is different in that it sees continuity as *prior*, not as something to be accomplished by the body, or by media or by theory, but as the condition in which all of these phenomena come into being in the first place. There are no gaps to bridge, and there never were.

Insistence on continuity need not come at the expense of difference. On the contrary, in the transactionism that I propose, differentiation is precisely what produces things and what makes things happen. This differentiation is at once cosmic and local. As Sean Carroll points out, as the entropy of the universe increases, "Complexity first goes up, then goes down," so that "today, in between the far past and the far future . . . the universe is medium-entropy but highly complex." This is because the early universe, near the Big Bang, is in a low-entropy state, unified and undifferentiated. As the universe moves toward its eventual high-entropy state, in which its current complexity will be blended and "diluted away," the "initially smooth configuration has become increasingly lumpy . . . as tiny perturbations in the density of matter have grown into planets, stars, and galaxies."[49]

As it is on the cosmic scale, so it is on a personal scale as well. We are lumps within lumps. What differentiates one thing from another (always contingently, always temporarily) is what a thing *does*, not what it "is." To be is to do. It is through this continual performance of differentiation that bodies, minds, and media come into being. To be responsible to the spatiotemporal continuity of the universe, the evolutionary continuity of life and mind, the social construction and regulation of behavior and identity, and the enactive continuity between media use and the flow of life is to acknowledge a persistent dynamic among things across spatiotemporal scales—scales made possible by complex formations of matter that emerge because of their structural robustness, their complexity, and their persistence in the context of entropy. These formations are always temporary, and some are more robust than others. Things are differentiated, then, by what they do (or more precisely by what they *are doing* for now) rather than what they are in any transcendent sense.

A commitment to naturalism in no way diminishes the necessity of the humanities. This book's most emphatic disciplinary contention is that the humanities are at present, and in fact must always be, essential tools for understanding the workings of the mind. Indeed, they may be the most effective tools that we can ever have for *scientific* understanding of the mind. Over millennia, the scholarly disciplines of the humanities have developed versatile and adaptable approaches to style, structure, meaning, implication, reference, expression, and representation in the arts. The hermeneutic aspects of these disciplines, or the ways in which they are *not* subject to the positivist rigors and abstract modeling of the "hard" sciences, make them better suited for feeling out the implications and subtleties of artworks than quantitative studies could ever be. This is not to say that there is no place for analytic and quantitative study of the arts. But if the problems of cognition and consciousness are so far ungrasped by quantitative science, this is partly because of the same variety of dualist division between logic and feeling, between model and world, and among mind, body, and environment that has introduced so many unnecessary problems into film and media theory. For the same reason that cognition and consciousness seem so slippery to the hard sciences, so too do principal problems of interpretation and affect posed by works of art. And yet we are able to engage with artworks in meaningful ways on a non-"logical" level, and arts practitioners are able to create artworks by way of feeling, rather than primarily through logistical planning. The position of this book is transdisciplinary rather than interdisciplinary, in the same sense in which transaction differs from interaction. To argue for continuity in the world is to call for foundational continuity among the disciplines. We must think beyond the conceptual boundaries between mind and world, world and diegesis, bodies and technologies, technologies and texts, humanities and sciences. Only then can we begin to do justice to the working of media in mind.

THE STRUCTURE OF THE BOOK

Media in Mind consists of six chapters. Chapters 1 through 3 can be thought of as a section that investigates bodily and psychological relationships with media and with the environment, showing how a transactionist approach can help in thinking through some fundamental problems of classical and contemporary media theory and can facilitate a naturalist understanding of media form and media use. Chapters 4 through 6 turn their attention more fully to media technologies. By way of a transactionist reconsideration of the concepts of the "platform" and the "interface" as they have been developed and employed in media theory, these chapters work to denaturalize conceptual gaps regarding the nominal inside of media, much as the first three chapters do for conceptual gaps regarding the nominal inside of the mind. This structure is not meant to imply that the mind and technology "sides" of media use ought to be taken as discrete from one another. To the contrary, I argue throughout *Media in Mind* against any such conceptual division of mind and media from one another and from their environmental context.

This book focuses mainly on cinema and video games. The emergence of these technologies represented two major transition points—the popularization and mass dissemination of moving images and that of reactive, computational entertainment media—that have been especially influential in how scholars have imagined the relationship between media and mind. Between the two, chronologically, was the emergence of television, a medium with its own ever-evolving ways of participating in the world, which requires its own (also ever-evolving) use practices and modes of bodily engagement. Although television and television theory are not primary focuses of this book, they—along with radio, virtual reality, cellular phones, personal computers, and so on—are no less parts of the wider story of media in mind.

Chapter 1 proposes Dewey's concept of the transaction as an approach to media theory. Through discussions of the video game *The Unfinished Swan* (Giant Sparrow, 2012), the films *Inside Out* (Pete Docter, 2015) and *L'Argent* (Robert Bresson, 1983), and two poems by Emily Dickinson, it illustrates the utility of a transactional understanding of media use and highlights some of the ways that media texts grapple with issues of continuity and discontinuity.

Chapter 2 focuses on the topic of perception as an active mode of engagement with the world and with media, arguing that the many ways in which we perceive, conceptualize, structure, and negotiate the world are varieties of feeling through our environments and feeling out our relationships to the objects in them. This includes vision, often thought of as a nontactile (and thus, somehow, as a more objective) sense. It also includes language and the other structures, including media, that we use to explore the parameters of our transactions with the world. The chapter argues for a mode of interpretation that is sensitive both to the transactional relationships among characters, objects, and environments in media, and to users' own transactional relationships with media, in the context of their own environments, bodies, and lives.

Whether they are conceived as pictorial, linguistic, or symbolic, mental representations are a foundational aspect of many theories of the mind and of media. Chapter 3 discusses the stakes of internal mental representations for media studies. It suggests that some media theorists and practitioners have intuited, by way of their close engagements with media, that perception might be more direct and active than has been commonly thought, and that this has troubled their relationships to the concept of internal mental representations, or to the "theater of the mind." This is explored through cases including the use of the videogame *Tetris* (Alexey Pajitnov, 1984) in psychological studies, the influence of cinema on Hugo Münsterberg's thinking about the nature of the mind, and the use of moving-image media in neuroscientific study, both as a stimulus and as a tool for visualizing results.

Chapter 4 engages with theoretical work on the figure of the platform, a term that the field of "platform studies" uses to describe the underpinnings of media—the physical hardware and sometimes the operating systems or other software—that make media possible but that are also treated as distinct from media texts. They are the containers, not the content. A platform is that which stores, presents, or "delivers" media content, shaping that content in the process, much as the representing mind is seen as that which contains and works with mental content. The field of platform studies, I argue, tends to enact a new and specific version of an old argument, the argument for "strong" emergence, which is at heart a justification for dividing the world into separate entities with discrete essences. Chapter 4 makes a case for the utility of a weakly emergent conception of the platform, which treats platforms as discursive, rather than ontological, formations.

If the operations of the platform, like those of the internal mind, are inaccessible, hidden, and symbolic, we are granted limited access to them by way of the interface, or the outward-facing surface of media. Some scholarship on the interface has complicated this picture, treating the interface not solely as a surface aspect of media but as a function of the relationships among media and their users. Theorists such as Johanna Drucker, Alexander Galloway, and Branden Hookway have expanded the boundaries of the interface as a theoretical figure, but I argue that these boundaries ought to be pushed still further. Chapter 5 proposes a transactionist understanding of the interface, drawing upon philosopher of science Karen Barad's concept of *intra-action*, which bears a strong resemblance to Dewey and Bentley's "transaction," but which puts particular emphasis on the performative differentiation of phenomena. Intra-action is a way of describing the "mutual constitution of entangled agencies," or how agencies emerge from their entanglement in such a way that "agencies are only distinct in relation to their mutual entanglement; they don't exist as individual elements."[50] Rather than things coming together to interact, intra-action is a dynamic, within a larger continuity, through which things can be seen to behave as if they were separate from one another. Galloway uses the neologism *intraface* to describe "an interface internal to the interface," which is "within the aesthetic," that allows for what is "outside" the medium to make itself present within the interface.[51] In order to extend the insights of scholars like Drucker, Galloway, and Hookway to a transactional account of media use, I propose turning the term outward, so that, rather than addressing a way in which the interface can bridge the gap between the aesthetic internal and the social external, it describes the ways that media, user, and context are contingently differentiated from one another by the dynamic among them. This everted conception of the intraface reflects the mutual entanglement central to Barad's concept of intra-action, and it further differentiates the intraface from the conventional model of the interface as a surface aspect of media. Rather than a point at which user and media come together, it represents a productive, performative, and always contingent separation of user *from* media.

This is always a structured separation—structured not only by media technologies but also by practices of media use, as well as the social investments of media users and the industrial investments of media makers. Returning to the purported external world, chapter 6 presents a case study of the Nintendo Game Boy, the first widely successful portable video game console. The case of the Game Boy represents a confluence of many of the strains of thought from throughout *Media in Mind*. The device is designed to be held in the hands, moved around, and moved *with* through the world. Its promotion and packaging encourages potential customers to think of it as a tool for transcending gaps among imagination, game world, and "real" world. As a device, it reflects a particular philosophy of technology, called "lateral thinking of withered technology," developed by the Game Boy's lead designer, Gunpei Yokoi.[52] The Game Boy is an act of material imagination, part of which is the act of Nintendo imagining its potential users' bodies and minds. Via the physical and computational structure of the Game Boy, Nintendo constructs what I call the "Vitruvian thumb," an idealized human (also physical and computational) counterpart to the console.

Media industries are in the business of selling people on the *idea* of gaps— between themselves and the world, between themselves and one another, between objects and services available for purchase—and then selling them "solutions," or ways to bridge those ostensible gaps, in order to better integrate themselves with the world, with one another, and with technology by way of the platforms, interfaces, and interactive "experiences" that they purchase at a premium. Interactional theories of media participate in this dynamic when they reinforce these gaps, though the conceptual solutions that they offer are generally quite different from the technological ones that media industries sell.

The book's conclusion steps back to take in a (much) wider view, and it offers some thoughts about media's ability to depict, characterize, and grapple with the concept of continuity in a cosmic context. Media use is a way of participating in a larger unity of which media technologies—and media forms—are parts. As are we. Looking back from the afterlife, a character in George Saunders's novel *Lincoln in the Bardo* says: "All things started as nothing, latent within a vast energy-broth, but then we named them, and loved them, and, in this way, brought them forth."[53] For there to be something, there has to be everything. But for there to be everything, there has to be something. Things only come into view, and into being, through active and ongoing performance of differentiation.

CHAPTER 1

Transactionism

A Theory of Media in Mind

Playing the video game *The Unfinished Swan* (Giant Sparrow, 2012), you are confronted by an undifferentiated white void.

The child Monroe hesitates, steps tentatively, tries to feel his weight in the world. Facing your television, you manipulate a PlayStation 4 controller with its many buttons and joysticks. You feel its weight in your hands. As you look at your screen, you see through Monroe's eyes, which is to say that you see nothing but white. Monroe hears his footsteps and the sound of his own voice, but he sees nothing, feels nothing to his touch. From far away come nautical sounds: a seagull, a chime (perhaps a buoy?), crashing surf. Monroe explores the actions available to him. He takes a few more steps. As you press the "X" button on your controller, Monroe jumps with a shout, hearing his feet strike the ground. You press your controller's right trigger button, and Monroe, surprising himself and you, hurls a sphere of black paint into the space ahead of him, followed by another and another. As they strike unseen surfaces, the paint balls splatter to reveal, in black and white, walls, a passage, trees, rocks, a bench, a path (see figure 1.1). Painting the world seems to bring it into being for Monroe, although it has in fact been there all along.

As with so many stories of creation, *The Unfinished Swan* is initiated by the division of dark from light, by the establishment of a fundamental contrast that will make all other distinctions, perceptual and conceptual, possible. These distinctions give rise to an impression of a world divided, a world composed of discrete objects, of anticipation and interaction, a world of relationships among *things*. But first there are perceptions that the child quickly learns to create, to organize, and to use. As the world seems to take shape, to resolve into separate things, so too does the child begin to take on a uniqueness, an innerness, and an intentionality that distance him from the world around him even as he becomes immersed in it.

Figure 1.1 In *The Unfinished Swan* (Giant Sparrow, 2012), the initial white screen is divided first into a contrast between black and white and then into spaces and the objects that occupy them.

The Unfinished Swan is played from a first-person optical point of view. With your right thumb, you control the tilt and pan of a virtual camera that corresponds to Monroe's perspective on the game space. With your left thumb, you control Monroe's motion forward, backward, and side to side, effectively dollying the virtual camera through the world of the game. In terms of genre, *The Unfinished Swan* could be classed as a "first-person shooter" (or FPS). In its play mechanics, it is most similar to games like *Doom* (id Software, 1993) and *Call of Duty* (Infinity Ward, 2003), in which a player navigates a dangerous environment and eliminates enemies with projectiles. I said earlier that you see nothing but white as you begin to play the game, but this is not strictly true. At the center of the screen is a small, circular reticle, which aids you in aiming the spheres of paint. You can see it, but there is no reason to believe that Monroe can. In another FPS the reticle might represent the crosshairs of an assault weapon. Rather than the violence and destruction typical of the genre, however, the "shooting" in *The Unfinished Swan* is a tool that players use in order to perceive and to make sense of the game world.

While the game is an unusual FPS, it is important not as an exception but as an exemplar. Through its unusual use of the shooting mechanic, *The Unfinished Swan* compels its players not only to be active in their creation of a perceptible game world, but to be conscious of the labor involved in that activity. By foregrounding the work of perception, the game reminds us that players of all video games actively create perception when they explore game spaces and probe the properties of game worlds. Perception of video games does not happen automatically, in other words. It must be achieved through players' skillful physical engagement with games as they move their in-game avatars, control virtual cameras, and interact with game objects and characters.

In this respect, *The Unfinished Swan* is an allegory of the ways people create perception and knowledge by inhabiting and moving through the world. From birth, we embark on a series of differentiations, dividing light from dark, soft from hard, loud from quiet, object from nonobject, available from off limits, food from nonfood, threat from nonthreat. Over time, these differentiations build on one another and become more specialized, but their exploratory and taxonomic basis never goes away. As philosopher of science Michael Polyani writes, "We keep expanding our body into the world, by assimilating to it sets of particulars which we integrate into reasonable entities. Thus do we form . . . an interpreted universe populated by entities."[1] The knowledge that we create is perceptual, conceptual, aesthetic, and tactical, all at once. It is also personal. We create it always by way of our particular bodies, with their particular structures and ways of accessing the resources of our environments, and positioned in particular ways by our sociocultural contexts and by the physical environments that we happen to occupy, in all of which contexts we learn, as psychologist Louise Barrett puts it, "to exploit our specific bodily resources."[2] We also do so in the contexts of systems of power that, as explicated by theorists too many to mention, seek to determine how those bodily resources are defined and exploited. Through this fraught and contingent process of inventing knowledge, as Polyani writes, a "reasonable" impression of discrete objects and beings is formed.

This impression soon attains a reflexive dimension. The "self" becomes something, if not prior to the existence of the body, then at least contained within the body, which acts as a barrier or vessel that shields the self from the continuity of the world. The self thus seen is discrete, private, and internal: a unit and a unity. Socialized into this impression, we may see ourselves as apart from the world around us, which enables us to act upon the world as if from outside it, and to see the things and beings that populate it as fundamentally separate from ourselves. This is not to say that we do not see ourselves as being in the world, but rather that we tend not to see the world as being in us. In this view, the environment surrounds us, but it does not constitute us. We reserve an inner aspect of being that is discontinuous with the outside world, and we thereby set ourselves apart from our environments. We afford this same courtesy, in varying degrees, to the beings and other things around us, granting them unity and (usually only for living things) degrees of subjectivity, intentionality, and consciousness.

This perspective erects legible conceptual boundaries between things, boundaries that help us to impose order on our surroundings and thus to exert control over them. But it also obscures the primordial entanglements and dynamics among ourselves, other beings and objects, and the environment that we share. This in turn obscures the individual and collective effects we can have on that environment, as well as the reciprocal ways in which changes in that environment are also changes in ourselves. Furthermore, it facilitates the imposition of a comparable conceptual order upon us, one that renders us countable and identifiable as units of use. There is real peril—ecological, political, moral—in treating the world as discontinuous, and yet there is also seductive ease in treating the world just so. That easy path should not be treated as the natural order of things, however; as a way of understanding the world, it is, like any other, a contingent, historically specific construction, produced by and productive for existing structures of power. The easier it is made to see oneself as apart from the environment and apart from others, the easier it is to be complacent in our own exploitation as working, thinking, and feeling beings, and the easier it is for us to ignore the ongoing, larger-scale ecological, social, and political disasters to which we each contribute every day.

Media are often accused of separating their users from the world and from the people around them. But media use can also cue us to our continuity with that world and those people in ways that we tend to overlook in everyday experience. By intimately—and visibly—acting with media technologies, media users exemplify the ways in which we continuously act *with* the world and with the things in it, including other people, rather than acting unilaterally upon them. Through the stories they tell and the formal techniques they employ, media can (and too often do) naturalize the logic of monadic individualism, obscuring the continuity of user and media even as this continuity remains the source of their persuasive power. But media can also be sites of resistance to perceptual and conceptual habits that obscure our entanglement with the world.

This is an ecological conception of media use, in that it is concerned with dynamic relationships among organisms and objects in the context of their shared environments. It sees both media users and media themselves (texts and technologies, forms and platforms) as mutually entangled aspects of that ecology, rather than as occupants of it. Neither is discrete from its context, and neither is discrete from the other. This perspective differs from other self-identified ecological theories of media, such as those proposed by Marshall McLuhan and Joseph D. Anderson, that erect conceptual divisions between media and the world or between the world and the mind. McLuhan characterizes media as an ecology in itself, rather than as a constituent part of a broader ecology, thereby sequestering media in space, time, and essence from the rest of the world. Beginning with spoken language, this division of media from world is what allows media to "observe" the world as though from outside it, and thus what allows media to exert influence upon culture. Speech, McLuhan writes, "gives the power of detachment from the environment that is also the power of great mobility in knowledge of the environment."[3] Rather than seeing media as apart from the environment, Anderson seeks to understand film within the ecology of human perception. While he restores the place of film in the environment, though, Anderson regards experience as a product of internal representations in the mind, not as the product of an active relationship with the environment. In Anderson's account, explored in more detail in chapter 3, even as media are restored to their place in the broader ecology, the mind is severed from its own position in that ecology.[4] For an ecological approach to media to be productive in seeing media as part of the world ecology, it needs to account for the primordial entanglement of its elements: media as an aspect of the environment, mind as an aspect of the lived world. Such an approach, in other words, needs to be transactional.

TRANSACTIONISM AND DEWEY'S *IN*

Media in Mind proposes an ecological approach to media use, media technology, and media theory that I call *transactionism*. Transactionism is first and foremost a commitment to naturalism, an acknowledgment that media and media users are constituent aspects of a broader reality, continuous with that reality and with one another. Through discussion of *The Unfinished Swan*, two poems by Emily Dickinson, and the films *Inside Out* (Pete Docter, 2015) and *L'Argent* (Robert Bresson, 1983), this chapter begins to feel out the variety of ways that media characterize relationships among bodies, minds, and the environment, and it begins to explore the implications that come with thinking of self, world, and media in transactional terms, an exploration that will continue throughout the rest of the book.

These implications may at first seem counterintuitive. Perception is not something that we do to media, nor is it something that media create in us. It is a quality of shared activity among users and media. Affect and emotion are likewise products of this dynamic, contained neither in media nor in their users. This view calls into question some of the most common metaphors used for describing media and for describing the mind. In particular, it troubles both the idea of the mind as a container and the idea of media having content. Susan Sontag railed against the latter when she wrote that "interpretation, based on the highly dubious theory that a work of art is composed of items of content, violates art. It makes art into an article for use, for arrangement into a mental scheme of categories."[5] The theory that a mind is composed of content is equally dubious and equally instrumentalizing.

The term "transactionism," as I am using it, builds upon ideas about the nature of knowledge proposed by the philosopher John Dewey. In the book *Knowing and the Known*, which Dewey cowrote with Arthur F. Bentley, Dewey and Bentley argue that knowing should be understood not as an action or an interaction but as a transaction, in that it is a reciprocal and continuous dynamic, and not a case of one entity acting upon another.[6] Over the course of his long career (Dewey lived from 1859 to 1952; his first published essay is from 1882 and his last from 1951),[7] Dewey developed a view of the world characterized by holism, continuity, and interrelation, a naturalist perspective that understood all things as aspects of one continuous reality and thus saw all things as connected and coconstitutive. Dewey's way of characterizing the mind fell out of favor in a twentieth century that largely preferred a more positivist, computational understanding of cognition, but since the 1980s it has been revived by philosophers, including Alva Noë and Mark Johnson, who follow Dewey in characterizing the mind as embodied, environmental, and situationally specific. Both Johnson and Noë follow Dewey also in characterizing art not as an exception to "normal" experience but as an exemplary form of experience.[8] As Dewey put it, art is a "refined and intensified" form of experience, spatiotemporally continuous with everyday life.[9]

Transactionism carries an ethical and a political charge, as it implies an obligation to media and to the world, including the beings and the objects that at once populate and constitute it. In making an argument for transactionism, I make a case for practices of media use, media making, and media theory that reach into the world in exploratory and contingent ways. If we think of all of these practices as forms of research into an ecology of which we and media are aspects, engagements with media can become sites of resistance against the normalizing power of disciplinary, aesthetic, and discursive control.

The title *Media in Mind* gestures toward metaphors of containment. To have something "in mind" means to be mindful of it, to ponder it, or to be conscious of it. To "have media in mind" is in this sense to think about media. But from a transactional perspective, the mind is not decisively possessed and contained, nor is it possessing of content. The mind is actively produced though continuous bodily activities in the world. Thus, there is no clear physical place or time where a mind begins or ends. It is of the brain, but not wholly of it. It is in the body, but not wholly within it. "Media in mind" thus has another meaning for the purposes of this book. If the mind extends across the environment, including the body and the objects around it, and is an aspect of what transpires among these things, then the media we use are participant parts of our minds. Media are not imported into the mind to be transformed into symbols and comprehended or otherwise reckoned with, nor do they act *on* the mind from without. They directly participate in the constitution of the mind.

Such an *in* is always reciprocal. We are in the world, and the world is in us. The only way to discover the character of this relationship is by feeling it out, by actively perceiving, exploring, and testing its contours. To do so is to probe the structures and limits of the world, and also to probe the structures and limits of what we call our selves. This is a developmental process that lasts for our entire lifetimes, although it is usually regarded as passive or transparent, which is to say it usually is not regarded at all. Media use can render it visible, and video games like *The Unfinished Swan* call their users' attention to perceptual exploration in their narratives, in their visual and sonic aesthetics, and in their gameplay.

To think of a spatiotemporally continuous whole is to think of relationships within that whole in terms of their continuity as well. Relationships in space, time, causality, and knowledge are never unidirectional, always mutual. Transactionism resists hard distinctions between what have traditionally been treated as subjects and objects, and between what we think of as nouns and verbs. To think transactionally is to see continuity among such categories as these:

- knower, knowing, known
- perceiver, perception, perceived
- user, use, that which is used
- stimulus, stimulation, response
- cause, event, effect
- player, play, game
- viewer, viewing, film

Inasmuch as we can hold these aspects of a causal relationship to be separate, we do so only for the sake of description, allowing us to think, or to argue, about action at a particular scale, seen from a particular perspective and with a particular set of rhetorical investments. As this chapter and those that follow show, a commitment to naturalism requires us to reconsider the status of images in media and in the mind, as well as our conceptions of media technologies, or platforms, and the ways that they function in user experience. My goal is not to discount existing descriptive tools for talking about media but rather to position those tools properly as epistemological framing devices, dependent on looking at media use from a particular perspective and at a particular scale. To do this responsibly, we must acknowledge the shared ecology in which media use occurs and to which media use contributes.

Every organism exists in an environment, every text occupies a context. At the same time, organisms are parts of their environments and texts are parts of their contexts. To trouble the conceptual distinction between a thing and the world around it—to recognize that the world is as much in the thing as the thing is in the world—is also to trouble the comfortable distinction between inner and outer aspects of being. The body, or the soul, or the brain, is not a container for the mind. Where, then, does a mind occur? Like Polyani and like Barrett, Dewey locates the mind not in a place (such as the body, the soul, or the brain), but in a process. He writes:

> To see the organism *in* nature, the nervous system in the organism, the brain in the nervous system . . . is to answer the problems which haunt philosophy. And when thus seen they will be seen to be *in*, not as marbles are in a box but as events are in history, in a moving, growing never finished process.[10]

The "problems which haunt philosophy" are rooted in habits of conceptually dividing the world into discrete objects and moments, and into distinct levels and sites of causality. Such divisions obscure the fact that the world, including the mind, is characterized by dynamic, continuous, never-ending processes of change. Within this system, the mind is both a quality and a cause. It participates in the world from within, and the world likewise participates in it. To more clearly see the relationship between media and mind, then, we must think not about the effects that media have on the mind but about the roles that media play in the mind.

Media are in our minds as events are in history.

Dewey's *in* embraces continuity while rejecting containment. This is an *in* closer in meaning to "across" or "throughout" than it is to "within." Events in history (human cultural history, the ecological history of the world, the physical history of the universe) follow from and lead into each other, are never discrete from one another in space or in time, and can never be divided into discrete causes. The same is true of the more local spatiotemporal continuity of brain, nervous system, organism, and environment. These are not separate units bouncing against one another like marbles clacking in a box. They do not act upon one another, or interact with each other, so much as they participate in transactions that include, and transform, the entire situation, including themselves.[11] This understanding of action troubles the concept of the discrete human self, replacing autonomy with blended, imbricated, and integrated participation in the world at large. All of these descriptors are, in fact, misleading, as they all imply a mixing or an intertwining of things that were previously separate. They were not. It is the continuity that is prior. The intertwining of self and world is primordial and eternal; what needs to be reintegrated is how we think about and describe that relationship. The "in" of *Media in Mind* is Dewey's.

In *Knowing and the Known*, Dewey and Bentley make a distinction among *action, interaction,* and *transaction* as ways of knowing, or of understanding the behavior of the world. Action, or self-action, is a prescientific model, in which things are seen as "possessing power of their own, under which they [act]." Self-action sees objects as discrete, independent units, each acting under its own power. A dropped ball, for instance, might be seen as internally compelled to seek out the earth, not drawn downward by the earth's gravitation and certainly not drawn together with the earth due to distortions in spacetime.

Challenged by Galileo, Newton, and others, self-action gives way to a model of interaction in which still-discrete things act upon one another within the context of shared environmental constraints. The ball is not compelled to seek out the earth; ball and earth draw each other nearer by way of gravitation. But the ball and the earth are still discrete things. Gravitation is a way of describing a relationship between separate entities rather than an aspect of their fundamental entanglement.

Lamenting that "epistemologies, logics, psychologies, and sociologies are still largely on a self-actional" or sometimes an interactional basis, Dewey and Bentley call for a transactional knowing that asserts "the right to see together, extensionally and durationally, much that is talked about conventionally as if it were composed of irreconcilable separates." Such an approach resists the still-dominant language of self-action, which "shatters the subjectmatter into fragments in advance of inquiry and thus destroys instead of furthering comprehensive observation for it."[12] To understand things transactionally is not to understand "items or characteristics of organisms alone," nor "items or characteristics of environments alone," but rather "the *activity* that occurs *of both together*."[13] Transaction goes beyond interaction and beyond what might be called the "interface" between things. Rather than thinking of a relationship *between*, transactional thought conceives of relationships *across*, so that one thing never acts unidirectionally upon another. Things and their environmental contexts always act together, any action always incorporates that which acts, and any knowledge always includes that which knows.

Media complicate this picture through their creation of seemingly discrete systems of representation and narrative, so it is important to see past the illusion of separation between media and the world and to be conscious of media's embeddedness in the world alongside brains, nervous systems, and bodies, and of the physical and psychological entanglements among people and media. If an ecological conception of the mind, such as the one Dewey describes, is an answer to the "problems which haunt philosophy," then to think ecologically about media use will be to answer (at least some of) the problems which haunt media theory.

PERCEPTUAL WORK IN *THE UNFINISHED SWAN*

The gameplay of *The Unfinished Swan* takes place inside a painting, the frame of which also frames the world that the game's players, and Monroe, must explore. The game opens with a brief expository sequence, told in the past tense and illustrated with line art. After his mother, a painter, died, Monroe was taken to an orphanage. He brought with him an unfinished picture of a swan, his mother's favorite of her own paintings. Later, discovering that the swan had disappeared, Monroe passed through a mysterious door into the world of the painting. As Monroe crossed this threshold . . . the gameplay begins and the narration's tense snaps from past to present. Now in control of Monroe and seeing the game world from his optical perspective, players are confronted by the blank white screen. Along with Monroe, they are tasked with making sense of and navigating the at-first invisible world.

Earlier, I called *The Unfinished Swan* an allegory of the way people create perception and knowledge by inhabiting and moving through the world. We can now see how the game goes beyond allegory. *The Unfinished Swan* both allegorizes and embodies transactional relationships. In the opening section of the game, both you (as a player) and Monroe (as a character) must acclimate to a new means of perception. For Monroe, seeing the world cannot be separated from throwing the paint. For you, seeing the world cannot be separated from pressing a button on your controller to make Monroe throw the paint. By making perception dependent upon these manual manipulations, and by thereby making you (and Monroe) conscious of working to perceive, the game renders visible the work required of all perception. Perception and knowledge can thus properly be seen as creative activities, as the production of something new via dynamic relationships within an environment. The game's narrative framing underscores this point. Monroe is depicted not only as exploring an environment but also as creating a piece of expressive media—a *work* of art—through the work of perception. Monroe aestheticizes the world by perceiving it, and he perceives it by aestheticizing it. The two are inseparable.

Mark Johnson calls for a twenty-first-century philosophy of the embodied mind that pursues Dewey's claim that (in Johnson's words) "art is experience in its most consummated, fully realized form." For Johnson, this would mean

> a philosophy that sees aesthetics as not just about art, beauty, and taste, but rather as about how human beings experience and make meaning. Aesthetics concerns all of the things that go into meaning—form, expression, communication, qualities, emotion, feeling, value, purpose, and more.[14]

As *The Unfinished Swan* demonstrates, Johnson's "and more" should be understood to include perception. By picking up a controller, turning on a console, and playing *The Unfinished Swan*, you enter into a new aesthetic relationship, and you thereby engage with new perceptual and enactive structures and challenges. The narrative of *The Unfinished Swan* is likewise initiated by Monroe's entering a new relationship with an aesthetic object—the painting—and thereby a new relationship to perception, action, and constraint. His confusion upon finding himself in the all-white space corresponds closely to that which you experience when the gameplay begins with nothing of the game world visible. Through the figure of Monroe, through your controller, and through your own bodily actions, you as a player are compelled to feel out the qualities of this world, including, first and most (button-)pressingly, how you can possibly navigate a space with no discernible features. In order to see the world of *The Unfinished Swan*, in other words, you must first *learn how to see* in it. This begins not with a passive, absorptive glance but with an active gesture of differentiation.

If you experiment with the game's paint-throwing mechanic, you will soon discover more sophisticated strategies for exploring the game's spaces. By throwing paint judiciously, you can reveal the paths and the affordances of the spaces around Monroe, mapping out the world of the game. If you throw too much paint, the environment will become saturated in black and its details nearly as indistinct as they were before the throwing began (the atmosphere remains white, so some objects in the open are still seen in silhouette). An attentive player will notice, too, that strafing back and forth while throwing paint allows you efficiently to reveal the environment while also traversing it, and that side-to-side ambulatory motion is further helpful in producing parallax effects in order to judge the dimensions of objects and to estimate distances. Monroe soon discovers a passage out of the square-cornered room in which the gameplay begins. He moves into spaces of increasing geometrical complexity: a stony alcove, a tree-lined path, stepping stones over a pond, and a castle. Ascending to the battlements, Monroe can look back and see the paint-spattered world that he has "created," a world made visible to him only by the perceptual work that he has undertaken in it, made visible on your screen by your own work as a player of the game, and made visible here in figure 1.2.

What is Monroe's relationship to the paint that he hurls into his environment? One way of characterizing it, an interactive way, would be to say that he throws the paint in order to alter the appearance of the world, allowing him to perceive and

Figure 1.2 *The Unfinished Swan*: a view from the battlements.

come to know its contours and to work with that knowledge in deciding his next moves—both where next to go and where next to throw paint. From this perspective, action and perception would be two separate things. Actions are things that one does, while perception is something that happens automatically. Actions are a way of moving through and altering the world, while perception is a way of absorbing it. Perception, in other words, is a passive phenomenon that constitutes the interface between an exterior world of objects and actions and an interior world of meanings and decisions.

I have been arguing for the alternative position that that perception is a kind of action, not a passive or receptive phenomenon. Philosopher Alva Noë has made a passionate and extensive case for this perspective. As Noë puts it, "Perception is not something that happens to us, or in us. It is something we do."[15] Perception, in the terms I have been using, is a material transaction among organisms, the things around them, and the environment that they share. It is a product of biological evolution, a result of the needs of developing organisms in relation to a dynamic world. These needs themselves develop relative to the capacities of the organism and the demands of the environment, and they also transform those very capacities and demands. Rather than being passive, then, perception is first and foremost functional. It is a way of probing the world for information, of feeling one's way through an environment and, over time, establishing structures of feeling, both perceptual and conceptual, that are suited to the structures and probabilities of that environment. The throwing of the paint, and the material of the paint itself, are *parts* of Monroe's act of perception.

Johnson writes that babies "must *learn* the perceptual and conceptual experiences that adults take for granted."[16] Monroe is himself but a child, still feeling out his place in his own world and exploring what Louise Barrett calls his specific bodily resources, when he is thrust into the new world of the painting with its new mode of perception. Players of the game are subjected to similar constraints, afforded narrower channels of action than they have in day-to-day life: a screen, joysticks and buttons, a control scheme. These are the available tools for feeling out the contours of the game's space. *The Unfinished Swan* defamiliarizes perception both for Monroe and for you, the player, via its paint-throwing mechanic. At the same time, not all is unfamiliar. Monroe does not have to learn again how to stand or to walk, for instance, and the game adheres to a familiar, standard FPS control scheme: two joysticks to move and look, "X" button to jump, and trigger button to fire. Like Monroe, players bring acquired bodily resources to bear on their negotiation of the world of *The Unfinished Swan*. This enactive familiarity is the stable ground against which the game's defamiliarization of perception plays out.

Encounters with media are little rebirths, occasions to relearn patterns of perception and understanding. All video games, and indeed all media, require their users to reckon with technological constraints and to negotiate new kinds of experience each time they play a game or watch a film or look at a painting. In this light, it is telling that the strategies for paint-throwing that emerge from playing *The*

Unfinished Swan include continuous strafing of the camera coupled with throwing a steady stream of paint balls into the environment. While it might be seen to parallel the scattershot gunfire of a more conventional FPS, this technique also bears more than a passing similarity to visual saccades, the rapid and constant involuntary scanning movements that human eyes make in order to facilitate perception of three-dimensional environments.[17] Indeed, as a player gains experience with the game, these manual saccades come to be so habitual as to be all but involuntary themselves, the camera-controlling right thumb jerking and twitching as if on its own, while the right index finger unleashes a constant hail of paint into the game space.

However, it is important to note that involuntary does not necessarily mean inactive or passive. *The Unfinished Swan* is one of many examples in this book of media that foreground qualities of media experience that we often take for granted. Requiring their users to do actively what other games might do automatically, these games and films prompt those users to pay closer attention to the kinds of perceptual and enactive processes that they always employ when using media and that they employ outside of media use as well. The effort of visual saccades may effectively be transparent from moment to moment, but it is effort all the same. To have to recreate saccades in a game not through involuntary eye movements but through voluntary hand motions makes the saccades tangible and visible—an effort of the thumb—and players' adaptation to the technique, in which the strafing motion becomes so constant as to be virtually automatic, illustrates how such a learned activity can become "transparent" in support of other, more conceptual or strategic pursuits.

As its narrative progresses, *The Unfinished Swan* modulates its player's relationship to the visibility of the game world. The game only sticks with the paint-throwing mechanic through the first of its four chapters. As Monroe makes his way through chapter 1, the world's perceptual qualities begin to change. These changes are explained by way of a secondary narrative, unveiled in pages of storybook text that Monroe discovers, that tell the story of "the King," who previously ruled this land and who sought to make changes to it in response to the demands of his subjects. As one page of text puts it, the subjects "were tired of white . . . tired of tripping, of banging their shins, of misplacing their homes." So the King "pledged to spend the next month painting shadows for his kingdom." After the player discovers this text, shadows of objects become visible, so that the presence of shapes can be inferred without throwing paint, although throwing paint still reveals their structures in more detail. Subsequently, some colored things become automatically visible, including blue water and red balloons. These are gradually joined by more colored objects, as well as some solid-black ones. By the end of chapter 1, the paint-throwing is all but obsolete, rendered unnecessary by the readily visible game world.

As chapter 2 of *The Unfinished Swan* begins, the game's throwing mechanic remains the same, but the paint is replaced by water, which Monroe uses to manipulate machinery and later to coax plants to grow, including leafy vines that he can climb to reach new areas. In its second half, the game all but abandons its early challenges to perception. It retains its FPS format, but its projectiles are now used to manipulate objects and to build structures in the game world. *The Unfinished Swan* becomes more conventional, less engaging, and less visually innovative in its later chapters. This arc is redeemed, in my opinion, if we think of the game as a developmental narrative. As Mark Johnson puts it, babies have to learn the perceptual experiences adults take for granted. Monroe develops his perceptual skills alongside the game's players, so that as he becomes accustomed to his new world, he can begin to take its visibility for granted. The later chapters of *The Unfinished Swan* seem to make perception automatic, but their narrative continuity with the first chapter, and the way that players must build their way up to the later chapters—narratively and perceptually—by making the world visible in the game's early stages, serves as a reminder that none of this happens automatically. The world is there for the seeing, but we will not see it unless we move through it. Perception does not just happen. It must be done.

MEDIA AND MIND IN ANALOGY

Media texts that challenge perceptual habits also challenge habits of thinking about media. In particular, they can help to break down conceptual dualisms that have attended media theory from its beginnings. If the mind is an "inner theater" in which conscious and unconscious operations take place in a symbolic or imagistic language of thought, a premise shared by psychoanalytic media theory, cognitivism, and classical psychological film theory, then the mind is discontinuous with the world at large. When David Bordwell writes that cognitivist film theory relies upon "mental representations," or Christian Metz writes of an "internal duality" of conscious and unconscious processes whose "characteristic operations are more or less accessible to introspection," or Hugo Münsterberg writes of "internal functions which create the meaning of the world around us," each of these theorists erects a boundary between inner and outer reality.[18] If a theory conceives of media forms as fictional or virtual, or as "content," then representations, both those in media texts and those in the theater of the mind, are also held apart from external reality, a theoretical maneuver that diminishes their presence and their power in the world.

The perceived resonance between images in media and images in the mind leads to periodic reconsiderations of how the mind works, which are often prompted by developments in media technology. This can be productive, as new media technologies furnish new metaphors, which in turn facilitate new perspectives on the nature of the mind. However, it can also be misleading, as it is easy to slip from arguing that qualities of a medium resemble qualities of the mind to arguing that the technics of that medium operate like the functioning of the mind.

The very newness of a new medium plays a part in this appeal. As Jay Bolter points out, technologies furnish ready ways of explaining nature in terms of culture. New technologies, especially the "defining technologies" of a time, are often regarded as analogous to the workings of the mysterious machinations of nature. "Plato compared the created universe to a spindle," writes Bolter, "Descartes thought of animals as clockwork mechanisms, and scientists in the nineteenth century and early twentieth century have regularly compared the universe to a heat engine."[19] By providing new sensations and suggesting new metaphors, new media experiences open up new avenues of speculative thinking about the mind. This newness can be persuasive in itself, as the stimulation of new media use gives rise to excitement about what these new modes of experience reveal about experience itself. As linguist and video game scholar James Paul Gee writes:

> Locke and Hume argued that the mind was like a blank slate on which experience wrote images and ideas, taking the technology of literacy as a guide for how to view the human mind. Much later, modern cognitive scientists argued that the mind worked like a digital computer calculating generalizations and deductions via a logic-like rule system.[20]

Between Locke's and Hume's slate and cognitivism's computer, cinema became a prominent metaphor for the working of the mind in the first half of the twentieth century. The metaphoric resonance between cinema and mind was noticed early and has been noticed often. In 1907, the philosopher Henri Bergson wrote that "Whether we would think becoming, or express it, or even perceive it, we hardly do anything else than set going a kind of cinematograph inside us . . . the mechanism of our ordinary knowledge is of a cinematographical kind."[21] This sort of metaphor tempts slippage between the appearance of a medium—what is on the screen or the page—and the technological underpinnings of the medium. To see something mind-like in the play of images in a medium need not imply something mind-like in the workings of the media technology, nor vice versa. If a film onscreen seems mind-like to a viewer, this does not necessarily imply that the projector is mechanically like the operation of the viewer's mind, nor that whatever underpins the viewer's mind is mechanically (or metaphorically) like the projector. Similarly, computational cognitive science sees the brain or mind as a "rule system," which must then have an input (perception) and an output (action) through which it interacts with the world. A pattern of reciprocal action is thereby initiated. The mind is thought of as mysterious and as somehow apart from the world. A medium appears that seems to resonate with the mind in unprecedented ways. The experience of the medium is adopted as a metaphor for the experience of the mind, and the mechanics of the medium are credited with being like the mechanics of the mind. The perceived mysterious interiority of the mind, via this equivalency, is imported into ways of thinking about the medium. The impression of both medium and mind as discrete from their continuity in the material world is thereby reinforced.

Isolating media and the mind from the "outside" world and from each other at once downplays their intimate relationship with, and overemphasizes their causal power over, one another. As a byproduct of setting both aside from the material world, theory can begin to see direct correspondences and causal relationships between media and mind that appear to bypass "reality" altogether, so that media seem to act directly upon the mind and vice versa. To Metz, for instance, the resonance between these two internal structures—in the film and in the mind—allows film to effectively circumvent external reality, tapping directly into a "disturbing seductive power" of conscious phantasy, whereby "we can see there . . . a production of the unconscious."[22] The theorist-filmmaker Dziga Vertov wrote that "musical, theatrical, and film-theatrical representations act, above all, on the viewer's or listener's subconscious, completely circumventing his protesting consciousness."[23] For Münsterberg, film is an externalization of the internal that objectifies our "mental act of attention" by drawing attention out into the world.[24] For Bordwell, "Narrative films utilize mental representations for their depicted events" and "draw on historically developed conventions that involve schemata and heuristics," meaning the conceptual categorization and hypothesis formation that viewers employ in comprehending films.[25] In each of these accounts, form in media appeals more or less directly to form in mind. In emphasizing cognitive processing, attention as a "mental act," or the production (or the "protesting") of the unconscious, each theorist demotes perception to a passive role, rendering it a conduit of sorts between the outside and the inside worlds, which are where the real action is. As chapter 2 will argue in more detail, conceiving of perception as active, embodied, and intertwined with the world and with the objects in it sheds new light on this tendency to erect rigid divisions among objective reality, subjective experience, and the content of media.

As I write this in the late 2010s, the contemporary "defining technologies" are, and have for some time been, digital technologies. The computer has been a prominent metaphor for the mind, in both cognitive science and in the popular imagination, since around the middle of the twentieth century. With the proliferation of video games since the 1970s, of home computing since the 1980s and 1990s, of digital modes of production, distribution, and exhibition in the film industry since around 2000, and of social media and handheld internet devices since the mid-2000s, digital metaphors have become increasingly prominent in the theory and philosophy of media use. Owing in part to the perceived intimacy and interactivity of new media, and also to a concurrent increase in interest in embodiment and materiality across the scholarly disciplines, metaphoric mappings of media onto the mind and body have asserted increasingly close equivalences between their source domains and their target domains. Rather than being like thought, media are a material in which thought occurs. Or, because they require new forms of activity (or require activity at all, if we are given to think of perception as a passive nonactivity) from the bodies of their users, new media incorporate those bodies into the processes by which they frame their subject matter, so that the core subject of a medium comes more prominently to be the body of its own user. Or, because they are dynamic and networked, digital media are more world-like than earlier media could ever be.

D. N. Rodowick writes in *Reading the Figural, or, Philosophy after the New Media* that "cinema and the electronic arts are . . . *ahead* of philosophy" in that "their invention, cultural form, and patterns of distribution and use are based on a set of concepts that recast the genealogy of visuality and the aesthetic in new contexts,"[26] a recasting that philosophy might then endeavor to follow. The phrase "philosophy after the new media" does not describe a mere periodization. Philosophy for Rodowick must be after new media, must take after the lead of new media as a mode of expression.

For Mark B. N. Hansen, digital media technologies mark a shift in the relationship between media and the body because media "lose their material specificity" when they are digital. This loss of specificity calls forth a more active role on the part of the media user, an embodied process of "selection" through which "the body . . . informs the medial interfaces." As a result, Hansen writes, the framing function of the interface is displaced back onto the body of the media user. "It is this displacement," writes Hansen, "that makes new media art 'new.' "[27] What Hansen describes as the nonspecific materiality of digital media elevates the body— specifically, the work performed by the body—to a newly central position in the work of media use. As Hansen writes, "Just as perception is compelled to rediscover its constitutive bodily basis, so too must art reaffirm its bodily origin."[28]

More recent work by Hansen, as well as by Steven Shaviro and others, considers contemporary media in light of the "process philosophy" of Alfred North Whitehead, seeking to eradicate the line between inner and outer experience in a fashion that resonates in many ways—though not in some key others—with the Deweyan concept of transaction. As Shaviro notes, Whitehead opposed the "bifurcation of nature," or the "schema according to which we radically separate sensory experience from the physical activities that generate that experience."[29] Hansen embeds his insistence on the bodily origins of art in a broader environmental context when he writes that Whitehead can help to clarify how "the shift catalyzed by twenty-first-century media—the shift from agent-centered perception to environmental sensibility—yields an enhanced human contact with worldly sensibility."[30]

While his process philosophy has been a key driver of antidualism in recent media theory, Whitehead's approach to continuity diverges from Dewey's in crucial ways that render Dewey's transactional perspective a more productive framework for thinking of the continuity of media and mind in naturalist terms. Dewey and Whitehead were contemporaries, born sixteen months apart—Dewey in 1859 in Vermont, and Whitehead across the Atlantic in 1861 in Kent. Dewey makes clear his affinity for what he calls Whitehead's "substitution for the idea of mechanism of the idea of organism," by which

> Every concrete reality is of the nature of an organism; that is, it is a whole which endures or has a history, which develops, and which as a whole both reflects into itself the life-history of other organisms and in some degree dominates the energies of its constituent parts.[31]

However, this organismal aspect of Whitehead's philosophy appears to be at odds with other commitments that he makes. In particular, Whitehead retains a Platonist notion of eternal, abstract entities, seemingly motivated by his methodological investment in the abstraction of logic and mathematics, on the one hand, and by his theism on the other. "The primordial created fact is the unconditioned conceptual valuation of the entire multiplicity of eternal objects," writes Whitehead. "This is the 'primordial nature' of God."[32] Of this line of thinking, Dewey writes, "Fundamentally it seems to me that Whitehead has substituted one dualism, that of eternal objects and of concrete actualities, for the older dualism of mind and matter. God seems to be a *deus ex machina* to bring together these dualistic terms."[33] Descartes famously posits the pineal gland as the conduit through which the mind interacts with the body. Following Dewey's assessment, God for Whitehead seems to occupy the place of the pineal gland as a way to rhetorically unify what is in fact an irreconcilable dualism.

Whitehead's mixture of organicism with theism and Platonic logic blurs the boundaries between living and nonliving, and between mind and nonmind. This results in a panpsychic perspective that sees *everything* as possessing a mind. Whitehead writes that

> living bodies can be pursued down to the edge of lifelessness. Also the functionings
> of inorganic matter remain intact amid the functionings of living matter. It seems that,
> in bodies that are obviously living, a coördination has been achieved that raises into
> prominence some functions inherent in the ultimate occasions. For lifeless matter, these
> functions thwart each other, and average out so as to produce a negligible total effect.[34]

For Whitehead, life and mind are eternal essences that suffuse all matter. Depending on how they are counterbalanced by the other aspects of that matter, these functions may or may not make themselves "obvious."

The panpsychic aspect of Whitehead's philosophy has resonated in media and cultural studies in part because it decentralizes the figure of the human in the context of the organisms, objects, and environments with which humans share the universe. This provides new avenues of thinking, for instance, about ecology and embodiment in an era of acute and ongoing environmental crisis. It resonates also with Hansen's conception of "today's media," which, he writes, "impact the general sensibility of the world prior to and as a condition for impacting human experience."[35] For Hansen, Whitehead's organismal mode of philosophy is "invaluable" in supplementing "phenomenological accounts of experience with an ontological conception of total environmental agency" so that phenomenology might "overcome its historical . . . correlation with human perception" in order to "become free to address worldly sensibility more generally, including the sensibility of inanimate entities."[36] While Hansen "wholly concur[s]" with Dewey's critique of Whitehead's "commitment to the prior existence of eternal objects," he finds an attenuated reading of Whitehead's ontology helpful in resituating media within a worldly sensibility that exerts "its impact not solely as a passive source and by being channeled through delimited subjective processes . . . but as an environmental agency enveloping such processes but exceeding them in its total scope."[37]

Regarding the sensibilities of inanimate entities, Shaviro writes, "I must accept that the categories I use to describe myself are also valid for other entities. . . . This means that every entity in the world has its own point of view, just as I do, and that each of them somehow *feels* the other entities with which it comes into contact, much as I do."[38] That Whitehead's dualist approach to antidualism informs Whitehead-inspired cultural and media studies is not a problem in and of itself, but it can have the strange effect of casting all matter (and sensibility of, and the experience of, all matter) in human terms. In my opinion, this gets things upside down. To attempt to deprivilege the human by granting human-like qualities to all things is to privilege human qualities and human experiences as standard. Maybe other things don't *want* to share human qualities and human experiences. Maybe other things don't *want* at all. Granting human-like experience to all things sets human modes of being and experiencing aside as abstract qualities that can be ported from one thing to the next. It is problematic enough to suggest that we can do this from one human to another. Human modes of experience (whether personal or collective or cultural) do not precede human bodies, lives, experiences, and relationships.

CONTAINERS AND THEIR DISCONTENTS

The language used in day-to-day speech to describe the mind—the way we "keep things in" the mind, or "are out of" our minds, or try to "see what is in" the mind of another person—both reflects and buttresses the tendency to conceive of the mind as a kind of enclosure or container. As Mark Johnson points out, this metaphor of containment is central to how we conceive interiority, exteriority, and the boundary between the two:

> Our encounter with containment and boundedness is one of the most pervasive features of our bodily experience. We are intimately aware of our bodies as three-dimensional containers into which we put certain things (food, water, air) and out of which other things emerge (food and water wastes, air, blood, etc.). From the beginning, we experience constant physical containment in our surroundings. . . . We manipulate objects, placing them in containers. . . . In each of these cases there are repeatable spatial and temporal organizations.[39]

By analogy to the impression of our bodies as bounded containers, mental phenomena are commonly described, across languages and cultures, via metaphors of containment, so that ideas are seen to have conceptual content and to themselves be contained by the mind. "These are not *inherent objective properties* of ideas and of the mind," write Johnson and George Lakoff. "They are *interactional properties*, and they reflect the way in which we *conceive* of mental phenomena by virtue of metaphor."[40] We are encouraged by the containment metaphor to see the mind as containing things—concepts, images, meanings—but also as being contained within us.

From here, it is not too far a leap to understanding our bodies as temporary containers for our "selves"—our minds, our souls—selves that may sometimes transcend the boundaries of their fleshy containers through thought, or that may be housed within those boundaries, to be released rather than eliminated on the occasion of the body's destruction. If the body is a mere container for the mind, it is Descartes's res extensa, an unthinking material:

> Although I certainly do possess a body with which I am very closely conjoined; never-theless, because, on the one hand, I have a clear and distinct idea of myself, in as far as I am only a thinking and unextended thing, and as, on the other hand, I possess a distinct idea of body, in as far as it is only an extended and unthinking thing, it is certain that I, [that is, my mind, by which I am what I am], is entirely and truly distinct from my body, and may exist without it.[41]

Like Descartes, Plato is clear about his belief in a transcendent, eternal soul, pre-existing and surviving the body, a soul that is contained within, or enchained by, a temporary, containing body. This belief is in keeping with Plato's wider distinction between the intelligible world of forms and the sensible world of perception. Plato writes of the soul using "the body as a means to study anything, either by seeing or hearing or any other sense—because to use the body as a means is to study a thing through sense—perception."[42] The body is a kind of conduit or apparatus that is employed by the mind. We are a mind, or a soul, looking out *through* the eyes of our body, hearing through its ears. Perception becomes the representation of the world, by our bodies, to our souls. This distinction leads Plato to see art as frivolous at best and dangerous at worst, as it has the ability to destabilize the positivist order imposed by cultural control.

The nineteenth-century poet Emily Dickinson was an especially probing theorist of the mind. Through her experimentation with language, Dickinson performed exploratory research on how minds could be characterized (in poetry) and provoked (through poetry). Meditating on the concept of the mind as a container, and of the power of the container as a metaphor, she writes:

> The Brain — is wider than the Sky —
> For — put them side by side —
> The one the other will contain
> With ease — and You — beside —
>
> The Brain is deeper than the sea —
> For — hold them — Blue to Blue —
> The one the other will absorb —
> As Sponges — Buckets — do —

The Brain is just the weight of God —
For — Heft them — Pound for Pound —
And they will differ — if they do —
As Syllable from Sound —[43]

The brain here is "wide" in its ability to contain concepts and images that encapsulate the immensity of nature as an idea. Confronted with the boundless sweep of the sky, the mind can contain it as a concept, much as a poem can contain it in the three letters *s-k-y*. Three more letters can contain "you," and your mind's containment of the concept of you is a recursive maneuver in which the container contains itself, or at least appears to do so. But your mind contains not you, yourself, but "you," the concept. This pattern continues to develop throughout the rest of the poem, in which internal imagery (the "blue" of the brain) corresponds to the external world (the blue of the sea), the concept of God comes to reside within the humble mind, and the mind itself comes to be godlike in its dominion over the concepts that it contains in the internal theater that it creates.

Dickinson asserts the power of the human mind to generate and to contain ideas, and also celebrates the brain as the material substrate of the abstractions that allow people to grapple conceptually with the world around them. "Brain" means mind to Dickinson, but it also means brain, the thing. Her final line, which aligns the brain with "syllable," while God (and, by extension, all of the natural world that has been invoked in the earlier stanzas) is aligned with "sound," emphasizes the centrality of the containment metaphor in the notion of the mind that the poem explores. Syllables are sounds given intentional structure, articulated for semantic content. They "contain" by making reference outward into the world, much as minds in dualist, Cartesian models refer outward from their subjective internal realms. So images or concepts have content and are contained by the mind, which is contained by the person, who is contained in the wider world but who also is capable of taking the world in, of conceiving of its features and thereby absorbing it, as a sponge or a bucket might absorb water, blue and all.

REACHING FOR THE WORLD

Following Dewey, Noë, and others, I have suggested that we think of perceiving and knowing as exploratory action rather than as absorptive containment. When *The Unfinished Swan* requires its players to produce visual perceptions of the game world by throwing balls of paint, it revisits a seeming contradiction between projective and introjective vision pointed out by Christian Metz:

I have the impression at once that, to use a common expression, I am "casting" my eyes on things, and that the latter, thus illuminated, come to be deposited within me. . . . A sort of stream called the look . . . must be sent out over the world, so that objects can come back up this stream in the opposite direction (but using it to find their way), arriving at last at our perception, which is now soft wax and no longer an emitting source.[44]

Metz calls the receptive mode of perception "soft wax," echoing Plato's suggestion that memory is like a wax tablet on which perceptions and thoughts are imprinted—a metaphoric equivalency between mind and media.[45] While Metz calls his impression a "banal fantasy," perhaps it contains more truth than he acknowledges. The contradiction at the heart of this account arises from holding perception and the perceived at a distance from one another, so that vision must cover a distance by being cast (or projected) out across it, and then must, on its return trip, cover that same gap between the outer and the inner world, arriving at a now-receptive apparatus. If we take perception to be a mode of continuous and active participation in the world, there is no such gap to mind, so to speak. Metz's contradiction is not in thinking of perception as something one actively does; it is in his separation of the act of perception into separate aspects, namely (active) casting of his eyes and (passive) reception of images.

Even in the cinema, this perception is never purely visual or audiovisual. In her phenomenological study of cinema, Jennifer Barker argues that cinematic experience should be understood in terms not just of vision and hearing but of tactility, or of bodily commitment, across the traditional, ostensibly discrete, sensory domains of vision, touch, taste, smell, and hearing. Barker writes in particular of "the imbrication of vision and touch," claiming that "it is the combination of our gaze at the movie screen and our muscular body's commitment to the film space that allows for our feeling of being there."[46] Here again is a problem highlighted by Metz, who wrote that it is "no accident that the main socially acceptable arts are based on the senses at a distance, and that those which depend on the senses of contact are often regarded as 'minor' arts."[47] Barker's formulation of vision as a tactile sense, a form of contact, resolves the tension in Metz's thinking between viewer and viewed, between vision and the other senses, by closing the gap between them. In place of that gap is direct feeling.

This direct feeling entails not only an intimate connection with the world but also an obligation to it. The world is here for the touching, and it is up to us to discover how to touch it. Given the differences in our bodies, our environments, and our sociocultural contexts, each of us can, and will, touch it differently. The world of *The Unfinished Swan* is there to be made visible through our paint-throwing and our exploration of its environments, just as the world of another game is there to be made visible by the simple act of turning the game on and exploring it. A film, likewise, must be watched and listened to in order to be seen and heard. These are all investments of time and energy on the part of media users. Media worlds, we might say, are there for us only inasmuch as we reach for them. This does not make them exceptional; it is an aspect of their worldly nature.

The film director Robert Bresson writes of his desire to "translate the invisible wind by the water it sculpts in passing."[48] To Bresson, a spiritual and religious film-maker, this surely means to expose the face of the divine as it makes itself apparent through the workings of the material world. But Bresson was also highly attuned to perception, action, vision, and hearing as material phenomena, and his films are both tribute and testimony to the interrelatedness of things, to the transactional relationships among objects, entities, perception, and environments. At the same time, Bresson's metaphor could describe relationships among any number of things—pointedly, the relationship between the world and the celluloid that records images of it in filming, but also the relationship between media and the mind. In this equation, which is the wind and which is the water? Is the mind the invisible wind that "sculpts" the sights and sounds of cinema? Or is the perception of cinema the wind that gives shape to the mind? The former interpretation is cognitivist, as it sees the mind as a framing force that performs an operation on the film text. The latter is more in line with strains of media theory that see film form as a discursive and psychological framework that imposes a perspective on the spectator. I would argue that these approaches look for answers in the wrong places. The mind is in the *dynamic* between things. It is the sculpting itself. And this sculpting is never unidirectional. It is just as well to say that the water sculpts the wind.

THE STORY OF THE BLIND MAN'S STICK

The dynamic that Bresson proposes, and to which he aspires in his filmmaking, is characterized by a relationship with invisibility. Vision has long been privileged as the dominant sense for orientation, for understanding, and for gaining insight about one's position in the world. For this reason, blindness, both literal and metaphoric, has come to be a recurring trope in explorations of perception, affect, and conceptualization. The figure of a blind man feeling his way through the world with a stick or a cane appears time and again in attempts to move beyond thinking of experience of the world, and of the world itself, in purely visual terms, and, further, in rethinking the physical boundaries of what we call experience. For instance, Merleau-Ponty writes that

> the blind man's stick has ceased to be an object for him, and is no longer perceived for itself: its point has become an area of sensitivity, extending the scope and active radius of the touch, and providing a parallel to sight . . . the length of the stick does not enter expressly as a middle term: the blind man is rather aware of it through the position of objects rather than of the position of objects through it.[49]

Similarly, the novelist Gregor von Rezzori opens his novel *An Ermine in Czernopol* with an account of a drunk man, functionally blind, feeling his way home from a midnight bar by probing the ground with his cane, only to find himself locked into a rail groove, by which he "then lets himself be led as if tethered to a pole."[50] The probing stick becomes a conduit through which the man's motion through the world is directed, a substitute for sight that also becomes the medium through which a "picture" of the world, and the possibilities for action in it, are formed.

The anthropologist Gregory Bateson frames the relationship between a blind man and his stick in terms of the self: "Consider a blind man with a stick," he writes. "Where does the blind man's self begin? At the tip of the stick? At the handle of the stick? Somewhere halfway up the stick?"[51] More recently, Alva Noë has suggested that the perceptual tapping of a blind man's stick is a productive metaphor for *all* perception, an indication that our senses, including vision, are produced not passively but by active engagement with the world at large.[52] And the cognitive archaeologist Lambros Malafouris writes that the metaphor of the stick, especially as applied by Bateson, serves as a reminder that "what we often see as a fixed human nature is more a flexible process of ongoing human becoming—a process still in progress and largely unfinished."[53] Not unlike a painting of a swan.

In each of these accounts, we find an assertion that to understand vision, we must first think about its context, but the literal and metaphoric power of vision is such that in order to think about its relationship to its context, we must imagine that context without it. Each of these writers seeks to narrow the conceptual gap between vision and the other senses. Vision is neither discrete, nor passive, nor internal, but an activity that is part of sighted people's way of being present in the world. The blending that occurs, the blurring of the boundaries between the perception of the object and that of the world (Merleau-Ponty), the borders of the "self" in the context of objects and environment (Bateson), the status of one's humanity in space and time (Malafouris), the relationships between the senses (Noë), and the status of volition in a world whose structures we can only ever dimly perceive (von Rezzori), all point to a further blurring of the distinction between "internal" and "external" experience.

The visible world of *The Unfinished Swan* is disclosed only as players bring about its visibility through systematic interaction with its surfaces. When the game begins, there is already a world there, but players cannot see it. It is audible and players can move through it in limited ways without ever throwing paint, but it is unnavigable without use of the paint-throwing mechanic. Throwing the paint, and throwing it effectively, is a prerequisite skill for players being able to make their way through the world and the narrative of the game. Perception of the environment and of the navigational and interactive possibilities it presents is contingent on players' ability to make it visible.

What difference, then, is there between throwing the paint and "feeling" through the game's world in a tactile sense? Isn't the paint in *The Unfinished Swan* like a blind person's cane, or like a hand cautiously extended outward into a dark room? Noë has suggested that "a blind person tap-tapping his or her way around a cluttered space, perceiving that space by touch, not all at once, but through time, by skillful probing and movement," ought to be "our paradigm for what perceiving is."[54] From this perspective, what players do in *The Unfinished Swan* is not so dramatically different from simply moving through the world of any video game, which, like the paint-throwing in *The Unfinished Swan*, brings new spaces and possibilities into view and into grasp. To navigate the world of a game is to trace its geographic and enactive contours. To move a virtual character's body laterally via the left control stick in an FPS, or to reframe a virtual camera via the right control stick in a third-person game, is likewise to probe the game world, unveiling its textures and limits. And then, how different is this from moving our own bodies through the wider world that we occupy? Don't we make perceptual events by bringing ourselves into the presence of the world's spaces and extending ourselves into them in any ways that our bodies permit—like a probe or a blind person's cane, like a thrown ball of paint, like a turn of the head or a saccade of the eyes? By foregrounding the active nature of perception, *The Unfinished Swan* calls attention not only to how active perception always is in games, but to how active perception is in general. Rather than establishing game-specific, exceptional kinds of perception, then, games like *The Unfinished Swan* in fact do just the opposite, revealing the continuity among media, and between media and the world, by disrupting players' habits and inviting them to consider perception anew. To do so is to trouble not only the figure of perception as a conduit from external world to the internal world of the mind, but to undermine the very notion of the mind as something with an inside and an outside.

INSIDE AND OUT

The films *Inside Out* and *L'Argent* are a study of the differences between interactional and transactional thinking in cinema. The former film was produced by the Disney subsidiary Pixar, which specializes in computer-generated animation and has close ties to Silicon Valley through its origins in Lucasfilm's computer division and subsequent investment by Apple founder Steve Jobs. *Inside Out* proposes a world composed of discrete, interacting parts, an ethos that pervades the film from its computerized mode of production to its conception of the human mind as a committee of entities interpreting information presented to them by the senses. *L'Argent*, the last film of Robert Bresson's long career, is more interested in action in the world, and specifically in the tension between the felt nature of ecological transactions between humans and their environments, on the one hand, and the highly structured and regulated nature of financial transactions, on the other. The films thereby articulate ideas about interactions and transactions both in their narratives and in their representational structures.

Inside Out tells the story of a girl named Riley and her uneasy adaptation to her family's move across the country to San Francisco. The film depicts Riley's internal life through anthropomorphized emotions Joy, Anger, Disgust, Fear, and Sadness, who sit in a control center in her brain, observing the events of the outside world on a screen and driving her subsequent reactions via a computerized interface. The emotions are represented as animated caricatures, each associated with a color and a gendered personality stereotype: Joy is an exuberant, pixyish woman who glows yellow, while Anger is a squat, square man with red skin who shoots fire from his scalp when he is enraged. Riley's behavior is depicted as a result of interactions, and sometimes arguments, between these discrete and competing drives. Much of the screen time is taken up not by Riley's story in the external world but by an adventure in which Joy and Sadness have to travel through a landscape that represents the space inside Riley's mind. This space is conceived on a mostly psychoanalytic model featuring, for example, a prison of the unconscious that houses traumatic memories and a train of thought visualized, rather inanely, as an actual locomotive.

Inside Out conceives of relations between humans and their environment along an interactionist paradigm, depicting its characters as physical shells for the workings of their minds, which transpire in an inner sphere and which guide the behavior of the characters. The screen on which the emotions view the world is a collective version of what philosopher Daniel Dennett calls the "Cartesian theater," or a view of the mind in which some kind of internal observing entity or "chief executive" watches and responds to the images brought into the mind by the senses.[55] This purported internal viewer is sometimes called a homunculus. In *Inside Out*, that which views internal images is not a single executive homunculus but five homunculi, a committee who collectively hash out what Riley will do next. *Inside Out* views action, whether physical action in the world or psychological action in the mind, as the work of autonomous entities acting upon one another. It further depicts memory as a recording medium in which images and sounds are encapsulated in transparent orbs that glow with colors corresponding to the emotions with which they are associated. A happy memory might be colored yellow for Joy, while a more melancholic one will take on a bluish cast, the color associated with Sadness. Later in the film, it is revealed that memories can change color over time, depending on which emotions handle them, and that not all memories last, as they are periodically evaluated for relevance and discarded by maintenance workers.

At every turn, *Inside Out* divides its world. Memories are treated as complete units, with beginnings and ends, snatched from the continuity of life and independent of one another. Humans are fundamentally disconnected from one another and from the objects and environments that surround them. Over the course of the film, it is revealed that all of the characters, including domestic animals like cats and dogs, have their own anthropomorphic or zoomorphic interior drives that determine their behavior. Each of these committees has its own screen through which it views the world, so that every "self" is divided from the world around it, and each self is divided into discrete actors in competition or cooperation with one another. Echoing the digital logic of the computer animation in which they are instantiated, these bits and pieces of characters and events come together, each acting according to its own granular nature, to produce the action of the film, in both the external realm of Riley's world and the internal realm of her mind. The relationship between the inner and the outer is presented via the logic of mediation, through the screen in Riley's mind and the console through which the emotions guide her behavior. *Inside Out* imagines action as interaction, perception as mediation, everything always at a remove from everything else.

By contrast, *L'Argent* concerns itself with transactions, both perceptual and financial, in the material world. A previously duped businessman disposes of a counterfeit bill by passing it off on a young man named Yvon. Yvon unwittingly attempts to spend the fake money, and he is arrested. As a result of the arrest and the time he spends in jail, his life begins to unravel. He loses his job and family, becomes involved in violent crime, and eventually murders the owners of a hotel for money and then, for obscure reasons, an entire family who have taken him under their wing at their rural farm. At the film's conclusion, he finally turns himself in to the police.

Throughout *L'Argent*, Yvon is depicted as a passive participant in the events that shape his life, present for their occurrence but unable to get a handle on the workings of the world around him. Yvon and the film itself seem to want to feel something about the world, to touch its material surfaces. Bresson's camera lingers on details of scenes in unconventional ways, taking in events from uncommon and at times confounding angles, such as a car chase filmed almost entirely in static shots of automobile pedals and a side-view mirror. Toward the end of the film, the editing becomes more elliptical, with the climactic action of the murders entirely elided from the film's visual depiction of events. In these ways, the film seems to be trying to feel its way toward an understanding of the world, its images and sounds the results of a tactile relationship in which none of the terms are taken for granted. The CGI worlds of *Inside Out*, both the inner and the outer world of Riley's appearance, are made up out of whole digital cloth. They are technological simulations in a way that is wholly appropriate to the film's own view of the mind as a kind of computational simulation. *L'Argent*, on the other hand, is more interested in tap-tapping its way around the world of its filming, in feeling out the contours of its spaces, occupants, and possibilities.

Bresson was a prolific writer of aphorisms about filmmaking, in which he laid out a set of principles for his own work. In his book *Notes on the Cinematographer*, Bresson sees a world whole, the principal intrigue of which is in its continuity: "one single mystery of persons and objects,"[56] as he calls it, in which the "cinematographer is making a voyage of discovery on an unknown planet."[57] The task of the cinematographer (by which Bresson means a director sensitive to the medium and to the world) is to fragment the world into moments, shots, sounds, to "see beings and things in their separate parts," a separation that is a product of the seeing and not in the things seen. Rather than attempting faithfully to recreate "the" world, or to create an illusion of realism, Bresson seeks to render things and beings "independent in order to give them a new dependence."[58] The transactional continuity of the world is transformed, via the work of filmmaking, into a cinematic transaction that produces new, but no less continuous, relationships between its textual form and the world at large. A thing is made of discrete parts, and a thing is a *thing*, only inasmuch as it is rhetorically framed to be so. Where we see clear divisions among things or clear distinctions of scale, there is nonetheless only spatiotemporal continuity. As *L'Argent* strives to be faithful, but not identical, to the continuity of the world, Yvon becomes a kind of proxy for the struggle of the artist to maintain a position of tactile engagement with an environment in which powerful forces—forces of habit and rhetoric and, most notably for *L'Argent*, forces of capital—conspire to differentiate the world, to modularize it and divide it from him.

It is thus fitting that the film's narrative revolves around the financial transaction, the one transactional model to which capitalism would reduce all others. If, as in the ideal of the competitive marketplace, money is taken to be the arbiter of rightness, not to mention righteousness, the financial transaction is a site at which (as in Dewey's transactional knowing) action includes the actor and the acted-upon, as the one is quantifiably depleted and the other equivalently enriched by the exchange. Currency becomes how one extends oneself out into the world, how one moves from the isolation of self-action to the worldly integration of transaction. This in turn effects a transformation of how we imagine the self, as the status and power of selfhood becomes identical with the status of the self as a bearer of currency. Selfhood, then, is measured as currency, so that the "money" of the film's title refers both to currency and to Yvon himself. As a bearer of illegitimate currency, Yvon is rendered illegitimate by the order of law.

Capitalism thrives on the abstraction of value into currency. The exchange of currency becomes the arbiter of value and is thus both a means of imposing a law of value and a tool by which to effect an abstraction of labor. As in Yvon's experience, financial transactions come to stand in for perceptual transactions, and the affected parties are ultimately reduced to seeing themselves along an interactional model, as self-motivated actors in perpetual competition with one another for limited, quantifiable resources and commodities, connected to one another only through the exceptional case that is the financial transaction. Brian Price sees just such a suppression of worldly feeling when he argues that, through Yvon's reticence throughout *L'Argent*, Bresson represents "the chain of exploitation at work in a capitalist economy as opposed to how various members of that chain feel about it."[59]

The members of that chain may feel differently at different times. When one has a bit of money in one's pocket, this interactional model can in fact be a flattering way to see oneself, an illusion on which capitalism is primed to prey. The radically free individual, moving in an interactional world populated by the same, may seem to be in a position of privilege, but this illusion of freedom is ultimately productive only of regulation, measurement, and control. Until the film's end, Yvon quietly resists this interpellation, but the structures of his social and economic world permit no such escape. In one sequence, Yvon follows a woman on her way out of town. The film here pulls back from its intimate gestural detail to wider shots that reveal the pastoral setting in which the subsequent action of the film takes place, leading up to Yvon's murder of the woman and her family. At the conclusion of *L'Argent*, Yvon presents himself to the police: "It was me that murdered the hotel couple for their money, and me that just killed a whole family." This is not just a confession to the law but a surrender to an order that he can no longer resist, an order in which money is the sole currency of transaction and in which a person like Yvon can only be this or that, criminal or not, subject to a law that is indifferent, if not downright hostile, to his inherent connections with the world around him.

If *L'Argent* wants to feel its way toward the surfaces of the world, *Inside Out* is more interested in modeling the processes that underlie those surfaces. But in doing so, it settles on a model of these processes as fundamentally discrete from the world outside the body, outside the mind. Riley's "self" becomes a container defined both by what it keeps in and by what it keeps out, so that each side—mind and world—is rendered virtual to the other.

Troubling the idea of a boundary between inside and out, restoring what Bresson calls the "one single mystery," Maurice Merleau-Ponty wrote that "inside and outside are inseparable. The world is wholly inside and I am wholly outside myself."[60] Like Bresson, Merleau-Ponty is here attuned to the perils of the containment metaphor, a convincing and convenient model that misrepresents the true nature of ecological being in the world.

REACHING FOR THE WORLD

Media texts and technologies are at once sites of research for their users and forms of research for their designers. To design a console or a projector or to create a video game or a film is to explore a position in the world, to initiate a speculative encounter among technology, environment, and organism. To use media is to perform research into their structures and constraints, always in the contexts of the structures and constraints of our own wider world of experience. To engage with media, whether as a creator or as a user, is to perform research into the nature and texture of experience of and beyond those media texts and technologies. If to research is to search forcefully, then research is a kind of probing action, like the action of the blind man's stick, a feeling out not merely of one's environment but always of one's relation to that environment. This probing is never disembodied but always a function of one's own physical presence, whether we are feeling our way through the world with a stick or with our eyes, feeling our way through a game world with a joystick or with thrown paint, or feeling our way through a concept with spoken language or with words on a page.

In another poem, Emily Dickinson conceives of the mind in a way radically different from the one she articulates in "The brain is wider than the sky." While that poem considers the mind as a container for concepts and perception, here Dickinson is more attuned to reciprocal action in the world:

> We grow accustomed to the Dark —
> When Light is put away —

As when the Neighbor holds the Lamp
To witness her Good bye —

A Moment — We uncertain step
For Newness of the night —
Then — fit our Vision to the Dark —
And meet the Road — erect —

And so of larger — Darknesses —
Those Evenings of the Brain —
When not a Moon disclose a sign —
Or Star — come out — within —

The Bravest — grope a little —
And sometimes hit a Tree
Directly in the Forehead —
But as they learn to see —

Either the Darkness alters —
Or something in the sight
Adjusts itself to Midnight —
And Life steps almost straight.[61]

Dickinson depicts an intertwined relationship between the body and the environment, not only in perceiving, but in conceiving of the most fundamental and concrete concerns, such as physical navigation, as well as existential "larger darknesses." To step onto a literal dark road is to feel one's way through a local, bounded problem (though always in the context of a wider environment), yet to grapple with the broader constraints of life itself is to feel out the relationship between the cosmic and the personal. To struggle against a cloud of depression, or against the looming specter of death, is to feel one's way through a body and a world constantly transforming. Through "We grow accustomed to the Dark," Dickinson provides yet another model for transactional thinking about how we feel through the world and through media—which are, after all, parts of the world, parts of our lives, and parts of our minds. We need only reach toward them.

CHAPTER 2

Feeling through the World

Skilled Perception in a Changing Environment

You look down a country road, seen onscreen in first-person perspective (figure 2.1). A horse-drawn carriage rushes past. Soon after, an open-topped motorcar barrels straight toward you, filling the screen at the moment of impact.

In its one-minute runtime, Cecil Hepworth's 1900 film *How It Feels to Be Run Over* encapsulates the promise and the delirium of new media experience. In its formal aspect, the film reverses the trajectory of the beginning of *The Unfinished Swan*. It opens on a black-and-white world, revealing a path extending into the depth of the image, a path to be taken in this case not by you but by the vehicles rushing toward you. In place of the structuring blackness of paint launched outward into the environment, the black motorcar bears down upon you from out in the environment, and when it reaches its target, it will extinguish, rather than establish, perception. In place of the initial white canvas of *The Unfinished Swan* is the final black screen of *How It Feels to Be Run Over*. The former is a void to be filled, the latter a void that has been emptied.

Despite these oppositions, the video game and the film share a deeper affinity. Each stages an encounter, in a nascent medium, that facilitates a new mode of presence and new conditions for perception. Each thematically maps feeling and vision onto one another, foregrounding the tactility of visual perception. And each calls attention to the transactional relationships among media and users, reminding us that things in the world—paint and cars, roads and rooms, films and video games— are not merely objects for perception but participants in perception. They become meaningful not by way of what they are or what we invest in them, but by how they participate, along with their users, in the context of a particular place and time.

This chapter characterizes perception as *feeling through the world*. As I use it, this phrase has at least two complementary senses. First, it describes a form of

Figure 2.1 *How It Feels to Be Run Over* (Cecil Hepworth, 1901): the approach and impact of the automobile.

environmental exploration. As in the story of the blind man's stick recounted in the previous chapter, this sense of feeling is not limited to the tactile but is meant to imply the active, probing nature of motion, emotion, and perception, including touch and also sight, smell, and so on. At the same time, the phrase "feeling through the world" is attuned to the bodily *and* environmental nature of felt experience. As I have been arguing, feeling is not an internal and discrete phenomenon but rather an aspect of transactions among bodies and their environments. We feel our way through the world, and it is by way of the world that we feel. These are two separate senses of "feeling through the world" only by habit of thought and by convention of language. On a more elemental level, they are two noncontradictory ways of describing the same phenomenon from different perspectives.

As the world changes, minds change with it. Or minds change with the times, not because they are newly altered or augmented from without but because they are constituted by changing bodies undergoing continuous experience in changing environments. Put another way, minds are ecological phenomena. The introduction of social pressure, an idea, a psychoactive drug, a new medium, or a tool can alter a mind in a narrow sense, but these should not be thought of as external influences upon the mind but rather as material participants in the mind, as contributing factors in what that mind is. In its physiological and psychological dimensions, media use is no less and no more a material transaction than is grasping a stick with a human hand. Even if it is not designed as a tool, say if its user picks it up from the ground where it has fallen from a tree, a stick used in this way is a technology. To lift the stick, to feel its weight, to put it to use is to perform a kind of research into the world, into oneself, and into the stick—to feel them all out by the ways that they touch, affect, and move through one another. Likewise, the development, exploration, and exploitation of new media technologies and texts represent a form of active research into their constraints, as well as the creation of new tools for probing the constraints of the environment and the creatures and other objects that populate it.

As chapter 1 began to illustrate, perception is active, embodied, and environmental. It is neither automatic nor passive. Perception, indeed, is a skill, and skills do not come to us from out of nowhere. They must be developed, and once acquired they remain contingent. Contexts change, as do bodies, and new challenges arise, and skills are only useful in the extent to which they are adaptable to new situations. Skills, in other words, are not transcendent or universal but situationally specific. "Acquiring" is not really the right word. Once you "have" a skill, it remains yours only inasmuch as you are able to adapt it to changing situations. The corporate language of "skill sets" and "retraining" treats skills, like workers, as interchangeable and replaceable units. In reality, skills are never so discrete. Jobs are not containers for workers, and workers are not containers for skills. Skills overlap and inform one another, and (again like workers) their true strength is not in their individuation but in their collectivity.

In a biological sense, skills are developmental. They are adaptations to the affordances and constraints of a particular body and to the availability over a lifetime of a particular set of tools and resources, and they are responses to the events that transpire in a particular environment. Even a skill such as perception, so primary that it can seemingly become transparent, is learned, and even such a skill develops and changes continually over the course of a lifetime. As mentioned in the previous chapter, psychologist Louise Barrett characterizes development as "learning to live in our bodies" when she argues that each person has to feel his or her way toward a sensorimotor way of being in the world:

> This is because all bodies are different. We learn how to exploit our specific bodily resources, and that requires "customized" learning strategies and developmental trajectories. . . . Development isn't an "inevitable march toward maturity" but something more fluid: a process that unfolds over time . . . as the result of the varying interplay of multiple internal and external influences.[1]

We feel our way through the months and years, developing the skills and pursuing the information we need to negotiate the challenges and opportunities, large and small, that we encounter. This requires familiarizing ourselves with bodies that are in varying degrees of structural flux over the courses of our lives.

We should not forget the babies that we were. We are no longer those babies, but those babies are now us. Development unfolds over time, as Barrett writes, and although it might be convenient to identify "stages" in this development, in truth it is continuous, from one moment to the next and throughout a lifetime. Building on his observation that babies must learn to perceive and conceive of the world, Mark Johnson characterizes adults as "big babies" in the sense that the "bodily ways by which infants and children find and make meaning are not transcended and left behind when children eventually grow into adulthood" but are rather employed in and refined into our adult acts of "conceptualization and reasoning."[2] The perceptual demands placed on us, and thus the things that we must do in order to perceive, change along with changes in our bodies, with the opportunities and limitations of the environments that we happen to inhabit, and with the actions, feelings, habits, desires, and bodies of the people we meet.

We must reckon, too, with the constraints of the media that we encounter. Media operate as much by way of introducing perceptual constraints on their users as they do by offering new opportunities for perception. In fact, they offer new opportunities for perception precisely by way of constraining their users. In order to play a game or watch a film, or even to idly observe the images from an ambient screen in a public place, a media user must engage the media rather than doing something else. Look here and not there, do this with your hands and not another thing, listen to this and not that. Commit your body, your effort, your time. This productive constraint pertains to media form as well. As early as 1933, Rudolf Arnheim argued that the perceptual constraints particular to the medium of film, the ways in which "the basic elements of the film medium" differ from "what we perceive 'in reality,'" are precisely what "provide film with its artistic resources."[3] Film's expressive power, in other words, is in what it takes away from its users. Ian Bogost makes a similar point about video games: "The power of games lies not in their capacity to deliver rewards or enjoyment, but in the structured constraint of their design, which opens abundant possible spaces for play."[4] As we shall see in more depth in chapters 4 and 5, users constrain media as well. This mutual constraint, and the new possibilities it brings about, sometimes goes by the name "emergence."

Media's constraints present challenges to their users' learned habits and skills. One of the fundamental pleasures of media use is in rising to the perceptual challenges that media present. Challenges of this kind can be more or less benign. Hollywood filmmaking tends to ease the perceptual burden on its audience, while avant-garde film intensifies it. Big-budget commercial video games tend to adhere to conventional modes of control, while art games often work to confound user expectations and break habits of gameplay. *The Unfinished Swan* is somewhere in the middle. It is by no means a game of the radical avant-garde, and its mapping of perception onto action soon becomes incidental to its narrative. The initial moments of *The Unfinished Swan*, however, are surprising, pleasurable, and productive in thinking through the active nature of perception in video games.

The connection between surprise, pleasure, and productivity in video games is sometimes described as "flow." A concept borrowed from the work of psychologist Mihaly Csikszentmihalyi, flow in video game studies describes the sensation of being balanced between challenge and proficiency, so that a player must continually improve his or her skills in a game to meet mounting challenges.[5] This chapter offers a Deweyan rereading of the concept of flow in light of a phenomenon that Dewey, decades before Csikszentmihalyi articulated the idea of flow, called "smooth-running functions."

Throughout this chapter, I discuss films and games that disrupt the smooth-running functions of perception and action in a variety of ways. As you might have surmised from what you have read thus far, I argue that this disruption is not unique to these films and games but is in fact something that all media do. Here I focus on exemplary cases that foreground their disruptions in ways that denaturalize the perception of media and prompt users to reconsider the historically contingent skills, conventions, and habits that shape their own ways of perceiving.

As the example of *The Unfinished Swan* has already shown, video game play can make users aware of skills, like perception, that they may tend to take for granted as automatic. In this chapter, this perception-revealing quality of media is further explored via a discussion of how media teach their users how to use them, and how they then, to varying degrees, work to complicate and confound those learned ways of feeling. *How It Feels to Be Run Over* addresses its contemporaneous viewers in a historical moment, the turn of the twentieth century, at which the lived perceptual environment was rapidly evolving. Video games like *QWOP* (Bennett Foddy, 2008) and *Microtone* (increpare, 2011) subvert player expectations, forcing them to develop new skills in order to move through and perceive their worlds. In the film *Certified Copy* (Abbas Kiarostami, 2010), we find characters engaged in a kind of mutual game in which they trouble the boundaries of their (and viewers') understanding of the relationships among the characters in the film and of the actions that the characters take. As the characters feel their way through their (diegetic) world, viewers feel out their own relationship to the film's ambiguous depiction of the relations and relationships among its characters. These new modes of being, or new ways of feeling through perception, action, and experience in media, can help us to rethink our relationship to volition, determinism, and action in our wider world. Working within the constraints of media, in other words, can help us to more clearly see, and to more effectively negotiate, that which constrains us and thereby constrains our possibilities for perception, action, and experience, every day of our lives.

HOW IT FEELS . . .

Released in an era of technological and perceptual upheaval, at the dawn both of cinema and of the motorcar, *How It Feels to Be Run Over* addresses an audience that is reassessing its ways of being present in the world. The illusions of the cinema offer new sensations and new ways of imagining space and time.[6] They place unprecedented perceptual demands on their audience, by "offering a new sort of stimulus" with an "accent on direct stimulation," as Tom Gunning puts it, and by demanding new modes of cognitive investment in comprehending their increasingly complex narratives.[7] Meanwhile, the mechanical world is accelerating all around, proliferated by new opportunities and new threats. Well into what has been called the "Second Industrial Revolution," people are immersed in what Davis S. Landes calls the "lusty childhood . . . of electrical power and motors; organic chemistry and synthetics; the internal-combustion engine and automotive devices; precision manufacture and assembly-line production."[8] In what Vaclav Smil terms an "age of synergy" lasting from about 1867 to 1914, "scientific advances, technical innovation, aggressive commercialization, and intensifying, and increasingly efficient, conversions of energy" feed into one another in unprecedented ways, creating a closely knit relationship among technology, commerce, and science that forms the basis for the "first truly global human impacts."[9]

More locally, and more personally, these sorts of changes unsettle the world of perception on a moment-to-moment basis. The changing contexts of everyday life, and the new media that reflect them and arise within them, make especially vivid the active nature of perceptual experience. The act of crossing a country road has been altered, intensified, and defamiliarized. So, too, has the act of seeing a road, a carriage, or a motorcar, which is now possible at a new kind of spatiotemporal distance, thanks to cinema. These changes to the world of perception further remind us that the meanings that we "find" in objects are not inherent to them or to us, nor do they occur in them or us in response to prodding by the other. They are produced in the transactions we share with objects—in how we approach them and in how they approach us. Increasingly, they approach us in rushes, on the street and on the screen. *How It Feels to Be Run Over* is attuned to this onslaught, which it both addresses and exploits in its provocation of its contemporary audience. Seen in retrospect, the film also reads as a meditation on its own technological and perceptual moment, an attempt to see and to feel with new technology and thereby to seize an opportunity, offered by this very newness, to explore the ways that new technologies structure seeing and feeling and how they thereby explore seeing and feeling themselves. As James Leo Cahill writes, this and other early British films that feature "choreographed accidents" function as "visual documentation of lines of technical research that dramatize their struggles with technology and contingency."[10] Karen Beckman emphasizes the tactile character of this documentation. *How It Feels to Be Run Over*, Beckman writes, "emphasizes cinema less as a medium of vision than as a feeling machine."[11]

In more detail now: in the single shot of *How It Feels to Be Run Over*, you look down an unpaved country road. A horse-drawn carriage approaches from around a bend, charges rapidly forward as if about to hit you, a narrative expectation and a resulting moment of suspense for which you might be primed by the film's title.

Then, relief as the carriage passes off the screen to the right, kicking up a cloud of dust as it goes by. But out of the haze emerges an open-topped automobile, headed straight for you. Its passengers gesticulate, urging you to move out of the car's way, but the camera stays put and the bumper of the car fills the screen, which cuts at the moment of impact to a series of handwritten title cards, white on black, reading "?? / !!! / ! / Oh! / Mother / will / be / pleased." Then, nothing.

The title *How It Feels to Be Run Over* promises vicarious experience, but what kind of experience does the film provide? If we regard film exclusively as a visual medium, we might resist the idea that this film could make us "feel" in a tactile or kinesthetic sense. But while *How It Looks to Be Run Over* might be a more accurate title for what the film *shows*, the film provokes more than a purely optical experience. At once, it participates in the technological "frenzy of the visible" that Jean-Louis Comolli has identified with the late nineteenth century, in which "movement becomes a visible mechanics" by way of the industrialization of motion, repetition, and reproduction, and it also reflects upon the anxiety of embodied presence in a changing technological environment.[12] As Vivian Sobchack writes, "our capacity . . . to touch, to smell, to taste, and . . . [to] feel our weight, dimension, gravity, and movement in the world" constantly informs our vision and hearing, "even at the movies."[13] The movement of the vehicles onscreen provokes the sight and the other bodily sensations associated with rapidly approaching objects in experience outside of the cinema, but the immobility of the camera is perhaps most powerfully felt in the way that it seems to constrain our own motion. The framing of the shot implies vicarious bodily presence in the world of the film, but you are powerless to move the camera out of the way of the car. The disconnect between your visual immersion in the scene and your inability to act to save yourself (or the camera) from the imminent impact is a fundamental source of the film's power. *How It Feels to Be Run Over* is concerned less with pain than with powerlessness.

In both its textual form and its technological format, then, the film foregrounds bodily encounters with new technologies. The horse-drawn carriage misses you, but the automobile hits you. (It is worth noting that the connotations of the phrase "run over" are evolving and expanding with technological change; when you are run over in the old way—trampled by a horse—you are being run, literally, over.) Two decades earlier, Eadweard Muybridge's zoopraxiscope study *Sallie Gardner at a Gallop* (1878) redefined the perception of animal locomotion by breaking it into discretely observable parts, objectifying organic action in a new way. Auguste and Louis Lumière's *Arrival of a Train at La Ciotat* (1895) famously, if apocryphally, incited panic in its viewers in their near-miss confrontation with an onscreen train.[14] *How It Feels to Be Run Over* intervenes in this historical moment, building suspense with the organic velocity of the horse-drawn carriage before realizing the threat of harm via the technological velocity of the automobile. But both velocities are ultimately aspects of the velocity of the image itself, as is the inertia of the film's framing. As Tom Gunning writes, when early films stage confrontations between moving objects and an immobile frame, "It is the framing itself, its marking of the act of display, that remains primary. The spectator is directly addressed, even confronted, by these plays with framing."[15] It is because the image of *How It Feels to Be Run Over* moves that we cannot; if we accept its perspective as a proxy for our embodiment in the diegesis, we assume its point of view but sacrifice our ability to move. The technological onslaught is twofold, with two technologies, car and camera, on a collision course. The approaching car provokes reflection on the mechanical action of the camera and on the tensions between its physical positioning (relative to the car) and our own (relative to the screen).

Perhaps it is no accident, so to speak, that Cecil Hepworth, the film's director, appears in the film as the driver of the car, turning over his usual spot behind the camera to business partner Henry Vassar Lawley and in the process trading control of one apparatus of modernity for control of another (one imagines also that Hepworth didn't mind keeping himself out of harm's way).[16] *How It Feels to Be Run Over* is ultimately concerned with how it feels to be fixed in place by a new technology of motion, whether we are pinned under the wheel of a newfangled automobile or positioned contra a moving image that is at once present and indifferent to us. That moving image is shaped by the makers of the film—in both Lawley's camerawork and Hepworth's steering of the car—and by the technological specificities and the industrial, cultural, and physical contingencies of its production, distribution, and exhibition.

How It Feels to Be Run Over participates in a matrix of relations among body, mind, technology, and ecology. Already in 1900 it typifies perceptual reorientations that emerging moving-image media call forth in their users. When we watch a film or show, or when we play a video game, we draw constantly on our previous experiences with that film, show, or game; our previous experiences with its medium and with media more generally; and our lifetime of experience outside of media. We are always, though not always consciously, incorporating what we perceive into our understanding of what we are experiencing and using that understanding to help us anticipate what may happen next. This anticipation is not just anticipation of large-scale elements of structure such as major narrative developments or genre conventions, but is anticipation also of more local qualities, such as how shots will look and sound and how they will be joined together by edits. All of these aspects of media are more noticeable, and thus can seem to be more self-reflexive, the less they conform to our learned—our felt—expectations. David Bordwell's cognitive film theory calls expectations of this kind "schemata."[17] Noel Burch writes of a "zero point of cinematic style" that cultivates and fulfills these expectations as a way of "rendering technique invisible" and naturalizing the filmic image.[18] Whatever the terminology you use to characterize it, this expectation is an ongoing dynamic, an evolving felt relationship to objects and an environment.

Having established such expectations, media can then modulate our relationships to them. For example, in the horror film *It Follows* (David Robert Mitchell, 2014), characters contract a curse in which a demonic entity disguised as a human pursues them, at a walking pace, at all times. They must constantly be on alert, looking out for figures striding toward them. As a result, we as viewers are cued to be attentive in new ways to the characters' surroundings. In particular, once we are aware of the looming threat (to the characters' lives, and also in the possibility that the film might startle or horrify us at any moment), our relationship to the depth of the film's compositions changes. The background becomes less of a backdrop or setting and more of an active space of potential danger. The background is foregrounded.

By resisting representational conventions, a film can likewise destabilize our learned perceptual expectations from its very beginning. In the vertiginous opening sequence of *Thou Wast Mild and Lovely* (Josephine Decker, 2014), two characters on a farm engage in a mock fight in which one pretends to stab the other with a headless fake chicken. After the characters exit the scene, the hand-held camera lingers. It tilts down to regard the rubber carcass where it has been left in the grass, then tilts back up to the horizon, but the focal depth of the shot does not change, so that the horizon, the surrounding trees, and a barn in the distance are extremely out of focus. The camera pans rightward along this blurry horizon, then moves forward, bouncing with the camera operator's steps, to regard a caged dog, which is seen in sharp focus, as it is at a similar distance from the lens as was the chicken carcass. As the camera approaches the dog, a voice-over intones: "For all my life, I missed my lover. I wanted my lover. I wanted to be near my lover." The dog returns the camera's gaze and begins to growl. As the voice-over continues, the dog becomes agitated and barks aggressively at the camera, and thus at us in the audience. This sequence refuses the clarity of the zero point of cinematic style in a number of ways. It stays with the scene after the characters leave, dissociating itself from their perspectives. By allowing its images to go out of focus, and through the camera's apparent indecision about where to look and *how* to look, the film refuses the visual clarity that "renders technique invisible." The voice-over enters with no clear source, suggesting but refusing to specify a relationship between the images we are seeing and the point of view of the speaker.

The sequence establishes a vicarious but ambiguous observational presence in the world of the film. Why is the dog barking? At what is it barking? From the perspective of the film's production, it is barking at a camera and its operator. From the point of view of film viewers, though, there is no clear answer. By establishing a bodily presence in the world of the film, but one apparently without a body, *Thou Wast Mild and Lovely* reactivates some of the power of early films like *How It Feels to Be Run Over*, resisting conventional schemata of expectation developed over the 114 years that separate the two films and forcing viewers to revisit their perceptual habits as film viewers. Reckoning with media is reckoning with objects and environments. Media become meaningful in how we feel our way through their constraints and possibilities—or, reciprocally, they become meaningful through how they constrain and inflect our feeling through the world.

In his theory of human evolution, Charles Darwin touches on topics related to the mind, such as emotion, aesthetics, and subjectivity. By asserting that human minds differ from the minds of other animals only by a matter of "degree and not of kind," Darwin credits nonhuman animals with forms of mindedness continuous with those of humans, and he further situates humans' mind in relation to their evolutionary history and their ecological niches.[19] This establishes minds as products of a long history of interaction (or, as I have been arguing, what Dewey would call transaction) among bodies and environments, structured by the simultaneous and overlapping demands of the environment on the organism and of the organism on the environment. In the twentieth century, conceptions of minds as products of ecological relationships among organisms and environments are elaborated in, for example, Dewey's philosophy, in Susanne Langer's theory of the biological function of feeling in art practice, in Gregory Bateson's cybernetic approach to anthropology, and in James J. Gibson's ecological perceptual psychology.[20]

Since around the turn of the twenty-first century, ecological thought about the mind has been taken up most provocatively by philosopher Alva Noë, who insists that perception, though it may appear passive and automatic, as though it furnishes sensations to us, is in fact always a mode of active participation in the environment. Experience requires not only our encountering the world but the world encountering us. "The world shows up for us," writes Noë. "But it doesn't show up for free. We achieve access to the world through skillful engagement."[21]

By constraining the enactive options of their players, including their means of perceptual engagement, video games highlight the relationship between perception and action in three key ways. First, video games regulate and isolate physical actions, requiring relatively localized gestures rather than the full-body action to which users are accustomed in everyday negotiation of the world. Games thereby compel players to relearn familiar actions in terms of gestural abstractions. To step forward in a game might be to push one's left thumb forward incrementally, while to crouch might be to press a controller button with one's right thumb. Both this enactive abstraction and the process of learning the mappings of available actions onto an interactive control scheme elicit probing, felt exploration of newfound behavioral constraints. While it is possible to explain a game's control scheme using words, it is not possible to truly learn how to play a game without in fact playing it. As we saw in chapter 1, when players of *The Unfinished Swan* discover new techniques for strafing through space and panning the game's camera in order to make their paint-throwing more effective, they, in effect, relearn how to perform the visual saccades that provide much of the richness of three-dimensional visual perception. The most effective practices for strafing, which surely vary from one player to the next, have to be felt out; they cannot merely be explained.

Second, video games highlight the relationship between perception and action by exposing players to unfamiliar perceptual environments. The worlds of video games are inherently new to players. To play a game for the first time is to encounter a new space, a new mode of presence, and new ways of moving and acting. The world at large is persistent and continuous, and—barring injury, intoxication, incapacitation, or disorientation—our bodily skill in negotiating our environment does not change dramatically from one moment to the next. Games are parts of that continuity that are new to us. The worlds of games are continuous with the "outside" world in the way a room is continuous with a house, or an organ is continuous with a body. Playing a game thus has something in common with exploring a new locale while simultaneously relearning bodily actions so fundamental that we take them for granted in daily life. It is common to say that a video game simulates a new experience, but this sells video games short. A video game *is* a new experience.

A third way that video games highlight the active nature of perception is by drawing attention to the role of skill development in navigating the world. We are already accustomed to thinking of video games as skill based, particularly because video games are so often structured around diegetic challenges like narrative goals, the scoring of points, and the accumulation of spoils. These visible and measurable skills build upon more fundamental abilities. Just as we must learn to stand and walk before we learn to dribble a basketball, and just as we must learn to dribble a basketball before we can explore the dynamics of *playing* basketball, we must establish and feel out our presence in video game worlds before we can begin to engage skillfully with the kinds of higher-level rules that we encounter *in* the game worlds. As we have already seen, the necessary skills for games go beyond their explicit gameplay challenges and include the mere manipulation of game characters and negotiation of game environments.

Some games, particularly mainstream big-budget games, work to make this process as intuitive and simple as possible, in an interactive equivalent of Burch's "zero point of film style." In fast-paced, first-person shooters like *Overwatch* (Blizzard Entertainment, 2016), a high premium is placed upon responsive controls and clear visual feedback. Some slower-paced games, like *The Unfinished Swan*, instead require players to rethink their enactive and perceptual relationships to their game worlds in order to navigate those worlds. Other games do this in more extreme ways, so that disorientation is not merely a theme but the principal challenge of the gameplay.

This aspect of games is the subject of a microgenre that might be called *simulatio ad absurdum*: games that purport to simulate activities but that in fact satirize the very notion of computer simulation. The game *QWOP*, for instance, is presented as a simulation of the 100-meter dash in the Olympic Games. In this two-dimensional side-scrolling game, the player is tasked with moving her character from left to right across the screen, but instead of using a directional joystick controller, you are required to articulate the athlete's thigh and calf muscles, each independently of the others, with the Q, W, O, and P keys on a computer keyboard. The game is an exercise in timing, not to mention frustration. In order to take a step forward, you must flex the relevant muscles, in the right combinations and for the right durations, to make the legs kick and support the character. Rather than simulating the act of running in the Olympics by taking for granted the onscreen character's felt familiarity with being able to run and walk "automatically," as ambulatory people can do from toddlerhood onward, the game dissects the act of running itself into component parts that ambulatory adults never, or almost never, think about while running, unless something is impeding their stride.

The timing necessary to pump the legs is extremely difficult to maintain, owing both to the bizarre granularity of the simulation and to *QWOP*'s awkward input scheme. The game is played with pairs of keys at opposite ends of the top line of letters on a standard QWERTY keyboard, with the thigh keys on the left (Q, W) and the calf keys on the right (O, P). This layout is physically awkward for players, who are faced with a choice of playing the game with their ring fingers and pinkies, or using their more dexterous index and middle fingers, in which case they have to hold their hands at an unusual distance from one another, with the unfamiliar-feeling elongated keys like "tab," "caps lock," and "return" lingering under their idle fingers. Grouping the command keys not by left leg and right leg, which would be more physiologically intuitive, but by type of muscle provides another source of confusion. Along with the fact that computer keyboards are not generally built, like game controllers, for precisely registering the relative timing of keystrokes, this all renders *QWOP*'s one-hundred-meter dash nearly impossible to finish. I certainly haven't got close. It is challenge enough to get past the starting line, and most attempts end with the character collapsed in a heap on the track. In figure 2.2, I more than triple my previous best effort for the day, proudly striding three meters before a mistimed firing of my avatar's left thigh muscle (W button) brings my race to an early end. It

Figure 2.2 A typical race ends in *QWOP* (Bennett Foddy, 2008).

is possible to finish the race in *QWOP*, but the game is not really a racing simulator. It is telling that the game is named not for the sport that it represents in its graphics, but for the confounding control scheme to which it subjects its players.

Another such satirical oversimulation, *Surgeon Simulator* (Bossa Studios, 2013), tasks its players to perform a series of complicated surgeries by way of a virtual hand. The principal challenge of the game is simply getting this hand to work, as the player is required to rotate and move the hand and to articulate each of its fingers independently of the others. When the game is played on a computer, the mouse controls the motion of the arm, the left mouse button lowers the arm (which raises itself when the button is released), and holding the right mouse button allows the hand to be rotated and flexed at the wrist. The A, W, E, and R keys on the keyboard each control a finger of the hand, and the space bar controls the thumb. The hand in the game is a left hand (see figure 2.3), but I think it is safe to say that the in-game doctor character is right-handed. The game seems to imply a user who is right-handed, as well (for more on how games and game technologies imagine the hands of their users, see chapter 6).

As with *QWOP*, play of *Surgeon Simulator* is characterized more by failure than by success. The surgeries become exercises in gory slapstick as the virtual hand knocks equipment to the floor, makes unintended incisions, and drops vital organs at critical moments. It is appropriate that the game is called *Surgeon Simulator* and not *Surgery Simulator*, as it is more concerned with the absurdity of simulating a body than it is with the mechanics of surgery. One can imagine a game designed to simulate the activity of surgery that is much more detailed—instructional, even— about the procedures of surgery and concurrently more automatic in its simulation of the surgeon's bodily actions. Video games necessarily abstract and summarize bodily action, and *QWOP* and *Surgeon Simulator* are no exceptions. By simulating

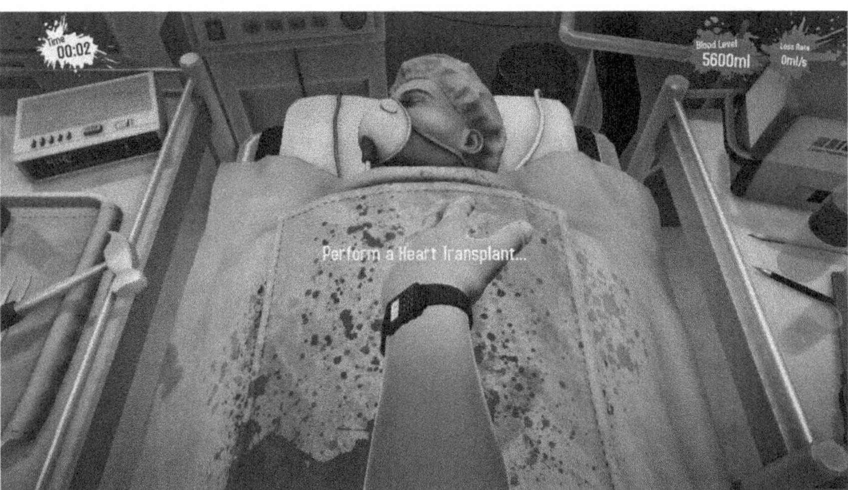

Figure 2.3 A typical surgery begins in *Surgeon Simulator* (Bossa Studios, 2013).

action with an absurd degree of granularity, though, these games denaturalize the relationship between what you do as a player and what your character does in the game, thereby pointing out the conventional and convenient varieties of simulated abstraction through which video games typically operate, in which the player is required to learn new skills for gameplay, but the character's body and basic bodily skills are taken for granted. I wrote earlier that the world of a video game is part of the wider world in the way an organ is part of a body. When *Surgeon Simulator* satirizes the idea of video game play as a mode of bodily simulation, it does so through the act of operating on a sedated body, as the player removes (and, most often, mutilates) its organs, and fumbles its way through that inner world, but always with the acknowledgment that the first fumbling is in tentatively feeling out the relationship between your actions and those of the oversimulated surgeon's hand.

Though they play as interactive jokes, these games productively render absurd the concept of simulation, emphasizing instead the roles that difficulty and failure can play in any form of art. As video game theorist Jesper Juul writes, "Failure forces us to reconsider what we are doing, to learn."[22] Any medium is capable of difficulty—through unfamiliarity, through obscurantism, through ambiguity— and these games exemplify the ways that difficulty can become an expressive tool, a structuring device, or a perceptual challenge, no matter the medium. Different artworks and different media go about teaching us how to see and to feel them in different ways.

LEARNING TO FEEL

The early stages of video games often present relatively safe and linear environments, settings in which players can explore and acclimate to the games' basic properties and control schemes. Later in the games, environments tend to become more complex, and challenges to require more fluid mastery of the controls. The gradually increasing geometric complexity of the early levels of *The Unfinished Swan* is but one example. The first-person shooter game *GoldenEye 007* (Rare, 1997), for instance, opens with the player-controlled James Bond (a digital approximation of his 1990s cinematic incarnation in the form of Pierce Brosnan) infiltrating a dam in Arkhangelsk, Russia. As the gameplay of *GoldenEye 007* is in first-person perspective, the polygonal Brosnan spends most of the game offscreen, except for his hands. At the beginning of each stage of the game, though, a disembodied camera approaches Bond, already in situ, circles behind him, and enters the back of his head. Polygon Bond fades away and players now occupy his optical point of view and control his motion, like otherworldly ghosts driving his body (which, in a Cartesian sense, they are). In the first mission of the game, Bond must fight his way onto the dam, proceed to a platform at its middle, and then bungee jump to safety, which is how everybody escaped from dangerous situations in the 1990s. The level's setting in a dam lends it an inherent spatial linearity, which efficiently narrativizes the level's *enactive* linearity in that it creates a linear path forward for Bond, with a predetermined series of mounting challenges arranged so as to train the player in core skills that will be necessary for negotiating the remainder of the game.

Rounding the first turn on his approach to the dam, Bond is confronted at close range by an enemy guard, who can be dispatched with pistol fire. As he approaches the dam, Bond encounters more guards farther away and finds a sniper rifle, giving the player a chance to try out the game's long-range targeting. Moving forward through the level, Bond faces enemy bunkers, alarms that can be tripped by enemies if they are not first destroyed by the player, and a moving truck that can be used for cover, all elements that will reappear in more complex and open-ended configurations in the game's later stages. The level introduces players of *Goldeneye 007* to the basics of the game's control scheme. It teaches them about skills that the remainder of the game will demand of them, such as targeting at a distance, effective use of resources, and particular kinds of strategic thinking. It helps players to begin to develop an intuition for how the game, and especially the enemy characters, will respond to their actions.

As players navigate the whole dam level, they also develop their own ways of making it perceptible to them. The sniper rifle can be used as a telescope, not only for eliminating enemies but for scoping out what lies ahead. Stray bullets leave marks on the walls, a quality that players can use to keep track of where they have been in the level. In later levels, where Bond must search through more complex and less linear areas, some players intentionally shoot the walls outside of rooms or warehouses as a way of keeping track of their progress and streamlining their work, an ad hoc way of using FPS projectiles to mark the game world in order to change their perception of it that anticipates the paint-throwing gameplay mechanic of *The Unfinished Swan* by fifteen years. The dam level of *GoldenEye 007* is designed to help players feel out their presence in the game world. With strategies like using the sniper rifle as a telescope or using bullet marks to keep track of their progress, players also feel their way toward strategies in the game world that may not have been anticipated by the game's designers.

GoldenEye 007 constructs an elaborate fictional world in which players participate by way of a recognizably human avatar. More abstract video games train their players' habits of action and perception, as well. Each level of the game *Microtone* (increpare, 2011) requires players to move a flat, black square around the surfaces of floating three-dimensional objects in order to collect X shapes. The square can only be moved to adjacent spaces on what appear to be orthogonal polyhedrons, and the square can never be moved out of the player's sight. Playing on a mobile device, a player touches one finger to the screen at the place to which she wants the square to move. If such a move is possible, the square inches its way to the destination, flipping edge over edge to get there. The square can only move along the surfaces of objects and cannot jump from one object to another.

This can lead to some seemingly impossible challenges, as in figure 2.4, where there seems to be no path from the square to the X. The square is stranded on the

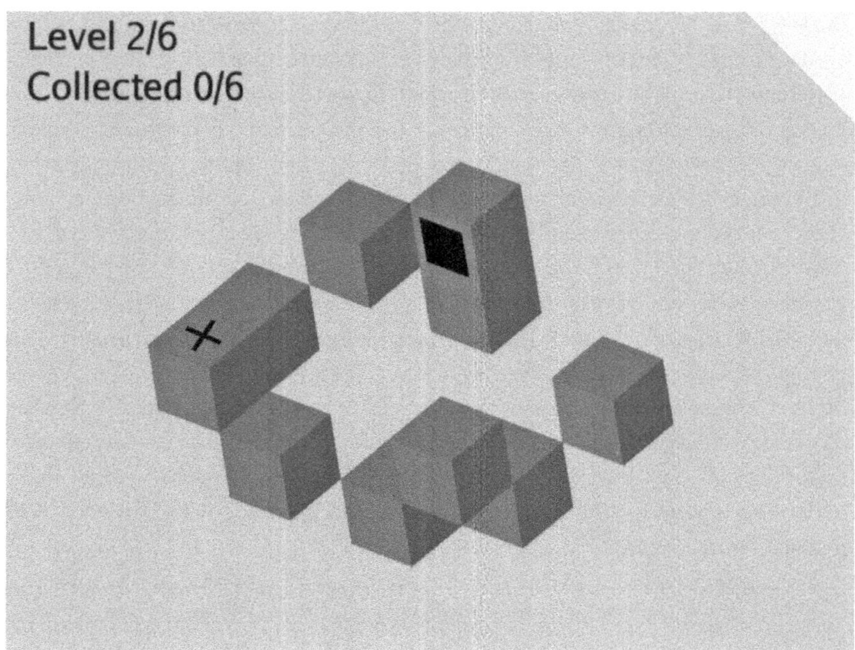

Figure 2.4 In *Microtone* (increpare, 2011), there seems to be no path by which the black square can make its way to the X.

rectangular solid at center top, while its target X is on the shape floating to screen left. However, the game's shapes are not actually orthogonal polyhedra, as they first seem to be, but rhombic dodecahedrons, which appear to be orthogonal shapes when viewed from particular angles but which are in fact far more complex. Figure 2.5 shows the same shapes as figure 2.4, as viewed from an oblique angle. To navigate the game's levels and to reach what had seemed to be inaccessible places, the player must rotate these objects, effectively changing the game's optical perspective. Rotating the shapes transforms their relation to one another and reveals previously hidden X shapes for the player to collect. On a mobile device, the shapes are rotated by dragging two fingers across the screen, which spins the objects in space. Viewed from another angle, the dodecahedrons will seem to resolve into different orthogonal shapes, revealing new pathways for the motion of the square.

There are a number of potential ways to describe this relationship between point of view and the shapes in the game. One is that the square is capable of navigating shapes that seem to be there but are not, that it moves through a world of seeming continuity, but that the game reveals this continuity to be an illusion. From the square's perspective, it moves along flat surfaces, but from our privileged point of view, we know better. Another way to describe it would be to say that rotating the shapes creates paths that were previously nonexistent. In this view, the player

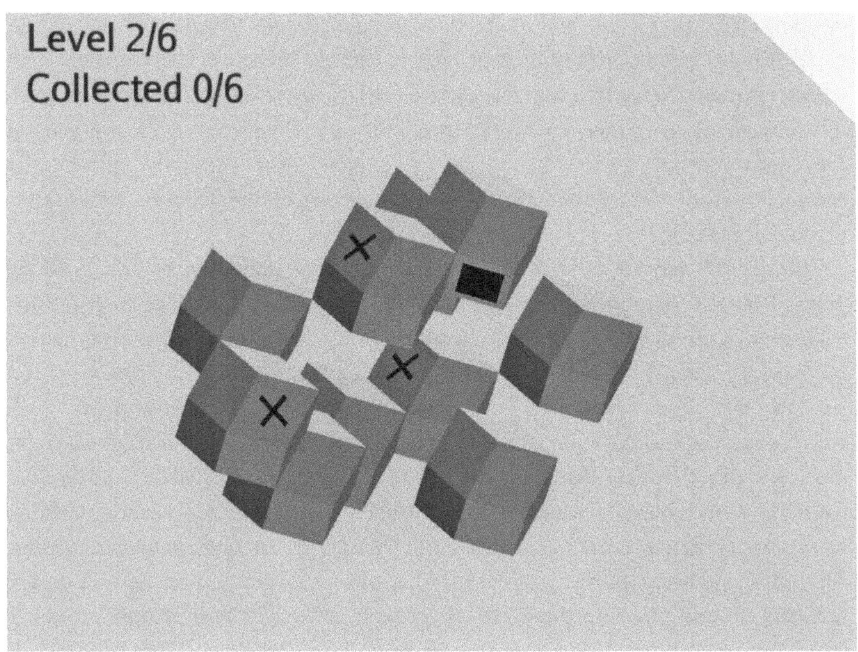

Figure 2.5 Rotating the objects reveals that they are more complex than they at first appear.

transforms the game world, then subsequently, accurately, perceives how it is now and moves the square accordingly.

Still another way, combining aspects of the first two, would be to say that the paths are created by their appearance. This is at once the most provocative and the most accurate characterization of *Microtone*. The game world that the square may navigate at any moment is the world as the player perceives it from a particular angle, and changing the player's perception of the world changes the square's possible paths of motion. But all of the potential paths of motion are already there. They simply cannot be taken if they are unseen, and to see them requires realizing them through physical manipulation. The principal challenge of the game is in adjusting to the possibilities offered by this mapping of perception onto virtual space. *Microtone* does for visual perception what *QWOP* and *Surgeon Simulator* do for simulation of muscular motion. In order to reconcile oneself to a game's challenges, one has to feel through what can be done in the game, and also feel through how it can be perceived, qualities that are never discrete from one another.

The back and forth of *Microtone*'s control scheme, in which players alternate between moving the square and rotating the objects across the surfaces of which it moves, can be awkward at first. With practice, though, what felt like two separate acts, of acting *in* the game and acting *on* the game, begin to flow fluidly into one another and come to feel more like one continuous activity. In its oscillation between one-fingered tapping and two-fingered swiping, *Microtone* foregrounds active perception as a core mechanic of its gameplay. In doing so, it brings into focus the kind of perceptual-enactive training that games like *Goldeneye 007* perform more invisibly. Perceiving *Microtone* reveals the possibilities of the game world in ways that are readily apparent, and the benefits of that perception are explicitly built into the reward structure of the gameplay, as it allows players to complete levels and advance through the game.

That games require physical action of their players is uncontroversial. Seeing perception as a variety of action helps us to see the new modes of perception that each new game demands of us. It also aids in thinking about continuity across media. Like games, films demand new modes of perception of their viewers and similarly train their viewers in how to watch them. The comfort and ease with which one might watch a film made in the classical Hollywood stylistic vernacular derives as much from industrial reluctance to challenge perceptual habits as it does from duly satisfied expectations of clear character motivation and narrative closure. In this way, much as do video games, Hollywood trains viewers to watch its films. Art-house and avant-garde films, each in their own ways, train them anew. Literary texts are no exception. In this sense, literacy, regardless of the medium, goes beyond comprehension. It is an ongoing process of negotiation, never finished, as the variety of media forms and technological formats, not to mention the context of a user's experience, never stop growing and pushing one another toward new formations. This is never a passive endeavor. It is only through skilled engagement with media that they become meaningful for us.

FLOW AND SMOOTH-RUNNING FUNCTIONS

In *Flow: The Psychology of Optimal Experience*, Mihaly Csikszentmihalyi develops the titular concept of "flow," a pleasurable and productive psychological state that he says can be achieved by competently performing challenging tasks. Among the sensations that characterize flow are a feeling of balance between mastery and challenge, a loss of self-consciousness, a transformation of temporal perception, and the merging of action and awareness, so that people in flow states "stop being aware of themselves as separate from the actions they are performing."[23] Csikszentmihalyi's flow puts a positive-psychology spin on a sensation described by Martin Heidegger in 1927. "When one is 'really' busy with something and totally immersed in it," writes Heidegger, "one is neither together only with the work, nor with the tools, nor with both 'together.'... In order to 'really' get to work, 'lost' in the world of tools and to handle them, the self must forget itself."[24]

Flow has become an influential concept in video game studies, taken up by video game scholars Katie Salen and Eric Zimmerman in their book *Rules of Play* and by Jesper Juul in his *Half-Real*. Salen and Zimmerman characterize flow as "an emotional and psychological state of focused and engaged happiness, when a person feels a sense of achievement and accomplishment, and a greater sense of self."[25] Although Salen, Zimmerman, and Juul argue that the appeal of video games goes beyond flow in important ways, they agree that the concept of flow as described by Csikszentmihalyi describes something crucial about video game play, and especially about the pleasures of games. Juul finds the term "flow" to be unduly limited in that it focuses on too narrow a conception of player enjoyment. There are "enjoyable aspects of games," he argues, "that cannot simply be explained as challenges. . . . The variation between challenges and lack of challenge is one of the ways in which a game can modulate its intensity."[26] To Salen and Zimmerman, flow is a phenomenon "not unique to games" that is "more about the player than the game" and is "but one of many possible tools"[27] available to game designers.

"Flow" also names a key concept in television studies, denoting what Raymond Williams calls the "characteristic organization, and therefore the characteristic experience," of broadcasting systems, a phenomenon that is "perhaps the defining characteristic of broadcasting, simultaneously as a technology and as a cultural form."[28] For Williams, flow is a quality of nondiscreteness among the "items" presented, so that programming is conceived not as "a program of discrete units with particular insertions, but a planned flow."[29] Williams's theory of flow predates that of Csikszentmihalyi, and the resonances between the two theories are clear. In each case, human action and experience is brought into accord with an environmental process. In the case of Csikszentmihalyi's flow, the flow state is achieved in and by the human actor, who rises to the demands of the situation, while in Williams's flow, the flow state is planned and programmed by a broadcaster. Flow for Williams is a state of the broadcast that induces a state in the viewer, a "given structure of feeling" in both broadcast and viewer.[30] The concept of televisual flow has been tested, critiqued, tweaked, and extended by generations of television scholars since Williams published these words in 1974, addressing nuances in and exceptions to its simultaneous characterization of television programming and of viewer experience.[31]

The video game studies interpretation of Csikszentmihalyi's flow and the television studies concept of flow, especially as originally articulated by Williams, both emphasize a loss of the feeling of separation between oneself and one's perceptions and actions. In this respect, flow resembles a phenomenon described by Dewey in the early twentieth century, about a decade before Heidegger wrote of the self that forgets itself. Writing about the skillful performance of precise and highly skilled tasks, Dewey writes,

> A piano player who had perfect mastery of his instrument would have no occasion to distinguish between his contribution and that of the piano. In well-formed, smooth-running functions of any sort,—skating, conversing, hearing music, enjoying a landscape,—there is no consciousness of separation of the method of the person and of the subject matter. In whole-hearted play and work there is the same phenomenon.[32]

Dewey's "whole-hearted play and work" bears similarity in particular to Csikszentmihalyi's flow, but as Dewey characterizes the phenomenon, it is not so much a pleasurable psychological sensation as a dynamic relationship between organism and environment. This is an important distinction. Csikszentmihalyi's model, like those of Salen, Zimmerman, and Juul, is interactional, while Dewey's is an early articulation of the kind of transactional connection among organism, action, and world that he would later describe in his elaboration of the transaction in *Knowing and the Known.*

Dewey's account is in this respect the inverse of the claims made by Csikszentmihalyi and carried forward by the video game theorists. Dewey avoids the problematic notion that people in states of flow lose awareness of themselves as "separate from the actions they are performing" by maintaining that such a separation never existed in the first place. In place of this prior separation is an enactive tension between organism and environment. In this way of understanding user-media transactions, the sensation that Csikszentmihalyi terms "flow" should not be regarded as an exceptional state achieved when we lose awareness of the separation between ourselves and our actions. Instead, something like a flow state ought to be regarded as the norm of day-to-day existence, characterizing the times when consciousness feels "transparent" rather than self-reflectively oriented. The true exception is in when we *lose* that smoothness and end up adjusting to, theorizing, analyzing, or having to make sense of unexpected perceptions or turns of events.

FEELING THROUGH A WORLD

Feeling through the world, we also feel our way toward conceptions of ourselves. At the beginning of Abbas Kiarostami's film *Certified Copy,* British author James Miller delivers a formal lecture on the relationship between copying and authenticity in art. He argues that copies are as authentic as originals, both because the act of copying is itself a form of origination and because original artworks are themselves copies of other things, a position that he further elaborates in more casual conversations throughout the rest of the film. James is visiting Tuscany for the release of the Italian translation (one kind of copy) of his book, itself titled *Certified Copy.* A French woman who has settled nearby offers to take him on a tour of the area. Ambiguously identified in the credits as "Elle," which could be either a name or a pronoun, she goes unnamed in the film itself. James takes her up on the offer, meeting her in a basement shop where she sells antiquities, some of them copies. The two apparently do not know each other and seem somewhat tense in one another's company from the beginning of their tour. As Elle drives them through the countryside between cities, she tells stories about her family and they bicker benignly about details until James insists that they be quiet and enjoy the scenery. The film offers us a copy this scenery, cutting to a moving shot, in the phantom-ride style, of the road, the countryside, and the passing cypress trees. If James is indeed enjoying the scenery, perhaps the film provides us with a copy of his enjoyment, as well.

Midway through the film, Elle and James stop for coffee. The cafe owner overhears their conversation and assumes that they are a married couple. Elle casually plays along with the misunderstanding, seemingly as an idle game. The game continues intermittently after she and James leave the cafe, and soon he is playing along as well. The more they discuss their "shared" past, the more muddled their relationship becomes, and Elle and James themselves appear to become uncertain about who they are, and who they have been, to one another. The day progresses, and the film itself seems gradually to become either complicit in or confused by the charade. By *Certified Copy*'s end, the couple are, for the most part, behaving as if it is a given that they are married. The film ends with Elle and James "revisiting" the hotel room where they spent (or perhaps did not spend) their honeymoon many years before. By this point, neither of them seems sure of where they stand relative to their pasts, presents, or possible futures. Any inconsistencies in their apparent fabrication of a shared past they now treat as lapses, or merely as differences, of memory. The structured reality that we might expect to underlie the film is deconstructed as the characters create a shared reality for themselves through their actions, and especially through conversation. As perceiving, feeling, and comprehending viewers of the film, we are asked to feel our way through its world, to (perhaps) understand what we can but, more importantly, to feel what we do.

And yet the film continually confounds expectations of clarity in both its narrative continuity and its formal construction. At one point, Elle, James, and a couple they have just met hold an impassioned discussion of a public statue that is readily present to them but that the viewers of the film never fully see. They are interested in the expressions of the characters it depicts, especially in the way that a female figure rests its head on a male figure's shoulder. Watching the film, we never see her head or his shoulder. They are always held off the edge of the frame, or behind the camera, and we only learn about the statue by watching the characters regard it and hearing them talk about it. Whatever understanding of the statue we can achieve is the result of our skillful, informed extrapolations from the characters' discussion, our limited understanding of the dispositions of the characters, two of whom speak their only lines in the film in this scene, and our own experience with public statuary.

We feel out the physical space of the film to the best of our ability, given the constraints within which we are made to work, and we might even feel that, in a way, we have sensed the statue, not firsthand, but through the characters who regard and describe it. The paths that viewers make through *Certified Copy* are not at all unlike the paths that players create through *Microtone* or *The Unfinished Swan*. They are unlike neither the road that Emily Dickinson's midnight walker "steps almost straight" to "meet . . . erect," nor the country road at the turn of the twentieth century in *How It Feels to Be Run Over*. In every case, to quote Noë again, "The world shows up for us. But it doesn't show up for free."[33] And it does not show itself to us. We create the possibilities and the limits of our worlds by feeling them out. We create pathways through the world by perceiving them.

MEDIA IN THE WORLD, THE WORLD IN PERCEPTION, PERCEPTION IN MEDIA

The turn of twentieth century was characterized by accelerating velocity and intensifying visuality, in the form of a rush of mechanical vehicles (in which to ride and by which to be hit), accelerating production, and newly moving media images, all of which transformed the perceptual ecology in fundamental ways. For every way that the Second Industrial Revolution facilitated new modes of perception, it created new perceptual constraints, posed new perceptual challenges, and demanded the development of new perceptual skills. Industrialization changed the world's way of participating in perception, disrupting the smooth-running functions of people whose chief worry in crossing the street had previously been an unseen horse, or perhaps a bicycle.

The acceleration continues, and in the twenty-first century, the status of the image and the status of motion—motion through the world and the motion of images—are similarly in flux. Interactive media like video games and virtual reality map action and perception onto one another in formations that are new in their technological particulars and the ways they constrain their users but are at the same time historically and physiologically rooted in earlier media and earlier practices of media use—in technique, in technology, and in their relationship to the embodied, active perception of their users.

How It Feels to Be Run Over reflects a confluence of perception, action, and mediation particular to its time. It asks its viewers to recognize something profoundly contemporary and perceptually new in the situation it depicts, and also to rise to the new perceptual demands placed on them by cinematic technology. Beyond this, it asks them to accept its use of the camera as a proxy for their embodied presence in the film's diegesis—to accept that they are not merely seeing but in fact fully experiencing the "feeling" of being run over. As I argued in the early part of this chapter, the deepest vulnerability of the film's audience is in its commitment to the motion of the image, not in the threat of bodily injury by the car.

This chapter has argued that changes to the environment are changes to perception, because the environment that we perceive is an actor in our perceptual experience. We perceive and act upon the environment not from within, in the sense of being contained by it, but in our functioning as constitutive and participatory aspects *of* it. As much as we are in it, it is in us. As the next chapter shows, this ecological understanding of perception calls into question the concept of internal mental representations, which have long been central to media theory's attempts to conceive of relationships between media and mind.

CHAPTER 3

Media and Radical Embodiment

Where Is Representation?

The video game *Tetris* (Alexiey Pajitnov, 1984) probably requires no introduction. Originally designed in the Soviet Union for a computer called the Electronika 60, the game spread rapidly around the world and across computer and video game platforms in the years that followed, in the process becoming one of the most popular and well-known video games ever made. Its popularity, and its portability across systems, owe in part to its simplicity; the game is readily accessible to players and to platforms alike. While the basic mechanics of *Tetris* are simple enough to learn, there is in principle no upper threshold to its progressively increasing difficulty. In this sense, *Tetris* represents a permanent challenge to its players, keeping them forever at the cutting edge of their own ability to play it. *Tetris*, seen in figure 3.1, is both a geometric puzzle-solving game and a fast-paced action game. In its challenge to players, it seems to straddle the distinction between the mental and the physical. For all of these reasons and more, *Tetris* has possibly seen more scholarly interest from across the disciplines than has any other video game. Debates about the physical and mental investment required of *Tetris* players are emblematic of wider scholarly and popular debates about the threshold between the mental (or internal) and the physical (or external) domains. As I argue in this chapter, *Tetris* and other media will be crucial in reframing those debates and especially in moving beyond the idea that such a threshold even exists.

This chapter shows how media have entered into, informed, and been informed by the idea of a distinction between the external world and the internal mind. Philosophical and popular understandings of the mind have long been dominated by the concept of an internal realm that is at a distance from the external world in one way or another: immaterial while the world is material, symbolic while the world is concrete, subjective while the world is objective. The previous chapter

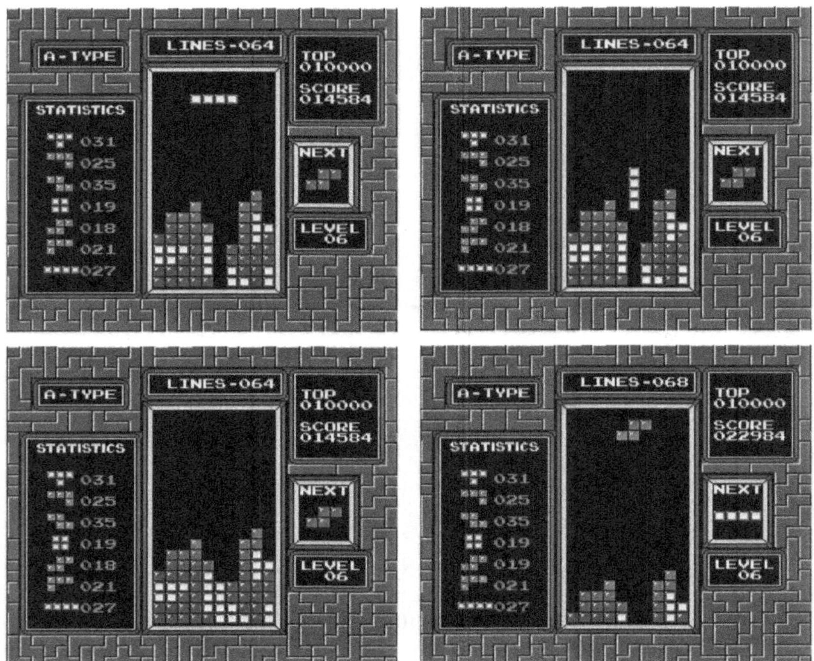

Figure 3.1 Achieving the eponymous "tetris" (four horizontal lines eliminated at once) in *Tetris* (Nintendo Entertainment System version, Bullet-Proof Software, 1987). *Top left*, the necessary linear shape, which will allow the player to complete the tetris, appears. *Top right*, the linear shape is rotated 90 degrees and aligned with the vertical column into which it will be placed. *Bottom left*, the linear shape drops into place. *Bottom right*, four lines disappear, and the player receives 8,400 points for the effort. About two seconds of gameplay are represented here.

discussed the implications that dualist models of the mind have for perception in and beyond media use. The current chapter turns its attention to the topic of representational content in media and in the mind. As in the previous chapter, I argue against dominant theoretical discontinuities and in favor of an understanding of media and mind that sees them from a naturalist perspective—that is, as constituent and intertwined, nondiscrete parts of a continuous material whole.

The idea that the mind works by way of internal representational content is known as *representationalism*. In this view, impressions of the external world enter the mind by way of perception (which, as we have seen, is usually regarded as a passive process and not an act), through which they are translated into representations characterized as the images, symbols, or language "of the mind." These private representations are the mind's content, and the inaccessible part of the mind—whether one calls it cognition, or the unconscious, or something else—operates via the manipulation of these representations according to rules similar to the rules of a language or a computer program. The idea of mental representations dates at least to antiquity and is evident today in how contemporary cognitive science treats cognition as a rule-based computational process. Over the millennia since Plato and Aristotle, the idea of mental representations has appeared in different forms across fields including psychology, philosophy of mind, psychoanalysis, cognitive science, and semiotics.

The appearance of moving-image media around the turn of the twentieth century gave representationalist thinking a new metaphor for the mechanism of internal representation, but it simultaneously posed new challenges for adherents of representationalism. Since the earliest days of film theory, scholars have seen qualities in media, or felt qualities in their own use of media, that have cued them to think about the mind in ways that push the boundaries of their dominant representationalist paradigms. However, these media scholars have largely responded to media's provocations along Kantian lines, ultimately distinguishing media use from other forms of experience and declaring it an exception to how the mind usually works. For Kant, aesthetic objects are "without any purpose," and the "mere form of purposiveness in the representation by which an object is given to us" is that by which we evaluate it in aesthetic terms.[1] In film theories put forward by Joseph D. Anderson and Kristin Thompson, as we shall see in more detail, experience of art is definitively distinguished from other experience by its nonevolutionary or noneveryday status. Like Kant's objects of aesthetic judgment, films are distinguished by their lack of purpose.

Setting media aside in this way makes media special—miraculous, really—in how they defy the normal order of things. This elevation can be a kind of damning containment, though, that puts media on a pedestal, deprives them of their materiality and their continuity with the rest of the world, and thereby deprives media use of its continuity with the rest of experience. Just as separating the mind from the world sets it aside as exceptional in a way that undermines its place and power in the ecology of which it is a constituent part, setting media aside as purposeless, nonevolutionary, or noneveryday severs them from their materiality and from their direct participation in the environment. The intuitive similarity between representations in media and the purported representations of the mind, it seems, gives rise to a defensive urge to partition both away from the continuity of the world. To the Cartesian wound is added a Kantian cut.

But what if, rather than saying media "content" is *like* mental "content," whether in its representational nature, its indexical relationship to things in the world, its self-contained underlying mechanics, or its discreteness from "real life," we instead did away with underlying assumptions of discreteness, internal representation, and "content" and focused instead on the direct relations—the continuity and the intimacy—among media, mind, and world? Recent developments in embodied cognitive science, especially in a growing subfield called "radical embodied cognition" (or REC), have foregrounded the role of both the body and the environment in the constitution of the mind. REC is *nonrepresentational*. It rejects representationalism in favor of an ecological mind that functions as part of the world, rather than facing inward toward a private theater of experience. I argue in this chapter that early media theorists like Hugo Münsterberg were also early, if tentative, REC researchers, dipping their toes in a nonrepresentationalist understanding of the mind by way of their engagement with media. REC emerged as an approach to cognition around the turn of the twenty-first century, but its historical antecedents include the work of Münsterberg's contemporary John Dewey, as well as that of Münsterberg's Harvard faculty sponsor, William James. Experimental cognitive science, psychology, and neuroscience have largely taken a different path in the last century than the one suggested by scholars like Dewey and James, and when scholars in these fields have employed moving-image and interactive media, including *Tetris*, it has largely been in the service of studying the mind within representationalist, interactional paradigms. These media theorists, in other words, have seen something in media that frees them, at least partially, from understanding the mind as locked into its own internal sphere of experience while, conversely, the sciences have often seen, in media representations, a confirmation of their own representationalist perspectives.

This chapter opens by discussing the important role that *Tetris* has played in philosophical debates about representationalism. This leads to a discussion of the ways that theoretical claims about media have been inflected by prior understandings of the mind, and conversely of how understandings of the nature of media texts and media technologies have found their way, via both metaphor and experimental application, into how philosophy and cognitive science conceive of the mind—in particular into the ways in which these fields conceive of the mind as a representational apparatus. The story of Münsterberg, a psychologist who turned to film theory late in his life, illustrates the ways that media can provoke their users to think about the mind in new ways, but also how those provocations are often contained and dispatched by setting media aside as an exception to everyday experience. A widely reported cognitive science study from 2011, I argue, exemplifies how science and philosophy of mind use representational media in ways that reinforce the existing assumptions of representationalism.

From Münsterberg's work in the early twentieth century through the semiotic, psychoanalytic, and cognitivist frameworks that largely characterize media theory from the second half of the century, representationalism has dominated media theory's conception of the minds of media users, and it has had powerful effects on how theory conceives of media use, media form, media technology, what media can do, and indeed what media *are*. Nonrepresentationalism, especially as articulated by Dewey and elaborated recently by scholars of REC, is thus a radical position relative not only to computational cognitive science but also to core assumptions of much media theory. It offers an opportunity to step outside of the theoretical feedback loop between media theory and representationalist theories of the mind, and it provides new ways to think about what media, media users, and media use achieve in the world, ways of thinking that rely on the idea of discrete "content" neither in media nor in the mind. As I have argued in the previous chapters, replacing content with continuity is necessary in restoring the place of media and their users in the ecology that they share. As we shall see in chapters 4 and 5, it further prompts a reexamination of language used to describe media technologies, such as "platforms," "apparatuses," and "interfaces," all of which have also been marked by representationalist media theory's reliance on discreteness and discontinuity in how it conceives of media, technology, mind, body, and world.

TETRIS: FROM THE EPISTEMIC TO THE PRAGMATIC

Since its debut in 1984, *Tetris* has been remade and rereleased dozens of times. While the specifics of the game vary from one version to the next, its core concept and mechanics remain the same. The description I will give here is specific to the Nintendo Entertainment System version of the game (Bullet-Proof Software, 1989) as played in the "A-Type" mode. Some variations of *Tetris* include endings to the game after a certain number of blocks are cleared, as in the NES "B-Type" mode, or the introduction of additional challenges such as "garbage blocks" that cannot be cleared, as in the Super Nintendo Entertainment System variant *Tetris Attack* (Intelligent Systems, 1995). The NES A-Type version is representative of the basic gameplay attributes common to most versions of the game, and it remains the standard for competitive *Tetris* play.[2] The mode's name distinguishes it from the B-Type mode, but for its popularity and familiarity A-Type might as well be an abbreviation for its status as the *Tetris* archetype.

Tetris is set in a two-dimensional abstract space. A series of shapes, each composed of four congruent square blocks joined edge to edge, descends from the top of a vertical corridor. These tetrominoes can take seven possible forms: a straight line, a block, a T shape, an L shape, a backward L, a Z, and a backward Z. They appear one at a time at the top of the screen and drop, as though pulled by gravity, toward screen bottom, where they accumulate in a pile. Using the game's controls, players can move the shapes left and right, rotate them clockwise and counterclockwise, and accelerate their descent. The goal of the game is to complete uninterrupted horizontal lines that fill the width of the corridor. When such a line is completed, it disappears and the lines above it drop into its place. After every tenth completed line, the blocks change color and their velocity increases. The game ends when the pile reaches the top of the screen, and the challenge to the player is to hold off the (inevitable) end of the game for as long as possible by strategically placing the falling tetrominoes. The player is rewarded with a score based on the difficulty of the moves completed in eliminating lines. A maneuver called a "tetris," achieved when a straight-line piece is placed on end to complete four horizontal lines at once, is the rarest in the game and yields the most points for the player (see figure 3.1).

In pursuing a high score, the player must respond with increasing rapidity to the appearance of new pieces, both determining where to place them and getting the pieces into position before they land at the top of the growing pile and are locked into place. There are three principal pieces of information with which a player of *Tetris* must reckon: (1) the current state of the pile in the game space;

(2) the current block and where it might best fit; and (3) the piece that will appear next, displayed in a box at screen right. In the context of the player's priorities (Eliminate lines wherever possible? Try to build up the conditions for a tetris?), the game becomes an increasingly urgent exercise in applying its deceptively simple gameplay rules and strategies to a relentless series of challenges. As the speed of the gameplay mounts, a player's hands move ever more quickly among the controls (joystick, directional pad, buttons, or keys) particular to that version of the game.

It is clear that playing *Tetris* is a physical task. But in what ways is it a mental one? And—crucially for our purposes here—what would such a distinction between physical and mental tasks mean in the context of *Tetris* gameplay? The game's hold on the imagination of game designers and players stretches over more than three decades, and new versions of *Tetris* are still appearing regularly as of 2018. The game has also become a popular tool for study of the mind. People who have been playing a lot of *Tetris* often report hallucinating images of the game as they fall asleep (I count myself among them), a phenomenon that has been dubbed the "Tetris effect" and that one study shows can even occur in amnesiacs who do not recall playing the game itself.[3] *Tetris* has been used with some success as a means for disrupting intrusive memories of traumatic events and preventing the memories from recurring,[4] and specifically as a treatment for the cumulative build-up of flashbacks in people suffering from post-traumatic stress disorder.[5] Computer scientists and mathematicians use the game as a way to compare the mathematical logic of the game program with the experiential expertise of the game's players.[6] The game has seen therapeutic success as a way of combating physical and psychological addictions.[7] It seems clear from all of this that *Tetris* is a psychologically powerful video game, or, more broadly, that it is emblematic of the powerful effects that video games can have in the psychological lives of their players.

Psychologically speaking, then, what does it take to play *Tetris* successfully? In a representationalist understanding of the mind, the game would appear to be an exercise in abstraction and mental rotation. A piece appears at the top of the corridor and players try to fit it into their understanding of the pile of blocks at the bottom, imagining what it would look like rotated and fit into potential resting places. One principal skill of *Tetris* play in this view would be that of rapidly translating the pieces into mental images and comparing them, in their various potential rotations, to mental images of the pile. The player would then attempt to perform the physical actions necessary to bring the game state into accord with her internal, strategic plans. In this view, there are at least two distinct but correlated skills involved in *Tetris*: the mental skill of assessing a gameplay situation and forming a plan and the physical skill of realizing that plan. The process is reciprocal: the game provides visual input to the player, who performs mental computations and then outputs behaviors by manipulating the controls, which then become the input for the game platform, which performs its own internal computations, outputting them back to the player again via graphics on the screen. Gameplay is a kind of feedback loop between two "black boxes," the player and the platform, whose internal computational machinations are inaccessible to one another, except by what can be inferred from their outward behavior.

If this sort of abstract mental rotation is one of the principal skills of *Tetris*, one would expect expert players of the game to be especially adept at mentally rotating tetrominoes. These players would be able to plan their moves more rapidly and get their tetrominoes into place more efficiently—that is, with fewer onscreen rotations—than do novice players. Comparing the behavior of expert and novice players, however, cognitive scientists David Kirsh and Paul Maglio find that expert *Tetris* players tend to perform more, rather than fewer, rotations of the falling tetrominoes than do less-skilled players.[8] Expert *Tetris* play is in fact often characterized by near-constant rotation of the tetrominoes. In Kirsch and Maglio's interpretation, expert players do not perform more, or more efficient, *mental* rotation tasks, for the simple reason that they do not have to. By rapidly rotating the pieces, expert players use the spatial rotation capacities of the game itself to facilitate their strategic thinking. To quote Kirsch and Maglio, "These actions are not used to implement a plan, or to implement a reaction; they are used to *change the world* in order to simplify the problem-solving task." The resources of the game are used by expert players to help them think about their tasks in the game—the rotations are "best understood as actions that *use the world* to improve cognition."[9]

Kirsh and Maglio interpret this result as a case of physical action being used to gather information for cognitive processing. They call this form of action "epistemic," in contrast to "pragmatic" action, which makes concrete progress toward a goal. In my perspective, this terminology confuses things, in that it erects what I see as an unnecessary distinction between types of action, depending on what the action is interpreted by an observer as being "for." Working from within a representationalist paradigm, the authors see the constant rotation of the pieces as an indication that cognition, which is by default an internal phenomenon, can extend outward to employ things in the world, conscripting material things into its operations when it is expedient to do so. Rotating tetrominoes is pragmatic when a player does it to move them into place but epistemic when she does it to externalize the task of mental rotation. Epistemic action, one imagines, ends at the moment when pragmatic action begins. In a follow-up study, Maglio and collaborators extend this line of reasoning, weighing the time and effort cost of performing physical actions (rotations) against the benefit of using "external information (the effects of additional rotations in *Tetris*) . . . to supplant internal computation (mental rotation)" and "balancing effort against potential gain" in a trade-off that they take to be emblematic not only of *Tetris* and activities in experimental settings, but of "real situations" as well.[10]

At least two unnecessary divisions are erected here: the distinction between epistemic and pragmatic action and another between media use and "real" situations. I would argue that better understanding of a situation *is* in fact progress toward negotiating it, and, further, that all situations ought to be understood as real. What Kirsh and Maglio call "epistemic action" is itself a variety of pragmatic action. If we do not hold knowledge or understanding aside from action in the world—that is, if we do away with the gap between the physical and the mental—it becomes clear that perceiving, knowing, and understanding are all forms of practical, strategic, skill-based action. From an evolutionary perspective, indeed, their material utility is precisely why these phenomena exist in the first place. How we understand the dynamic between knowledge and action depends on where (or if) we draw lines between mind and world.

Kirsch and Maglio's work on *Tetris* has become a foundational study in the field of embodied cognitive science, which seeks to rethink just these lines. As we have already begun to see, however, there is a significant difference between rendering the line between cognition and the external world movable, as "epistemic action" would do, and doing away with this line altogether, as advocated by Dewey's naturalist approach to the mind and more recently by theories of radical embodied cognition. Approaches like that of Kirsch and Maglio, which, following Daniel D. Hutto and Erik Myin, I will call "conservative embodied cognition" (CEC), import the body and the environment into cognition while maintaining a representationalist perspective that sees cognition in terms of content.[11] By contrast, REC, as Hutto and Myin put it, sees cognition as "concrete patterns of environmental situated organismic activity, nothing more or less."[12] While CEC allows that the body and the environment can sometimes be employed in cognition, REC sees the body, in the environment, as both the site and the source of cognition.

EMBODIED COGNITION: CONSERVATIVE OR RADICAL?

From the perspective of conservative embodied cognition, the computational mind is extended outward from its internal sphere when, for example, someone uses a pen and paper to do a math problem. If she is thus able to work an equation that she could not complete purely "in the head," without the pen and paper, CEC asks, aren't the pen and paper as much a part of the computing mind as the brain is?[13] In their seminal essay on this *cognitive extension*, Andy Clark and David J. Chalmers cite Kirsch and Maglio's *Tetris* study as evidence that "cognitive processes ain't (all) in the head" and that in some cases "the human organism is linked with an external entity in a two-way interaction, creating a *coupled system* that can be seen as a cognitive system in its own right."[14] In working an equation, person, pen, and paper all work together to solve the problem.

To Clark and Chalmers, this extension of the mind into the world is a phenomenon that *sometimes* happens in cognition. Their perspective preserves a discrete internal realm to which cognition is native—the place where cognition lives—but provides a way of thinking about how minds can, in particular cases like that of working a math problem on a piece of paper, reach out into and employ the external world in order to improve their efficiency. As Clark puts it, cognition can "exploit real-world action so as to reduce computational load."[15] This perspective preserves Kirsch and Maglio's distinction between what happens in the mind and what happens out in the "real world" or in "real situations." For Kirsch and Maglio, epistemic action, typically mental and internal, can become physical and external. For Clark and Chalmers, physical things, which usually participate in the world of action, can participate in cognition through participation in a coupled system. In each case, a gap between mind and world is bridged when the mind reaches out and conscripts material things into its computational operations. The boundary between internal and external is blurred by way of action: the mind acting (by way of the body) on the world, the world contributing to the working of the mind. In terms of Dewey's distinction between self-action, interaction, and transaction outlined in chapter 1, these models of embodied cognition are interactive. They conceive of the cognizing human and the things with which she is coupled as discrete entities that come together, reciprocally acting in such a way that the interaction between them constitutes a cognitive system "in its own right."

If this variety of embodied, extended cognitive science is interactional, what would a transactional model of embodied cognitive science look like? I would argue that REC provides us with just this. Cognition, first, would be understood less as an extending *out* than an extending *across*, in which no "internal" aspect of experience or action is discrete from the environment in which it occurs. The actions performed by players of *Tetris*, whether novices or experts, would always be both epistemic and pragmatic, as knowledge and action cannot be decoupled. The task of the gameplay is merely to play *Tetris*, responding to its challenges as they arise. The task is not to create a parallel internal game, full of hypotheticals and mental rotation tasks, while also playing the game itself—in effect playing two games of *Tetris* at once, one mental and one physical. That the task of playing *Tetris* is playing *Tetris* may sound like a tautology, but the long history of debate around *Tetris* gameplay shows that it needs to be stated outright. Rather than trying to figure out how players coordinate between their mental and their physical relationships to the game, I have been suggesting that we think of the mental and physical tasks of playing *Tetris* as fundamentally indistinguishable from one another. Doing so not only eliminates the distinction between mental and physical action for *Tetris* players, but does the same for how we can rethink the gap between players and the game.

The task of playing *Tetris* is not in the player alone, but in the transactions between the player and the game. This is not a quality unique to interactive media, nor to moving image media. In their aesthetic forms and in their mechanics, media have long provoked reflection, and even anxiety, about the relationship between the outer and the inner world, and about the implications that media forms and technologies have for the presumed sanctity of the inner, private, subjective self. As we saw in chapter 2, the appearance of new media provokes new ways of thinking about perception. By the same token, new media such as film around the turn of the twentieth century and video games around the turn of the twenty-first provoke new felt relationships to representation and new ways of thinking about the roles that representations play (or do not play) in the mind.

This chapter's topic may hit closer to home than that of chapter 2. That chapter's position—that perception is active rather than passive—can in fact be flattering: perception does not just happen to (or in) us—it is something we do, something we achieve. It is a skill for which we do not often enough give ourselves credit. But the idea that there is no discrete, inner realm of experience, no private "self" discontinuous with the material world, is more apt to be regarded as a threat to the ways in which many of us value our own identities. Since the dawn of cinema, in academic film theory and in popular and literary accounts of the effects of media technologies, we see a history of thinkers coming up against the challenges that media present to representationalism and, often, shying away from this confrontation's radical implications for the nature of the mind and thus for the nature of media.

MEDIA AND MIND: A POETIC ANALOGY

In the opening stanza of his thirty-seven-part poem "Cinema," from 1926, Eugene Jolas draws an analogy between the mechanics of a motion picture device and the workings of his own mind and body:

> eyes blinded
> motors turning in my tired brain
> mechanical wheels of my nerves
> refrain of irony
> cry silence[16]

It is unclear whether Jolas refers here to a camera, a projector, or a more general cinematic apparatus inclusive of both. However we imagine this apparatus, it is clear that Jolas's sense of his body—eyes, brain, nerves—and of his ways of relating to the world—seeing, feeling, crying—have been upended by the appearance of moving-image media technologies. In his language, the organic takes on a mechanical aspect, while the mechanical encroaches on the world of feeling, both into physical sensation and into his narrator's exhausted, ironic reaction to the mounting co-acceleration of technology and perception.

In the opening lines of his 2012 book *Plato's Camera*, philosopher Paul Churchland also draws an analogy between cameras, bodies, and brains:

That the *eye* is a camera is now a commonplace. It most surely is a camera, and we understand in great detail how it works . . . The learning brain, by contrast, very slowly constructs a representation, or "takes a picture" of the landscape or configuration of the *abstract universals*, the *temporal invariants*, and the *enduring symmetries* that structure the objective universe of its experience.[17]

Where Jolas's poem despairs at the prospect of perceptual subjectivity being displaced or transformed by representational media, Churchland sees the analogy between camera and brain as a promising framework through which to investigate and characterize the construction of representations that correspond to the "objective universe" of experience.

The poet and the philosopher both intervene at the boundary between inner experience and outer world. Like many media theorists before and after him, Jolas appears to feel disoriented not only by the new sensations offered by film but more fundamentally by how film seems to upset the order of perception, affect, and presence as regards the division between the inner and outer worlds. This stanza can be read as an account of a machine taking over the narrator's mind and body, or as the reflective voice of a camera or projector expressing its own frenzied take on the world, or it could be both, an evocation of a new kind of fraught and hybridized identity that has come into the world by way of people's new entanglements—by way, that is, of their transactions—with cinematic technology.

While Jolas portrays the comforting, familiar boundedness of the mind as being troubled by the new medium, Churchland makes a metaphoric connection to illustrate the operation of the brain. In the brain, as in the eye, Churchland sees something camera-like, a similarity that pertains less to the mechanics of how the mind and the camera work than to what they achieve—in this case, taking a picture, or constructing an abstract "image" of sorts from the particulars with which they are confronted. Like so many theorists of the mind before him, Churchland draws on an analogy to media (wax, slates, books, computers, film, photographs) that is in some respect mind-like, and he uses this analogy as a tool in his attempts to eliminate the gap between the inner mind and the outer world. Churchland's perspective on the mind is called "eliminative materialism." He does not see the mind as discrete from, but rather as an aspect of, the material world. For Churchland, the mind is identical with the brain, so for him, the picture-making of a film apparatus is not analogous to internal mental representations but to the material operation of the brain in the context of its environment. The brain is a camera with no operator, no projector, and no audience.

Historically, however, the mind has largely been understood not as identical with the brain but as the property or product of an immaterial soul. In this context, the "pictures" taken by the mind must also have an observing party to whom they are presented. Aristotle writes that "to the thinking soul, images serve as present sensations. . . . This is why the soul never thinks without an image."[18] (While Aristotle may have codified the idea of circular reasoning, he was by no means immune to it himself.)[19] Since Aristotle, representationalism has dominated thought about thought. Two thousand years later, Thomas Hobbes describes abstract mental images as data upon which the mind performs logical operations, or ratiocinates. "By ratiocination, I mean computation," he writes. "Ratiocination . . . is the same with Addition and Subtraction."[20] Mainstream contemporary cognitive science follows Hobbes in viewing the mind as a computational apparatus that performs operations on abstract symbols.

The influence of representationalist cognitive science on media studies is exemplified in David Bordwell's cognitivist approach to film, which he writes is committed to "*constructivist* explanations in terms of *mental representations* functioning in the context of *social action*."[21] Ironically, this approach corresponds in its representationalism with the semiotic and psychoanalytic models of signification that Bordwell emphatically rejects in formulating his cognitivist perspective. Mental representations in cognitivism, which will have some relationship "outward" to both cinematic images and to social behaviors, are not unlike the distinctions that contemporary media theory makes between hidden structures and processes, such as *langue* (the underlying structure of language) in semiotics and the unconscious in psychoanalysis, on the one hand, and how they give rise to structured manifestations in *parole* (language as actually spoken) and the conscious mind. Like semiotic and psychoanalytic approaches to media, cognitivist media theory, as articulated by Bordwell, is representationalist and dualist at its very foundation.

The idea of pictures or symbols in the brain is problematic, however, in that an internal representation would seem to require an internal observer. As psychologist Richard L. Gregory writes, the idea of pictures in the brain requires "something like an eye in the brain to see its pictures. But then this internal eye would need another eye to see its pictures—then another eye . . . an infinite sequence of eyes and pictures without getting anywhere."[22] In response to the committee of homunculi in *Inside Out*, we might ask: what's going on in *their* heads? Mental "pictures" need not be visual. Internal representations are often characterized as symbolic or linguistic, as in what philosopher Jerry Fodor calls "mentalese," or the language of thought.[23] Alternatively, what if the inner observer is a kind of "pure" or "true" unified self that directly "sees" the mind's images? This would cut off the recursion that worries Gregory. Still, the core question remains: if mental representation is linguistic or pictorial, who or what, in the mind, is doing the "telling" or "showing" and who or what is doing the "listening" or "seeing"?

For Churchland, the mind's representations are better understood as physical impressions of the world, not as internal images with an internal observer. The "Plato's camera" of Churchland's title is the brain, a recording medium that, when exposed to the world via the senses, extrapolates "abstract universals" or generalizations about the structures and processes that surround us and shape our lives. "The brain of each creature typically undergoes this 'picture taking' process only once," writes Churchland, "so as to produce the enduring background conceptual framework with which it will interpret its sensory experience for the rest of its life."[24] This is a lifelong process characterized by a kind of impression upon the brain, much like the impression of an image on film, which is always a diachronic process, even for "still" photography, and always a summary, not a complete record, of an interval in time and space.

In Churchland's perspective, the brain and the mind are one and the same thing. For this reason, the "Plato's camera" of the brain is a representing instrument, but it is not characterized by the sorts of internal representations that trouble Gregory. To Churchland, there is a treelike picture in the brain, but his model requires no internal eye to see it, as the treelike picture itself also *is* the brain. The "picture" made by this camera, then, is not pictographic at all, but rather indexical. One thing in the world (the brain) points to another (the tree). "Interiority" in the sense of symbolic computation does not factor for Churchland. The brain happens to be inside the body, but this physical interiority does not imply that what occurs in the brain happens in a discrete interior sphere. The brain is a material thing, continuous with the material world. As the mind, for Churchland, is the same thing as the brain, the mind is in a sense physically interior to the body, but it is in no sense discrete from the material world. The Platonic work of the brain is the construction of a physical indexical structure by which the brain points to *trees* as a category, and the organism is better equipped to deal with particular trees, should the need fortuitously arise.

Churchland sees an analogy between the functioning of the photographic apparatus and the functioning of the brain. Likewise, many early film theorists identified in the new medium qualities that they recognized as being like the mind, or as having a special relationship to the mind, or both. Psychologist Hugo Münsterberg wrote of cinema's ability to participate in mental events that "in the ordinary [live] theater would go on in our mind alone . . . as if reality has lost its own continuous connection and become shaped by the demands of our soul."[25] The theorist-filmmaker Germaine Dulac writes of what she calls the "visual idea," or "inspiration evolving in continuity" formed in the cinematic text *and* in its viewers by way of the moving image. For Dulac, the capacity to generate the "visual idea" is unique to cinema. Earlier representational forms, Dulac writes, have in the wake of cinema been obligated to imitate film ability to "concentrate impressions":

> Can we not deduce from this that, since literature and theatre, which have wanted to enter into and still do enter into the visual idea, have had to submit to the laws of the cinema, it is because they are not fit to collaborate with us? . . . Should not cinema . . . lead us toward the visual idea composed of movement and life, toward the conception of an art of the eye, made of a perceptual inspiration evolving in its continuity and reaching, just as music does, our thought and feelings?[26]

Dulac and Münsterberg each propose an intimate relationship in which cinema and the mind overlap. What is happening on the screen, in these accounts, seems to be happening for us, seems almost to be called into being by us (or by the demands of our souls), and to be uncannily suited to us. As Dulac writes, it *collaborates* with us.

For Münsterberg and Dulac, theorizing about new media facilitates new ways of understanding experience. Decades before Kirsch and Maglio, Clark and Chalmers, both Münsterberg and Dulac propose versions of extended cognition in their descriptions of interactions with media. Also like those later theorists, who only allow that experience is *sometimes* extended, they remain dedicated to more conventional models of the mind in their accounts of experience in general. To Dulac and Münsterberg, media use represents a special kind of mental experience, an exception to the internal representation by which the mind usually works.

Eugene Jolas's poetic analogy in "Cinema" is fittingly imprecise. It reflects an impression of being at once extended by and constrained or altered by a technology, of being both moved by the new capacities that the technology can afford and simultaneously dehumanized by the ways it can make human hardware—those organic eyes, brains, and nerves—seem obsolete. Like the perspective established in *How It Feels to Be Run Over*, Jolas's poem expresses exultation (and a degree of exaltation) in equal measure with anxiety. Am I enhanced or obsolesced by the onrush of new technology? Can it be both ways? As the film theorist Jean-Louis Comolli writes, "The photograph stands at once as the triumph and the grave of the eye."[27] Technology can make our sensoria seem more vivid than they have ever been, but is this enhancement or replacement? Can optical technologies make unaided vision obsolete? Can our brains be taken over by what Jolas calls the turning motors of media?

The promise of media as exceptional and transformational, as giving rise to entirely new kinds of experience, is founded on representationalism. So, too, is the related anxiety that media might exert outside influence on the mind, polluting or compromising it. By comparison, a perspective that sees media as part of the existing continuity of experience may seem pedestrian and undramatic. To the contrary, though, media in this view have a power in the mind that is foundational rather than exceptional, constitutive rather than transformational. By doing away with representationalism, radical embodied cognition equips us to think beyond the brain and the body and to consider how media participate in experience and thus in the very making of our minds.

Paul Churchland's dedication to materialism is instructive, though his exclusive focus on the brain is overly reductive. As philosopher W. Teed Rockwell writes, identifying the mind exclusively with the brain (seeing the mind *as* the brain), which is known as identity theory, preserves Cartesian dualism by substituting a distinction between brain and body for Descartes's distinction between soul and body. "Descartes said the soul was *in* the brain," writes Rockwell, "and identity theorists say the soul *is* the brain."[28] To say that human experience happens in the brain is like saying a video game happens in the circuitry of a console. A brain is necessary for human experience and circuitry is necessary for a console game, but a game happens on the screen, in the speakers, throughout the console and the controller (circuitry and all), in the world and indeed in the player (brain and all). And experience does happen in the brain, but not with the brain as its container or its sole substrate. Experience is "in the brain" in the way sunlight is "in the sky." Which it is—but more properly the sky is in the sunlight. The brain is in experience.

Philosopher Anthony Chemero has shown how conservative embodied cognition, as Hutto and Myin term it, came about as a reaction to, and an attempt to correct, computationalism's detachment of mental activity from the body and the environment. CEC does this by introducing consideration of the body into a philosophy of mind that remains in the computationalist/representationalist tradition. By explaining the role of the body and the environment within the terms established by computationalism, CEC preserves mental representations by rooting them in bodily sensation and action. These "action-oriented representations" are developed through the organism's ever-increasing history of experience in the physical world. Past sensations and observations are seen as being stored as data and used in computational reasoning about present and possible future situations. While nominally less abstracted or symbolic in form than non-"embodied" mental representations, these are internal representations nonetheless.[29]

We can see a similar maneuver in attempts to introduce embodiment into representationalist paradigms for media theory. Joseph D. Anderson's book *The Reality of Illusion*, for instance, proposes a model for cognitive film theory based largely on psychologist James J. Gibson's ecological, biological account of human perception, a steadfastly nonrepresentationalist view of the mind. However, Anderson runs into a dilemma when he attempts to reconcile Gibson's perspective with a cognitivist framework for film theory along the representationalist lines proposed by David Bordwell. In dealing with the illusory nature of motion pictures that "were not parts of our environment as we developed our capacities for perception," Anderson concludes that "here [in the case of cinema] it is necessary to introduce the concept of computation even though Gibson might not like the idea."[30] This is more than a mere quibble with a detail of Gibson's perspective. Anderson abandons a core aspect of Gibson's theory, perhaps *the* core aspect, opting instead for an ultimately Cartesian model of perception, or at least of film perception. Anderson then takes this as an opportunity to extend his version of computationalism to perception in general while maintaining that film structures our perception in uniquely illusory ways. Scott Richmond has more recently proposed an elegant theory of "proprioceptive aesthetics" that extends Gibson's concept of ecological perception to media not through the lens of cognitivism but through phenomenology. Richmond thereby avoids the representationalist commitments that hold cinematic experience apart from the rest of experience. Part of cinema's "aesthetic work," writes Richmond, is in "modulating and elaborating my modes of relation to the world, and, in the same move, to myself."[31]

The exceptional nonevolutionary status that Anderson extends to film parallels the Kantian idea of "aesthetic perception" developed in Kristin Thompson's film theory. To Thompson, "Because everyday perception is habitual and strives for a maximum of efficiency and ease, aesthetic perception does the opposite."[32] As for Anderson, works of art for Thompson are illusions that go against everyday perception and elicit perception of a different kind. Thinking of aesthetic experience as fundamentally inefficient, or as tied up in inefficient things, does not necessarily devalue it, but it does sever its connection to everyday experience. It creates a discontinuity of kind among artworks and other objects and thus naturalizes the cultural and monetary valuation of art as something "other," nonfunctional, and subject to different modes of control and commodification than are the rest of the objects that make up the environment. It also creates a gulf between the "safe" playfulness of aesthetic experience and the seriousness (and the serious risks) of everyday experience. Aesthetic experience can therefore only inform everyday experience indirectly, through how we conceive of it. Art cannot speak directly to life, but only by way of metaphorical connections that we make between the realm of the aesthetic and the realm of the everyday.

Rather than positing a special exception when confronted with a problem like the seemingly nonfunctional illusions of art, why not look to unusual and surprising aspects of art, cinema, and media experience as expansions of the range of "everyday" experience? Despite the fact that contemporary media did not exist in the early evolutionary environment, and despite the fact that they may seem illusory, inefficient, unhabitual, and difficult, media have powerful functions within the continuity of our lives. Thinking in terms of function, much as Richmond does in his conception of "aesthetic work," is key to REC's nonrepresentational conception of the embodied mind.

Chemero shows how the distinction between representationalism and nonrepresentationalism in philosophy of mind corresponds roughly to a distinction made in early psychology between frameworks known as structuralism and functionalism. Structuralism seeks to measure psychological phenomena and break them down into their component structures, favoring lab-based experimentation and abstraction. Functionalism is more interested in the functioning of minds relative to the lived environment, and it tends toward specificity rather than generalization. The structuralist psychological tradition was developed largely by Wilhelm Wundt, and its origins can be traced to the influence of thinkers such as Kant and Descartes. The origins of functionalism are most associated with William James, who developed his pragmatic approach to the mind under the influence of Darwin's evolutionary theory.[33] Wundtian psychological structuralism, especially via the structuralist linguistics of Ferdinand de Saussure and its influence on Claude Lévi-Strauss, Roland Barthes, and others, has had a profound historical influence on media theory. Functionalism has, thus far, exerted less influence on the field.

As a protégé of both Wundt and James, Hugo Münsterberg occupies a particularly complex position relative to this epistemological schism. Over a long career as a psychologist and a short career as a film theorist, Münsterberg responded to the appeals of both structuralist and functionalist thinking. His writing on film reflects the contentious relationship between these competing models of the mind and the effects that this relationship had on the formulation of early media theory.

Münsterberg's experience of cinema seems to have provoked him to reconsider some of his basic beliefs about the mind, notably to question a fundamental dualism in his understanding of perception. Ambiguities in his film theory, however, reflect how difficult it can be, both conceptually and disciplinarily, to transition to a new paradigm of thought.

HUGO MÜNSTERBERG AND THE EXTERNALIZATION OF ATTENTION

In 1900, Münsterberg dedicated his *Fundamentals of Psychology* "to [my] dear colleague at Harvard University, William James, in sincere respect and cordial friendship."[34] For more than a decade, Münsterberg had been migrating away from his mentor Wilhelm Wundt's experiment-driven structuralist approach to psychology and toward the functionalist ecological approach espoused by James. Even as he was pursuing his doctoral studies, which he completed under Wundt in 1885, Münsterberg clashed with his adviser about the philosophical underpinnings of the work they were doing. After beginning a lectureship in Freiburg in 1887, Münsterberg continued to gravitate toward functionalism, and within a few years, he had accepted an invitation from James to join him at Harvard, where he established an experimental psychological laboratory.[35] Despite their respect and cordial friendship, however, James and Münsterberg did not always see eye to eye.

Although Münsterberg worked in a largely functionalist academic department at Harvard under the initial sponsorship of James, his interest in experimental lab work and his later contributions to applied and industrial psychology reflected a continuing interest in measurement and abstraction that was not entirely compatible with James's functionalist approach to psychology. Münsterberg occupied a middle territory that was ultimately well liked by neither James nor Wundt. In 1893, the year after his arrival at Harvard, Münsterberg demonstrated his analytical methodologies at the Chicago World's Fair. James disparagingly called the exhibition "Münsterberg's circus."[36]

Toward the end of his career and his life, Münsterberg attended his first-ever film screening, of *Neptune's Daughter* (Herbert Brenan, 1914).[37] This experience appears to have reshaped Münsterberg's thinking about the mind, or perhaps to have troubled it in a way that led him to reassess his understanding of the relationships between minds, bodies, and environments. Two years later, he published a seminal work of film theory, *The Photoplay: A Psychological Study*. Sadly (and dramatically) he died that same year while lecturing in front of about sixty Radcliffe students. A lengthy and sensational notice in the next day's issue of the *Boston Sunday Post* featured an entire section titled "Students Scream."[38] In his elaboration of cinematic experience, Münsterberg gestures toward ideas about how media, body, and environment contribute to the constitution of the mind. Suspended between the influences of his mentors and collaborators Wundt and James, Münsterberg attempts to account for both the pragmatic function and the structural form of film in shaping the experience of the cinemagoer:

> Of all internal functions which create the meaning of the world around us, the most central is the attention. The chaos of the surrounding impressions is organized into a real cosmos of experience by our selection of that which is significant and of consequence. This is true for life and stage alike. Our attention must be drawn now here, now there, if we want to bind together that which is scattered in the space before us.[39]

Münsterberg goes on to assert that the cinema is uniquely capable of directing minds, especially through devices such as the close-up, which has "objectified in our world of perception our mental act of attention" via its guidance of our attention to particular details of the mise-en-scène.[40] The cinema can thereby produce a form of subjectivity that is external to our bodies. It can extend our act of attention into the world outside of our bodies by dictating which features of a scene we perceive. The close-up, in effect, *pays attention for us.*

Figure 3.2 visualizes the difference between everyday attention and cinematic attention for Münsterberg. In everyday attention (the left-hand image), the person perceives the outside world, and those perceptions are actively organized, within the theater of the mind, into what Münsterberg calls an "internal cosmos of experience." Attention is directed toward mental representations, and perception is external to this "internal cosmos." Perception would then have to be one or more of the following: (*a*) part of the mind, but external to the *internal* or subjective part of the mind; (*b*) part of the body, but located in a part of the body where the mind is not; or (*c*) external to the body itself. No matter which of these is the case, this model entails a dualism between internal attention and external perception. Internal experience is abstracted from reality in that it refers outward *to* it. This model of experience is in keeping with the representationalist paradigm of Wundt's structuralism.

In cinematic attention (the right-hand image), however, attention has been externalized by cinema. In Münsterberg's words, attention has been objectified

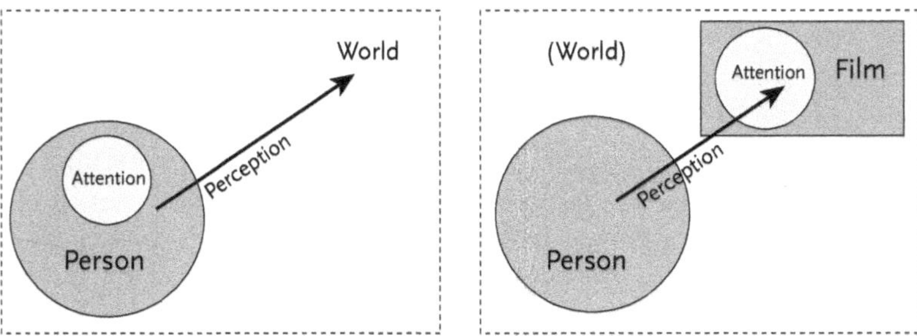

Figure 3.2 A visualization of everyday attention (*left*) and cinematic attention (*right*) as described by Münsterberg.

"in our world of perception." This is how Münsterberg accounts for film's ability to shape our understanding and interpretation of the events that it depicts. Notably, it also eliminates the dualism between internal and external experience that we saw in Münsterberg's account of noncinematic attention. Cinematic attention does not call for a discrete, inner, abstracted account of experience but rather renders attention a meaningful *part* of the "world of perception." Münsterberg's consideration of cinema effects a paradigm shift in his account of the mind. He is a structuralist for everyday experience but a functionalist for cinematic experience.

The educational theorist Lev Vygotsky, also writing in the early twentieth century, echoes Münsterberg in his discussion of what he calls "indirect" or mediated memory. Vygotsky characterizes behavior as a "*direct* relation to the task set before the organism," which he visualizes as an unbroken link between stimulus and response.

The stimulus is an environmental event or challenge, and the response is an organismic reaction to the environmental development. However, when a sign operation such as mediation enters into the picture, Vygotsky writes, the relationship changes:

> The structure of sign images requires an intermediate link between the stimulus and the response. This intermediate link is a second order stimulus [that] creates a new relation between S and R . . . the simple stimulus-response process is replaced by a complex, mediated act, which we picture as:

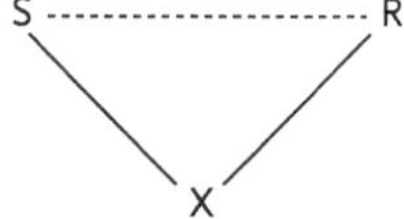

> In this new process the direct impulse to react is inhibited, and an auxiliary stimulus that facilitates the completion of the operation by indirect means is incorporated. . . . This auxiliary stimulus . . . transfers the psychological operation to higher and qualitatively new forms and permits humans, by the aid of extrinsic stimuli, *to control their behavior from the outside.*[41]

Like Münsterberg, Vygotsky sees mediation as a phenomenon that *comes between* the perceiving subject and the objective world and that thereby disrupts the interiority of the subject. What was once internal and inaccessible is externalized and thereby made accessible and manipulable. For Münsterberg, this means that media can direct or dictate attention. For Vygotsky, this externalized subjectivity "leads humans to a specific structure of behavior that breaks away from biological development and creates new forms of culturally-based psychological processes."[42]

In each case, these new forms of psychological functioning represent a break from, rather than a variation on, previous modes of experience. Vygotsky explicitly claims that aesthetic experience exists, by necessity, in *isolation* from the continuity of experience in general, a point on which he agrees with "Münsterberg's psychological theory, according to which isolation is an indispensable condition for aesthetic experience . . . because it guarantees a strictly central release of the affects generated by art and ensures that these affects are not expressed by any other external action."[43] Both Vygotsky and Münsterberg formulate general models of the mind that rely on discrete, internal, abstracted forms of experience, but this discreteness and internality is troubled by the stimulating effects that media can have on their users. In each case, and in keeping with the historical marginalization and sequestering of aesthetic experience from "normal" or "real" experience, the psychologists set aesthetic experience aside as an important and intriguing exception. And in both cases, the aesthetic, that is, that which provokes aesthetic experience, must itself necessarily be set aside as discrete, as isolated from the flow of everyday experience, in order to "speak" to the aesthetic sensibility of its users.

This reasoning ought to be inverted. What may seem to be exceptional about experience of media can help us to see through some of the illusions of subjectivity, and Münsterberg's and Vygotsky's models of the media-using mind are perhaps more accurate representations of everyday experience than the authors suspect. Their models of media use were closer than they may have realized to the tradition of James and Dewey, and they anticipated the ecological psychology of Gibson as well as more recent nonrepresentational radical embodied models of cognition.

For a theorist in Münsterberg's position, influenced by both functionalist and structuralist thinking, it is easy to see how such a perspective might prove attractive. Münsterberg found the cinema to be a hyperreal intensification of the world as we experience it in day-to-day life, a freeing of the world from its spatiotemporal constraints that allows it to be "clothed in the forms of our own consciousness." This transformation, specific to film, is at once an unprecedented achievement and the summation of a more general historical trajectory in aesthetics. Münsterberg continues, ecstatically: "The mind has triumphed over matter, and the pictures roll on with the ease of musical tones. It is a superb enjoyment which no other art can furnish us."[44]

Münsterberg hints at a bidirectional exchange that goes unmentioned. The transformation that he ascribes to film is a triumph of mind over matter. Film is the site of the mind's reorganization of objective, external reality. It is the mind's version of things. But, simultaneously, just the opposite is happening. Film *is* a part of the massive outer world, and its own weight can be felt in the very sensation that Münsterberg describes as the pictures rolling on with the ease of musical tones. To Münsterberg, as Karla Oeler puts it, "The close-up harmonizes with the intention of the spectator."[45] Here Münsterberg echoes John Dewey's concept of "smooth-running functions," which I argued in chapter 2 is a better way of understanding the "flow" that media can produce in their users, the sensation of being swept along in an intuitive-seeming, psychologically active, but somehow effortless-feeling process as stimulated by engagement with a media object. Münsterberg was fifty-three years old when he died in 1916. As with Dewey, it is unrealistic to wish that Münsterberg could have lived long enough to play video games, but it is intriguing to speculate about his potential commentary on the complex narratives and experimental films of the 1920s, not to mention on the sound and color film that followed, and the new directions in which they could have coaxed his understanding of the mind.

RECONSTRUCTING REPRESENTATIONS

Mainstream cognitive science and neuroscience tend to approach the mind from a priori representationalist perspectives and thus to perceive mental representations where they go looking for them. Popular reception of cognitive science tends toward representationalism, as well, in a way that romanticizes the "mind's eye" and mystifies cognitive science and neuroscience as kinds of technological divination into the hidden world of subjectivity. In both cases, the discursive power of images in media comes to stand in for the purported power of images in the mind. Additionally, images used as stimuli and for visualizing results enter into existing visual discourses about the nature of the mind, discourses that go well beyond the bounds of experimental science.[46] For this reason, it is important to consider the ways that these images resonate with how perception, memory, and internal representations have historically been depicted in media, and to consider popular conceptions of media themselves as extensions of our perception into previously inaccessible places (such as the brain and the mind) and into the past, that hazy realm where early media emerged and where memories—our own and those of others—are from.

In a 2011 study that was picked up widely in the popular press, researchers at the University of California, Berkeley, attempted to reconstruct film clips solely from information about the brains of subjects who were watching the clips.[47] The researchers amassed an archive of around eighteen million clips, each of them one second long. Each clip was correlated to probable corresponding states in the visual cortex according to previously collected data. Subjects were then exposed to a separate set of longer scenes not represented in the clip library. Using only functional magnetic resonance imaging (fMRI) to measure changes to blood flow in the visual cortices of the subjects, the researchers attempted to reconstruct the film clips that the subjects had been viewing (fMRI provides a more dynamic representation of the functioning of the brain than does MRI, which takes more static snapshots of the brain at a particular moment). For each second of fMRI data, a computer predicted the one hundred most likely matches from the eighteen-million-clip library. These one hundred most likely comparable clips were then averaged to produce a visual estimation of what the subjects might be viewing. The reconstructions are a kind of algorithmic bricolage, the computer's attempt to hash out a passable emulation of the original clips through selection and blending of the resources it had available.

Especially given that they could look like anything at all, the resulting images are indeed similar to the originals. The similarity is especially striking when the images are observed in motion.[48] Humanoid shapes move against backgrounds that suggest the settings of the original clips. Word-like forms appear in place of title cards. Velocity and screen direction are largely consistent between stimulus and constructed image. The study caught the public imagination, and the results were widely construed as reconstructions of the internal mental images that viewers produce when watching films. A press release from the lab referred to the brain's "coding" of visual information, portraying the experiment as "a critical step toward obtaining reconstructions of internal states such as imagery, dreams and so on."[49] As coauthor Jack Gallant put it, "This is a major leap toward reconstructing internal imagery. We are opening a window into the movies in our minds."[50] While the study itself appears neutral as to the status of subjective internal representations (its focus is on the physical activity of the brain), the popular interpretation of its results reflects the pervasiveness of the idea of the internal theater of the mind. Viewed without the assumption of mental representations, the results seem instead to suggest a somewhat consistent relationship between screen imagery and brain activity, as evidenced by the development of a tool that can predict what kinds of brain activity will result from exposure to particular onscreen images.

The composite images are clearly constructions, but what, if anything, do they *reconstruct*? The algorithm builds backward from activation states in the visual cortex toward images that provoked them. It characterizes a material relationship between viewers and film, rather than a representational process "internal" to users of media. If we think back to the diagrams for Münsterberg's model of cinematic attention in figure 3.2, this study tells us something about the "perception" arrow, but not about the "attention" circle. It does not reconstruct subjective mental images, but rather approximates objective physical images: not images in the mind, but the original onscreen images of the clips. Seen as limited to media stimuli and their physical effects, the study reveals itself as less psychological than forensic. For that matter, the sequential presentation of fMRI data, the archive of clips used in the reconstructions, and the study's reconstructions of film images are all themselves media representations. This study is permeated by representations, perhaps everywhere but where it is purported to find them.

As the visually compelling reconstructed images do much of the rhetorical heavy lifting in this study, it is important to note their resonances with other kinds of cinematic imagery. The reconstructions are texturally similar, for instance, to conventional cinematic representations of dream states, hallucinations, and memories. When French impressionist and surrealist filmmakers, including Germaine Dulac, experimented in the 1920s with cinematic depictions of subjectivity, they soon began to use soft focus, blurring effects, spatiotemporal distortion, and superimposition, techniques that persist as contemporary standard, and sometimes clichéd, signifiers of subjectivity in the cinema. All of these qualities are in evidence in the reconstructed clips.

Further, the clips exhibit an obscure, indistinct quality that is often associated with older or degraded media. The reconstructions were described in the press as a

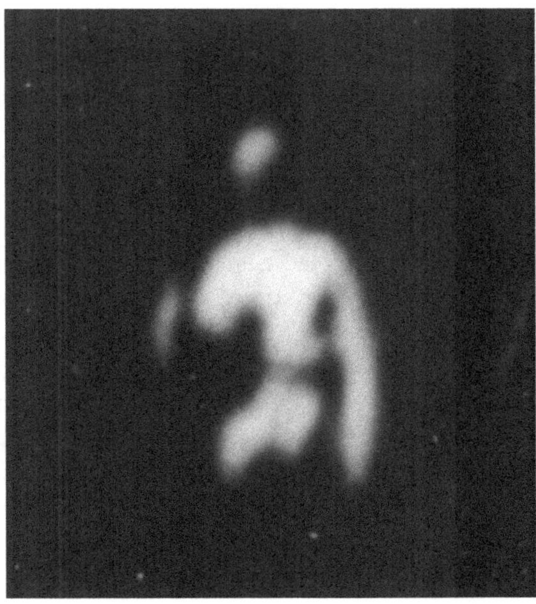

Figure 3.3 *Monkeyshines No. 1* (William K. L. Dickson and William Heise, 1890).

"haunting, almost dream-like version of the video as seen by the mind's eye."[51] From a contemporary perspective, early media recordings such as Edison Manufacturing Company's *Monkeyshines* kinetoscope experiments, carried out in 1889 and 1890 (figure 3.3), are dreamlike in a visually similar way, marked by what philosopher Martin Hägglund calls a "hauntological" spectrality, or a "relation to what is *no longer or not yet.*"[52] In applying Hägglund's historical insight to cinema, cultural theorist Mark Fisher writes that we can "distinguish two directions in hauntology. The first refers to that which is (in actuality is) *no longer*, but which is still effective as a virtuality.... The second refers to that which (in actuality) has *not yet* happened, but which is already effective in the virtual (an attractor, an anticipation shaping current behavior)."[53] *Monkeyshines* at the time of its production is the latter, an anticipatory step toward the more elaborately realized cinema to come a few years later. Seen in retrospect from the present, it is the former: a vision of actions undertaken over a century ago by people who are now dead, recorded by technology long obsolesced, but "still effective as a virtuality."

Despite all of its spectrality, *Monkeyshines* persists as a material thing. It is because of the material persistence of *Monkeyshines* that its spectrality is possible. Similarly, in the reconstructed clips from the Berkeley study we can see both a record of what once occurred, the specific instances in which these clips were played some time around 2011, and the responses in the visual cortices of the subjects. If we interpret the clips as reconstructions of mental representations, they gain further hauntological dimensions. They are thus connected to the *no longer* of the subjects' fleeting mental representations, snatched both from the passage of time and from the obscure internality of the subjects' minds, and to the *not yet* of a time possibly to come when the representational content of minds might be laid bare by brain-scanning technology. A haunting prospect indeed.

The study's reconstructed clips resonate with a complex of long-standing cinematic and extracinematic ideas of what subjectivity, and of what memory, "looks" like—an idea that has influenced thinking both about the nature of subjective experience and about the subjectivity, or the memory, of media themselves. The rhetorical framing of the images as an unprecedented look into a previously obscure realm further aligns the study with the rhetoric of early modern visual and acoustic media, which, as Carolyn Marvin has demonstrated, combined technological innovation with a kind of "cognitive imperialism" that created new, mediated domains in order to extend dominant colonial reach.[54] For Marvin, this constitutes an extension of imperialist influence around the globe that naturalizes the discourse of the cultures that happen to wield the power of communication and optical technologies. As media technologies are extended into observation and visualization of neurological phenomena, including the ostensible depiction of internal states, it is important to avoid the representationalist counterpart to the colonialist confirmation bias that rendered the illusory benevolence of technologies like the telegraph—a specter that we might call imperial cognitivism.

NEVER UNCOUPLED

Expert *Tetris* play does not demonstrate the difference between epistemic and pragmatic action; it demonstrates that the epistemic *is* pragmatic. Münsterberg's theory of attention does not demonstrate a special quality of perception specific to media use; it demonstrates how media use exemplifies a quality of *all* perception. And the Berkeley study does not reveal subjective images internal to the mind; it reflects the material continuity of brain, body, and environment. In each case, conceptual discontinuities have been inserted due to prior commitments to representationalist thinking. As a result, relationships between *Tetris* and players, between films and viewers, and between stimuli and test subjects are understood in interactional terms. The Cartesian wound remains unhealed.

In what Andy Clark calls cognitive coupling, perception "acts as a constantly available channel that productively couples agent and environment rather than as a kind of 'veil of transduction' whereby world-originating signals must be converted into a persisting inner model of the external scene."[55] While Clark always reserves a place for noncoupled cognition, carefully characterizing cognitive extension as something that *can* happen, I have argued that we are never "uncoupled" from our environment. Our minds are thus always extended, not in Clark's sense of extending outward from the body or from the brain, grasping and using the world, but in the sense of extending across space and time, emerging from the continuity of the world. In this perspective, coupling can be a useful way to describe a local dynamic, a productive relationship between two or more things, but it should always be understood as a descriptive convenience.

The language used to attribute discreteness to things, and the conditions in which things can then encounter one another, is an instrument of discursive power and control. Chapters 4 and 5 discuss how the figures of the "platform" and the "interface" have functioned in media studies' recent engagements with media technologies. Both figures represent ways of partitioning dynamic relationships within media and among media, their users, and the wider environment, always in service of particular rhetorical investments. Conceived transactionally, relationships among things are never really cases of things unilaterally acting upon, or employing, one another. Rather, they are aspects of a continuous broader dynamic characterized by direct and fundamentally entangled relations. This direct perceptual, affective, and enactive presence in the environment stands in contrast to the modes of presence proposed by dualist, representationalist models of the mind, whether in philosophy of mind, psychology, or media studies. Transactions between ourselves and our environments, the necessary conditions for us to perceive, feel, and act, are themselves the sites and sources of meaning, and that meaning is shaped by the parameters of our environments and the particularities of our bodies. In order to think about the roles—practical, meaningful, causal—that art and media can play in such a system, we will need to look more closely at the roles that media technologies play in that system. The intelligence of humans and the intelligence of media technologies are fundamentally intertwined, inseparable aspects of deeper, larger, longer processes of becoming.

Over the first three chapters, we have descended into the ostensible depths of the interior mind. We now move laterally, from the depths of internal representation to the likewise obscure technological depths of what is called the "platform." From here we will work our way upward, back toward the light of day.

CHAPTER 4

Platforms as Emergence

Platforms, it seems, are everywhere these days. The *word* "platform" certainly is. We are assured that platforms are the future, that the parties that develop and own them will have outsize control over the channels through which people communicate, innovate, and invest their resources. Increasingly, as in a wave of elections and referenda around the globe in the mid-2010s, media platforms shape and channel what passes for "knowledge" and "facts." In politics, the party platform seems to have yielded some of its power to the technological platform. With all of the optimism and anxiety swirling around it, it is perhaps not surprising that the platform is a contested figure, defined differently and assigned different boundaries, qualities, and potentials depending on the disciplinary, ideological, and material investments of those using the term.

"Platform" is applied denotatively to media technology in a wide range of ways. Sometimes it refers to physical hardware, sometimes to software code, and sometimes to a combination of the two. Software architecture like Facebook's can be a platform, but so can hardware like Sony's PlayStation 4 console. A distribution system for streaming media, like Netflix, can be considered a platform, as can the iPhone's combination of hardware and operating system, considered as a whole. What distinguishes these platforms from nonplatforms are their facilitative functions. They make possible further media, or user experiences, or exchanges of value (social, informational, monetary) that rely upon and are channeled through them. Platforms are infrastructural and regulatory. And, like the theater of the mind, they are structures that facilitate "content."

This chapter traces philosophical, disciplinary, and ideological valences that have largely gone unremarked not only in the enthusiastic industrial discourse about the profit potential of "platform businesses,"[1] but also in theoretical and critical works that characterize aspects of media technology, at varying scales, as platforms, in particular in the developing subdiscipline of "platform studies." To define something as a platform, I argue, is to ask your audience to accept it (*a*) as a *thing*, as a discrete object distinct from its surroundings, and (*b*) as possessing a particular and limited set of qualities, functions, and potential meanings. One of this chapter's central contentions is that such an understanding of platforms is an implicit argument for what has been called "strong" emergence, or the idea that separate things can come together to constitute a new thing distinct from its component parts. That new thing may share qualities with its component parts, but it is distinguished by qualities inherent to it and not to them. This way of ascribing essences, and thus of establishing Platonic or Cartesian discontinuities among things and their contexts, is sometimes called "substance dualism." In chapters 2 and 3, we have seen such a system at work in dualist models of the mind. In this chapter and the next, we will see its counterpart in dualist conceptions of media technology.

The external and internal boundaries of purported platforms are, upon closer examination, always fuzzier than they at first seem. Indeterminism about its objects creeps into platform studies. I argue that this illustrates the utility of the term "platform" as a descriptor, instead, of what are called *weakly* emergent phenomena—that is, emergent dynamics characterized not by their newness but merely by their unexpectedness. Think of the weather or of traffic—difficult to model, seemingly endlessly variable, and forever capable of surprising us.

Philosopher David J. Chalmers writes that strong emergence occurs when a "high-level phenomenon arises from [a] low-level domain, but truths concerning that phenomenon are not *deducible* even in principle from truths in the low-level domain." In weak emergence, a "high-level phenomenon arises from [a] low-level domain, but truths concerning that phenomenon are *unexpected* given the principles governing the low-level domain."[2] Strong emergence implies something essential and unknowable, while weak emergence reflects a changing relationship to knowledge. Strong emergence is an ontological claim, while weak emergence is an epistemological one. For Chalmers, a proud self-proclaimed dualist, "There is exactly one clear case of a strongly emergent phenomenon, and that is the phenomenon of consciousness."[3]

The field of platform studies has been effective in refocusing scholarly attention to the specificities of media technologies, but a tendency to substance dualism has isolated its objects of study from their continuity with their users and with their use. This chapter makes its case for a weakly emergent conception of the platform as an alternative to platform studies' interactionist tendencies. While a transactional understanding of the platform disrupts the medium specificity and disciplinary specificity of a narrower conception of the term, it does so in the service of a more integrative and productive account of what platforms are, how they are constituted, and what they can do. The chapter examines some of the ways that technological platforms and situations of emergence have been characterized both in media and in media theory. The fuzzy material and conceptual boundaries of these forms are illustrated through the example of a shot from the film *What Time Is It There?* (Tsai Ming-liang, 2001) that highlights the entanglement of media technologies and troubles the idea of media as containers or as content. This is followed by a discussion of the indistinct boundaries among "levels" in different theoretical conceptions of hardware and software platforms. I argue that the fuzziness of the distinctions among components and levels of platforms corresponds to a similar fuzziness in thinking about components and levels of emergence in life and mind. In both cases, the horizontal divisions (among parts) and the vertical divisions (among levels) are consistently drawn according to the rhetorical, disciplinary, and other resource investments of the parties doing the describing.

WHAT IS A PLATFORM (FOR)?

The term "platform" was adopted into the English language from the Middle French *platte-forme*, meaning "flat form," around the middle of the sixteenth century. It is used in English both to indicate a physical "raised, level surface," and, in a more metaphoric sense, to designate a "plan of action, scheme," or "design." Interestingly, the term seems to have first been used in English in the latter, more metaphoric sense, though its use to describe a material structure soon followed.[4]

In its current proliferation of media and technology discourse, the figure of the platform is most often presented as an ontology ("*this* kind of thing is a platform") when I would argue that it is in fact an imperative epistemological statement ("*think of this dynamic as* a platform") rooted in particular industrial, political, and disciplinary investments. To designate a platform is to draw a boundary, in space and in time, around part of a boundless dynamic and assert that what is within that line is stable and self-contained. It naturalizes that thing, not in the sense of claiming that it always was, but in urging us to take its wholeness and utility for granted going forward. This taking for granted is at the heart of a definition of the platform provided by Ian Bogost and Nick Montfort in their book *Racing the Beam*, a study of the Atari Video Computer System console that proposes a rationale and an agenda for platform studies as a discipline. "Whatever the programmer takes for granted when developing," Bogost and Montfort write, "and whatever, from another side, the user is required to have working in order to use particular software, is the platform."[5]

Despite its nominal orientation toward a control-driven future, the platform thus conceived is an inherently backward-looking construct, in the sense that it treats its object as prior, as something that exists now, that has come into being, and that has been established as substantially unified and complete. As we have seen in the previous chapters, this is also a common way of understanding the mind. The mind is seen as something that originated from the world, and that in many ways remains rooted in it, but that is also fundamentally different from it, that has become separated from the world in a way that allows it to act *upon* the world as if from without. This mind is contained by the world but is then further contained within particular material conditions (a body, a brain, a cortex) that liberate it from some of the constraints that pertain to the rest of the world, so that the mind is in the world but the world is not in the mind. A mind, in this way of understanding it, would be a strongly emergent phenomenon.

Facilitated by their dualism, such ways of conceiving of the mind can normalize what a mind is, establishing an idealized standard mind against which other minds can be judged as sufficient or deficient. Such purported deficiencies are often explained in ways that reattach or tether the mind to the material world from which it would ideally float free: a damaged brain; an abject body of inferior race, gender, sexuality, morality, or ability; an excess of "bodily" hormones, often racialized or coded as gendered, that compromise the logical purity of the mind or brain; a perverse attachment to fetishized objects that subverts the mind's independence; the "shame" of intoxication or addiction. The mind thus conceived is a leaky vessel—leaky not like a bucket but leaky like a boat, compromised because it lets too much of the world in.

The connection that I am drawing between conceptions of the mind as a container and of technological platforms as containers is not only a metaphoric equivalence. If the mind is understood as an aspect of the continuity of the physical world, then "media" ought to be so understood as well. As in Dewey's insistence on seeing the parts of the brain in continuity with the whole brain, organism, and nature, a transactional understanding of media will not draw rigid lines between media and users, nor will it do so among the components of media systems, nor between media technologies and media "content." For this reason, I seek to reclaim the term "platform" in its connection to material continuity. A platform in this sense is not a discrete thing in itself but one way to describe how an articulation of matter and energy functions, as viewed from a particular perspective. Even in its sense as a "plan of action, scheme," or "design," then, we ought to treat the platform as no less continuous with the material world than we would a raised, level surface. A railroad platform does not float free of the ground below it. It is an extension of terra firma that relies on the ground in a primordial way. Likewise, even our grandest designs and most outlandish fantasies are always *parts* of the material world.

Different disciplinary and industrial approaches to the figure of the media platform draw different lines around what such a platform is. As noted earlier, a platform might be software or hardware, an operating system, a media device, a computational media device specifically (to the exclusion of other media devices), or something else altogether. Common to strongly-emergent conceptions of the platform is an assertion that *something* is settled, stable, and unified. The argument for a platform is a figure-ground argument. In visual and other modes of perception, a perceiver understands figures, or objects, only by contrast to the context in which they are grounded. Figure stands out from ground. When a figure and a ground move relative to one another, as when a person walks across a room, an onlooker typically perceives the figure as being in motion and the ground as stationary. Perceptual differentiation of figure from ground seems to be a probabilistic process in which perceptual cues "bias observers to see one region as occluding another."[6] Attention tends to focus, then, on the figures, while the ground is taken for granted.

Figure 4.1 Detail from *A Hole Is to Dig* by Ruth Krauss and Maurice Sendak.

Figure occludes ground not only visually but conceptually as well. When we are asked to understand something as a platform, we are asked to accept it as a ground against which figures move. Its stability taken for granted, the platform recedes from view and the "content" that it makes possible commands our attention. The Apple iPad is a powerful portable computing platform, we are told, that makes amazing (or, in Apple's own hyperbolic rhetoric, "magical and revolutionary")[7] software applications and user experiences possible. The PlayStation series of video game platforms, developed by Sony, promises its designers the power to create immersive virtual worlds and its players the power to become immersed in them.

A platform tells its users, "You can stand on me, I am stable." In the children's picture book *A Hole Is to Dig*, writer Ruth Krauss and illustrator Maurice Sendak present an image of that most primordial of platforms, the terrestrial ground itself (figure 4.1). Billed as "a book of first definitions," *A Hole Is to Dig* provides its young readers with the twin reassurances of priorness and purpose. The world—the ground—is already there, and you need not worry about it going anywhere. Further, it is there *for you* in a personal sense. In Sendak's illustration, the ground curves upward as if to meet the feet of the two figures, who are thus elevated and enabled to gaze and gesture from their platform toward some distant detail invisible to us.[8] This is enough for a child, for now. One hopes that a later lesson will further specify: the world is there for you, *for you*. That is, from your perspective, the world seems to be there for you. For others, it seems as if it is there for them.

Empathy for others and care for the environment is born in acknowledgment that a ground is in fact shared by the figures and is itself no less dynamic and contingent than they are. Ideally, we would acknowledge that the figure-ground distinction doesn't make much sense outside of describing (relatively) local practicalities, in particular in describing the ways human perception has evolved to exploit the spatiotemporal scale, or the perceptual niche, that humans happen to occupy. As the physics of relativity has shown, the figure-ground distinction is always perspectival. Figure only exists if you take something to be ground, and ground only if you take something to be figure. In the end, everything is both potential figure and potential ground.

The strongly-emergent conception of the technological platform asks us to take *a* ground for granted again—a ground provided and defined for us by technological stakeholders. The proliferation of personal and personalizable devices designed to make their users feel like the centers of the universe again is a testament to this. Arguments for the infantilizing flattery of media technique and technology have been made many times before, as in John Berger's argument that, in Renaissance perspective, "perspective makes the single eye the centre of the visible world. . . . The visible world is arranged for the spectator as the universe was once thought to be arranged for God"[9] and in Jean-Louis Baudry's equation of the cinematic exhibition space with an artificial womb.[10]

As Constance Penley points out, however, such theoretical frameworks too often construct totalizing arguments about media effects that efface difference both among media apparatuses and among the minds, bodies, and identities of media users. In the case of apparatus theory like that of Baudry and of Christian Metz, this is due to limitations of the ways in which the theorists apply psychoanalytic concepts to cinematic perception. Penley finds apparatus theory's political aspect, its "important stress on the cinema as an *institution*," valuable, and she hopes to see it retained in an approach to the cinematic apparatus that is less totalizing, more capable of reckoning with difference.[11] The discipline of platform studies differentiates itself from its forebear, apparatus theory, by largely abstaining from overt political entanglements and focusing on the technological specificities of media platforms and their relationships to media form. While studies of platforms often address the cultural and industrial contexts in which platforms came to be, in its treatment of the platform itself as a whole with which users (both programmers and players), strongly emergent platform thinking re-establishes boundaries between thing and context, self and world, inside and outside.

An understanding of platforms as epistemological, rather than ontological, formations can be mobilized in at least three politically relevant ways. First, it calls into question the ethics and implications of designating something, or someone, as a unitary or a discrete object, definable as a collection of components in a particular formation, that has inherent qualities that emerge from the collection of those components in that particular form. You can look to no component of a thing's composition (skin, genitals, brain, processor, projector) as the essence of what the thing as a whole is, nor can you look to a thing as a "whole" in order to locate its essence. Second, it allows for a more integrated consideration of the work and the material resources that go into the production and operation of platforms, emphasizing platforms' continuity with the industrial and sociocultural practices in which they participate. And third, an epistemological interpretation of the platform places emphasis on conceptual, perceptual, and experiential newness, rather than on the designation of a thing as new in essence. Rather than defining what is (already) new, it celebrates what could be, seeking always to find new transactional possibilities rather than foreclosing them through interactional thinking.

Pursuing theoretical models that reflect platforms' material history, their connection to the labor involved in making and using them, and their participation in their sociocultural, industrial, and material contexts, scholars including Tarleton Gillespie, Caetlin Benson-Allott, Marc Steinberg, and Nathan Altice have traced the etymology and use history of the concept of the platform across a variety of languages and contexts. Their accounts have in common a sense of the expansive range of the term as it applies not only to computational media technologies, but to industrial management strategies (Steinberg), to the discursive positioning of cultural intermediaries and content hosts like Google and Youtube (Gillespie), and to increased scholarly interest in questions of "how *things* and *matter* produce action and meaning in the world" (Benson-Allott).[12] Increasingly, scholars consider also the degree to which human beings might be considered to be platforms or parts of platforms, as when Altice writes that "It is worthwhile to step back and evaluate the human and ecological 'platforms' that fuel and feed the development of our consoles and computers."[13] All of this work pushes the boundaries of the platform out into the world and, crucially, allows the world to further permeate the figure of the platform. These expansions of the platform blur conceptual boundaries around what can be considered a platform, as well as disciplinary boundaries around what can be considered platform studies. In both respects, they point promisingly toward an epistemological, or a weakly emergent, or a transactional conception of the platform. In such a conception, platforms, whether computational or cinematic, industrial or biological, are never discrete from one another, and they only come into being as platforms through their identification as such. Their entanglement precedes their existence.

ENTANGLED PLATFORMS

In a shot from the film *What Time Is It There?* (Tsai Ming-liang, 2001), a young man named Hsiao-kang sits alone in a dark Taipei bedroom, facing a television screen that supplies the room's only light (figure 4.2). He hugs a pillow. A cigarette is perched between his fingers, its long ash dangling precariously. Playing on the TV screen is François Truffaut's 1959 film *The 400 Blows*. That film's protagonist, an adolescent boy named Antoine Doinel, squirms gleefully inside an amusement park drum ride, pinned to its side by centripetal force. As he struggles to raise his leg, his image on Hsiao-kang's screen comes to echo that of Hsiao-kang on our

Figure 4.2 Hsiao-kang watches *The 400 Blows* (François Truffaut, 1959) in *What Time Is It There?* (Tsai Ming-liang, 2001).

screen. Like the scene that I asked you to imagine in this book's introduction, of yourself watching a film, playing a game, or reading a book, this shot from *What Time Is It There?* is a matrix of iterative circuits, both technological and perceptual. The smoke from Hsiao-kang's cigarette is not separate from the atmosphere of the room. It is part of the atmosphere. It is *of* the atmosphere, and the atmosphere is of it and of other things. The technologies, the bodies, the spaces, and the perceptions that this shot presents and represents are no less entangled and coconstitutive.

Hsiao-kang's cathode-ray tube television draws images on its screen with a concealed electronic gun that scans repeatedly across its phosphor-coated glass surface, firing a stream of electrons that illuminate it from within. This series of horizontal lines of light, drawn in rapid succession sometime around the year 2000 and simultaneously recorded by Tsai's camera, is cued by a series of electrical signals from a videocassette recorder, which produces them in response to a magnetic signal encoded on a videotape. This magnetic encoding is a transcription of images from a motion picture filmstrip, from which it is transferred imperfectly (transfers are always imperfect): the film's original 2.35:1 aspect ratio is cropped to 4:3, its frame rate is transferred via a "three-two pulldown" process so that the twenty-four-frames-per-second film can be played on Taiwan's thirty-frames-per-second NTSC video standard, and so on. The images in the copy of *The 400 Blows* that was used to produce the videotape transfer have their own distant origins in a film camera's sampling of light that radiated from our sun and was reflected at oblique angles, eight minutes later, by surfaces in France in the late 1950s, a sampling that produced a record of the workings of another machine—an amusement park ride—that, like Truffaut's camera and like Hsiao-kang's VCR, is propelled by cyclical mechanics, and that exerted physical force on the body of young Jean-Pierre Léaud, the actor who plays Doinel. Truffaut's camera is mounted to the ride, so that Léaud/Doinel stays center screen, which creates the illusion that the ride and the boy remain still while the world cycles around them. Opposite the TV screen, Hsiao-kang is equally still, though the motion of the films (both *What Time Is It There?* and *The 400 Blows*) remind us that he is also in constant motion, even when he appears still. Vivian Sobchack calls this "the *first* movement of the camera," which is "so fundamental that it is often not regarded as movement at all . . . this is the movement that commutes static photographic images into onscreen moving images through camera and projector."[14] In other words, we are cued by the motion of figures onscreen not to perceive the motion of the technological ground, of the media platform, as motion at all. But the moving image is constantly in motion, even when neither its characters nor its framing moves in a perceptible way. So, always, are you and I and the rooms we occupy and the ground beneath us. The room in Taipei is dark, save for the light from the TV, which is to say that Hsiao-kang's face is illuminated by the Parisian sun.

Hsiao-kang watches *The 400 Blows*, and so does Lee Kang-sheng, the actor who plays him. So too does Tsai's camera, which samples the light from the TV, both in the image it produces on the TV screen and on the surfaces of the room and the actor that it illuminates. I am watching *What Time Is It There?* on a laptop screen in 2016. The film is displayed here by a software program that reads binary data from a digital file and translates it into transistor signals that stimulate liquid crystals between two thin panes of glass, rendering an image that I now and again freeze-frame, with the press of a button, in order to "translate it" (always incompletely, inadequately) into prose. Keystrokes render prose, though the keystroke "command-shift-3" renders an image, and the resulting screenshot, drawn from the succession images that constitutes the film, is transformed again, finally reaching you as an image in a book (figure 4.2).

In this matrix of objects and dynamics, environments and events, people and places, fictions and realities, ranging from East Asia to Western Europe to the southeastern United States to wherever these words find you, over a period of more than fifty years, where can we draw lines that render its elements discrete? Such questions were relevant even as *The 400 Blows* was still under production. Does Doinel struggle against the centripetal force of the ride, or is it merely Léaud's performance that does this? Does Léaud alone push against the force of the ride, or does the actor perform *along with* the ride, in his depiction of Doinel? Does the mechanical power of the ride then constitute part of Léaud's performance (but not of Doinel's actions)? Does Truffaut's camera move with the ride, or does the ride move with the camera?

Hsiao-kang would not be able to view *The 400 Blows* if any technological element of the relationship among the VCR, the videotape, the TV, and a power source, was not present to him. Nor could be the video be seen if Hsiao-kang were not present to it. Nor could I see Hsiao-kang if Tsai's camera were absent, nor if I were. You could not see figure 4.2 if this book were not present to you, nor would it be seen by you if you were not present to it. I'm glad you're here. All of these overlapping transactions perform work together, across space and time, and each of them both transforms its participants and creates the conditions for further transactions to occur. While it may seem straightforward enough to talk about the interfaces between technological components—say, between Hsiao-kang's VCR and his television, or between Truffaut's camera and the film on which it records images—these relationships are complicated by being embedded in broader dynamics that are at once technological, cultural, industrial, and psychological. Looking at my laptop screen, I enter into a relationship with (for example) a transaction between an amusement park ride and a movie camera that occurred over fifty years ago and thousands of miles away. This relationship traverses and is inflected by what seem to be many intermediary relationships: between me and the image from *What Time Is It There?* on my laptop, between that image and its mise en abyme of *The 400 Blows*, between *The 400 Blows* itself and the profilmic events that it depicts. And yet my relationship to young Jean-Pierre Léaud in this moment also feels, somehow, direct. This feeling is not in me, any more than it is in *What Time Is It There?* It is an aspect of a transaction that includes both of us. If we were to draw a conceptual line around me and the film, we might say that the film and I, taken together, are a platform for those things that the film and I make together: perception, narrative comprehension, emotion, interpretation.

PLATFORMS AND APPARATUSES

I have been using "platform" to describe phenomena that occur across a range of sites, from software to hardware to organisms to inanimate matter, and in the transactions among them. As noted earlier, this is a broader conception of the term than is found in in more restrictive conceptions of platform studies, which define the field as concerned chiefly with the relationship between computational software and hardware on which it is run. Formally initiating the field, Bogost and Montfort propose platform studies as a way of thinking about computational media exclusively:

> There have already been many studies of digital media dealing with the reception and operation of computer programs, with their interfaces, and with their forms and functions. But studies have seldom delved in to the code of these programs, and they have almost never investigated the platforms that are the basis of creative computing. Serious and in-depth consideration of circuits, chips, peripherals, and how they are integrated and used is a largely unexplored territory for both critic and creator.[15]

The authors point out that such platforms underpin all varieties of computer-based media and not just games. In investigating the "basis of creative computing," Bogost and Montfort identify the levels of analysis that occur at and above the level of the platform:

reception/operation
interface
form/function
code
platform

For a video game, the levels of "interface" and "reception/operation" refer to the game's interactive scheme and to the activities of the player, respectively. "Form/function" refers to game content: visual depictions of the game world, the unfolding of the game narrative, and so on. "Code" is the programming for a particular game, the software that is translated, by the console or the computer, into the game as represented on the form/function level. Underlying all of this is the platform, the physical hardware on which the game is played.[16]

This list is not only a taxonomy of subdisciplines but also an interpretation of an object of study, a vertical slice of the bottom-to-top structure of how computational media like video games function both in technology and in use. Moving up through the list, each level does not necessarily lead to the next, as in a reductive system. Instead, each requires the introduction of a new element in order to form the structure that supports the phenomena above it. Each of these resulting levels becomes a platform for a higher level of function only with the addition of something new from outside the system, an animating energy, as it were. A game console alone is merely a nonfunctional, if physically complex, material object—not unlike a dead body. A console plus code has the capacity to create phenomena on the level of form/function. This level, with the addition of human participation, creates the potential for metaeffects such as would be found on the level of reception/operation: perception, comprehension, interpretation. Between these two levels is the interface, a term whose intricacies and implications are engaged in depth in chapter 5.

Saying that this is not a reductive system is another way of saying that it is a system of emergence in which discrete things come together to produce also-discrete new things at a higher "level." The concept of "things coming together" assumes agreement that there are separate things, agreement about what the boundaries of those things are, and agreement about how it is possible for those things to come together and what happens when they do. Depending on how you look, the lines between levels, as well as the distinctions between elements that are said to come together *at* levels, can be drawn differently. Katie Salen and Eric Zimmerman, for example, provide an alternative perspective on the relationships that occur below the level that Bogost and Montfort call form/function:

applications and files
operating system
machine language code
binary information
electronic signals[17]

"Applications and files" roughly corresponds to Bogost and Montfort's "code." The operating system is software that facilitates user navigation between programs and allows software applications and files to communicate with the machine code, which is instantiated in the physical operations of the platform. The operating system, when one is present (as in computers and in modern video game consoles) would appear also to fall under Bogost and Montfort's category of code. The three remaining categories are aspects of Bogost and Montfort's platform level, but "machine language code" in Salen and Zimmerman's model straddles the boundary between platform and code as articulated by Bogost and Montfort. In explicating these lower levels, Salen and Zimmerman quote a passage by historian Paul N. Edwards. While Salen and Zimmerman truncate the passage, I here restore it to its original length, as Edwards's full phrasing further illuminates the differences between Salen and Zimmerman's and Bogost and Montfort's accounts of processes at the platform level:

> The operation of computing machinery can be described at a number of levels. The "lowest" of these is the electronics of hardware: electronic switches, resistors, magnetic storage devices, and so on. Descriptions are causal and physical: electrons, currents, voltages. The second level is digital logic. The hardware electronics are designed to represent logical or mathematical operations, such as "AND" or the addition of binary digits or "bits"; the hardware itself is thus described as a set of logic "gates." Descriptions are logical, not physical, but they are still tied to the hardware itself, whose structure determines how each operation affects its successors. At a third level lies the "machine language" of the programs that "run" on a particular machine. Machine language consists of the binary representations of program instructions—the language the machine itself "speaks." Machine language also remains tied to a particular machine; programs written in one machine's language generally will not run on a different machine. However, machine-language programs are not a fixed part of the hardware (like its logic gates), determined by its physical structure; they are user-determined instructions.[18]

What Bogost and Montfort call the platform level is for Edwards subdivided into physical machinery, the electrical signals that run through it, the binary information that emerges from the patterns of activation of the hardware, and the encoding of basic-level logical commands into a "language" that operates by way of the on-off logic gates in the machine's electronics.

These alternative descriptions of what happens at the "platform" level correspond to differing accounts of what then occurs at the levels above the platform. Salen and Zimmerman's analysis is oriented toward the atomic construction of logical operations, binary functions that operate on the lowest levels of hardware and give rise to progressively higher-level logical processes, culminating, ultimately, in the rules that govern gameplay. Salen and Zimmerman make a distinction between what they call operational and constitutive (*sic*) rules in video games. Operational rules are the overt rules of a game, such as what the goal is or how points are scored. Constitutive rules are the less-obvious rules, like a game's physics and collision models, that structure the space in which the operational rules are enacted. Bogost and Montfort's approach is more immediately concerned with "how the hardware and software of platforms influences, facilitates, or constrains particular forms of computational expression."[19] It is concerned, in other words, with the representational affordances and limitations of the device. Salen and Zimmerman's perspective engages most fully with logical structures, Bogost and Montfort's with expressive possibilities. Neither does so to the exclusion of the other. These parallel orientations to the emergent nature of expressive computations, rather, provide context for one another in thinking about how video game players are positioned by, and how they engage with and use, video games. While they conceive the territorial boundaries of media use in similar ways, they differ in the internal boundaries by which they subdivide the territory.

The comparison in Table 4.1 makes clear that the "levels" of computational media are not clear-cut and that the distinction between platform and "content," as between figure and ground, is a discursive maneuver and not a quality of things in themselves. As it is to the mind, the container metaphor is inadequate to the transactional continuity of media, technology, user, and world. Inadequate, but also persuasive and pervasive, it is tied up in the idea that things are discrete from one another and the world, and that they possess, or contain, their own unique essences. It is tied up, in other words, in strong emergence.

Table 4.1: THE "LEVELS" OF COMPUTATIONAL MEDIA

Bogost and Montfort	Salen and Zimmerman	Edwards
	Implicit rules (social practices)	
Reception/operation	Gameplay	
Interface		
	Operational rules	
Form/function		
	Constitutive rules	
Code	Applications and files	
	Operating system	
	Machine code	Machine language program
Platform		Machine language
	Binary system	Digital logic
	Electronic signals	Electronic signals
	Physical machinery	Physical machinery

Consider the following three passages. They are written, respectively, by a theological philosopher, a physicist, and a filmmaker. Blaise Pascal writes:

> A town, a country-place, is from afar a town and a country-place. But, as we draw near, there are houses, trees, tiles, leaves, grass, ants, limbs of ants, in infinity. All this is contained under the name of country-place.[20]

Erwin Schrödinger writes:

> [Each] of us has the undisputable impression that the sum total of his own experience and memory forms a unit, quite distinct from that of any other person. He refers to it as 'I.' *What is this 'I'?* . . . If you analyse it closely you will, I think, find that it is just a little bit more than a collection of single data (experiences and memories), namely the canvas *upon which* they are collected. And you will, on close introspection, find that, what you really mean by 'I', is that ground-stuff upon which they are collected.[21]

And Robert Bresson writes:

> The true is not encrusted in the living persons or real objects you use. It is an air of truth that their images take on when you set them together in a certain order. *Vice versa*, the air of truth their images take on when you set them together in a certain order confers on these persons and objects a reality.[22]

Each of these writers is concerned with relationships among scale, holism, taxonomy, and identity. In short, they are concerned with the possibility of emergence and with relationships between matter and meaning. They write from different spiritual perspectives, Pascal and Bresson as Catholics and Schrödinger as a skeptical scientist with sympathies toward the Vedanta philosophy of Hinduism. Each is invested in the correspondence between a system and its parts, and in how a system can itself be part of a larger-scale system, whether it is a country-place, the semantic category "country-place," the concept "I," the self as an actor in the world, the sequential ordering of cinematic material, or the "air of truth" that cinema can establish.

If I say "country-place," I refer to a place in its collectivity, as a discursive unit, viewed from a particular scale. The term's ability to imply "houses, trees, tiles, leaves, grass, ants, limbs of ants" without directly referring to them is crucial to its utility as a semantic category. But "country-place" can have other resonances: it can connote escape, or ownership, or coziness, for example, in ways that seem to go beyond any of its parts. The term is a conceptual analogue of what physicist Robert B. Laughlin calls physical protectorates, stable structures that "formally grow out" of their components "but are in a real sense independent of them."[23] When I speak of a "country-place," I do not have to speak of—nor need I think of—its component parts. If I do want to speak of them, if I have a reason to make reference to a particular house or tree, or to a particular limb of a particular ant, I need to speak at another scale. To use a term that is at once cinematic and linguistic, I need to reframe.

To reframe the spatiotemporal scale of reference *to* a system is also to reconsider the scale of causality *in* the system. In the opening sequence of the film *Blue Velvet* (David Lynch, 1986), for instance, a hyperidealized depiction of American suburbia is punctured when a man, first seen watering his lawn, collapses from a stroke (figure 4.3). Through a series of cuts and forward-tracking movements, the camera pushes its way downward through the grass, revealing a writhing mass of insects in the soil below and suggesting a biological horror lurking beneath the aseptic veneer of the suburban lawn and beneath "suburbia" as a concept. The insects undermine the utopian image of suburbia that the film has efficiently established, in which insects are banished from sight in favor of the geometric reassurance of manicured lawns, uniform architecture, and pastel hues. Their appearance thrusts rudely into view the biological timescale that is the backdrop for human lives, that looms behind any one mortal being with an indifferent rustle and hum. The film intimates that all of this life and death is at work in suburbia, if not in "suburbia." There are always processes swirling above and below a supposed protectorate, smaller and bigger, constitutive and entropic, indifferent, that not only trouble the status of the thing or the event as a discrete entity, but denaturalize the very concept of the protectorate itself. Your scale cannot protect you forever. A country-place is a material thing *and* a collection of material things. A country-place is also a series of events past, ongoing, and potential, as well as a constituent part, itself, of a region and perhaps a nation, an ecosphere, a planet, all of which are, viewed at the right temporal scale, not things at all but rather processes.

Pascal writes of a spatial system, Schrödinger of an experiential one. The filmmaker Bresson touches on relationships between being and knowing. Each writer is concerned both with the material system (countryside, "I," cinema) to which he refers and with the denotative systems that facilitate that act of reference. How do things work at different scales, they ask, and how can we think and talk at different scales about them working at different scales? Each writer grapples with levels of emergence, thinking about the scales at which we might argue that things happen and units exist. These are the levels of spatiotemporal scale and causality at which systems seem to enter a degree of stability, discreteness, and—perhaps—autonomy. In physical structures these would be Laughlin's protectorates. For computer scientist Douglas Hofstadter, thinking about circuits of recursive action in technology and in the mind, they are "strange loops" or "paradoxical level-crossing feedback loops."[24] Neuroanthropologist Terrence W. Deacon, writing about the self-organizing functions of matter, calls such structures "ratchets."[25] In media technology, these semistable units might seem to include "platforms" or "apparatuses" like video game consoles, film projectors, and other exhibition devices, but also their component parts such as chips, power supplies, sprockets, aperture plates, and

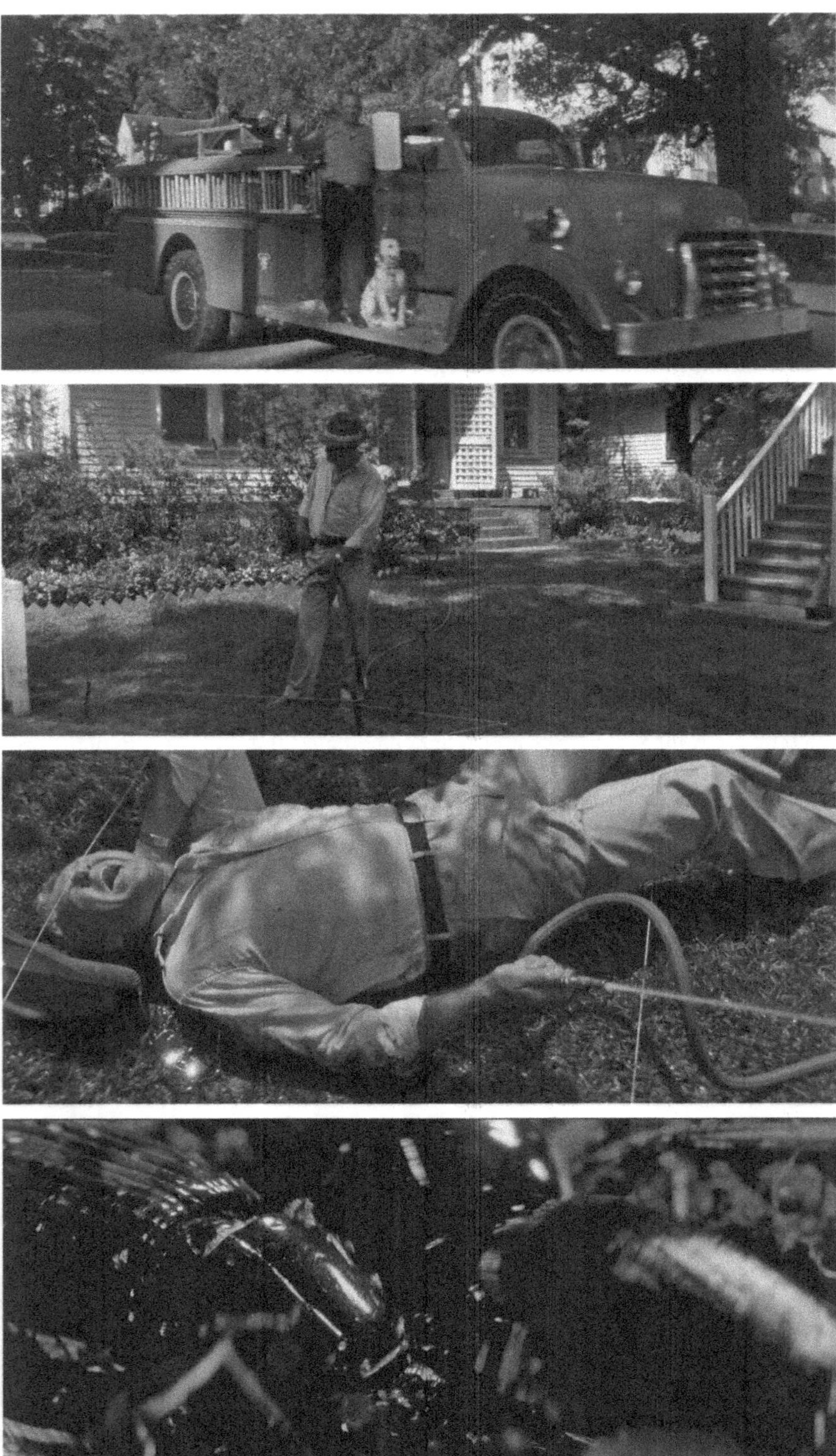

Figure 4.3 In *Blue Velvet* (David Lynch, 1986), from top: suburbia as "suburbia"; Tom Beaumont waters his lawn; he collapses; insects writhe in the grass and mud. Throughout the sequence, shot distances get progressively closer.

reels, which can be seen as modular "units" in their own right, not unlike the organs of the body. Like the organs of the body, however, they are physically intertwined and mutually reliant in their functioning. We see them as separate or modular only because they are told and sold to us in that way.

For Pascal, the naming of an object—a "country-place" or any of its constituent parts—is first a question of perspectival orientation. From a distance, we see things in their collectivity, while in closer proximity we are more inclined to perceive their local features. Lynch's camera *moves* to approach the insect scale. Seen from a closer vantage point, these features might appear to be totalities in themselves. This scaling effect pertains to conceptual as well as to physiological proximity. The "closer" one gets to an idea or to a concept or to a text, the bigger, the more prominent, and the more causally relevant its constituent parts come to seem. Likewise, as one backs away and looks at something from a distance, previously imperceptible higher-level properties might come to seem both structurally stable and causally active. In Pascal's theological worldview, causality is unified on the highest level, so that local phenomena are fractal instantiations of a higher process. "God has established prayer [to] communicate to His creatures the dignity of causality," writes Pascal, a devout Catholic to whom the workings of nature are ultimately the workings of a universal causality.[26] To see the limb of an ant on a blade of grass in a countryside is to see scalar aspects of a unified, universal process in which causes, ultimately, come from above and not below. Note that this is the opposite of theories like Chalmers's in which the strong emergence of consciousness affords some creatures *downward* causality. For Pascal, prayer provides humans with a degree of upward causality, but this is always a causality that trickles back down to the local through the ultimate causality of a divine being. Pascal's ant is quite different from the insects that instantiate the tonal shift near the beginning of *Blue Velvet*. The appearance of those insects indicates the presence of another kind of universal causality, one of cosmic indifference rather than of Pascal's "dignity."

Through cuts, track, and zooms, cinema has proven adept at moving from one spatial and discursive scale to another. Recall that, to Hugo Münsterberg, the close-up objectifies the attention of the audience by foregrounding aspects of the mise-en-scène. For Münsterberg, this is largely a way for film to focalize the audience's mind on particular narrative developments, so that we might "suddenly neglect everything in the room and look only at the hand which carries the dagger."[27] When *Blue Velvet* cuts to its writhing insects, it is not so much to advance the film's narrative as to expand its spatiotemporal framing and its conception of causality by way of spatially discontinuous cuts. The zoom lens can effect similar apparent changes in visual and conceptual proximity while also calling attention to the spatiotemporal continuity between the wider and the narrower scale. In the opening shot of *The Conversation* (Francis Ford Coppola, 1972), for instance, San Francisco's Union Square is seen in a high-angle, extreme long shot, the entire length and breadth of the block visible. The square is packed with people walking, sitting, performing, and milling about. From this perspective, they look like so many ants. Over a period of three minutes, the camera slowly zooms in on the scene, eventually picking out Harry Caul, the film's protagonist, and following him in long shot as he traverses the square.

Rather than the horror of what lies below the human scale, as unleashed by the cut to the insects in *Blue Velvet*, the slow-zoom opening of *The Conversation* points to a perspectival threat from above, the threat of surveillance, judgment, and interpretation. *Blue Velvet*'s cuts imply a scalar disjunct. "Suburbia" is blissfully unaware of the insects, but the insects, too, are oblivious of and indifferent to suburbia, even as they, or their progeny, will eventually consume it and its residents. The unbroken zoom in *The Conversation* foregrounds not only the scalar continuity among Caul, Union Square as a whole (people, leaves, grass, ants, limbs of ants), and the position of Caul's implied observers, but also the active threat of looming, unseen powers from above, powers that might at any moment intervene in or—perhaps worse— misinterpret one's actions. Caul is a surveillance expert who is obsessed with his own security. While the zoom-gaze at the beginning of the film belongs to his own surveillance team, Caul himself later becomes a subject of malevolent surveillance. At the end if the film, he is left desperately searching for some sign of how, let alone why, he is being surveilled, a search in which he destroys one of his only personal possessions, a statue of the Virgin Mary, seemingly sacrificing it to the higher threat of an unseen power that has robbed him of his own dignity of causality, disaffording him all private speech—prayer or otherwise.

Caul seems to feel his transactional participation in the world around him, moving smoothly through the traffic of Union Square at the beginning of the film, being gradually supplanted by a model of self-action in which an unseen power acts, as if unilaterally, *upon* him. In a seemingly paradoxical turn, this causal discontinuity is established through the formal continuity of the zoom, while the causal continuity of *Blue Velvet* is established through the formal discontinuity of cuts. *Blue Velvet*'s insects are not so much a detail of the scene, as a zoom might imply, or as Münsterberg's model of the close-up might have it, as they are a reminder of the cosmic context that binds the world of the film to our own, and the lives on the screen—both human and insect—to ours. I have been calling the insects indifferent, or representative of cosmic indifference, but it is perhaps more accurate to call them *undifferent*, reflective of a deeper commonality, continuity, and nondifferentiation. The horror of *Blue Velvet*'s opening is not in what lies beneath, but in that there is no beneath at all. This is a horror, however, only if our sense of self relies on the notion of strongly emergent entities like "I" and "suburbia."

While Pascal refers outward to higher causes, Schrödinger is concerned with self-reference and self-awareness. "I," for Schrödinger, is ultimately a material thing, the "ground-stuff" that is the material site of experience and memory. A life, as lived and as remembered, occurs in the continuous relations between a body and the physical world of which it is a part. If experiences and memory are "single data," or are the actions we undertake and the post hoc structures and interpretations that we impose on what we have experienced, these are bound together, or "collected," by their inscription on (or in, or *by*) the material world. But what is this "ground-stuff"? Does Schrödinger simply mean the body? I don't believe so. He seems to mean the stuff of the world, of which a body is one temporary articulation. The mind, in this view, should ultimately be seen as the universe thinking about itself.

This raises the question of what can think. If the universe thinks about itself through (or more properly *as*) sentient creatures, does it think about itself through inanimate things as well? Can it think by way of media? To Jean Epstein, any machine has its own "intelligence," born of its particular sensitivities to the world. The "complexity of the inner structure and interactions of a mechanical organism," he wrote in 1946, two years after Schrödinger, "leads to the individualization of the machine and impels . . . a tinge of unpredictability which signals the very beginning of what we call . . . freedom, will, or soul."[28] Among machines, the cinematograph is special to Epstein in that it "inscribes its own character within its representations of the universe with such originality that it makes the representation not simply a record or copy . . . [but] the seed of a philosophy that strays far enough from common opinions so as to be called an antiphilosophy."[29] Epstein views cinema's representations as a kind of mechanical philosophy that has the potential to liberate human philosophy from illusions about the nature of space-time.

What Bresson calls the "air of truth" taken on by a film is a notion or a feeling that arises from the relationship between a film and those who watch it. Contrary to André Bazin's claim that the "photographic image is the object itself, the object freed from the conditions of time and space that govern it . . . it *is* the model," Bresson offers a constructive model of cinematic truth—a truth that comes not from the photochemical origins or the indexical referentiality of the image but rather from the articulation of filmic material.[30] For Bresson, film makes a truth, or rather an air of truth, which implies a viewer upon whom an impression is made and through whose reciprocal use of the film the air of truth emerges. This impression of a truth, Bresson writes, confers a new life and a new reality on the (already) living persons and real objects used in the filming. These real things and these living people are themselves transformed, via the organization and articulation of their images, and their subsequent display for an audience, into something both epistemologically ("an air of truth") and ontologically ("a reality") new.

For Bresson, film does something like what the collection of experience does for Schrödinger. It confers on the world that it occupies a new kind of reality, a conceptual reality, a truth something like the "skillful engagement" that Alva Noë cites as essential to "achieve access to the world." In transactions of the observing, participating self (whether Schrödinger's experiencing, remembering "I" or Bresson's cinema-ordering "you") in the world at large, truths, meanings, and realities are produced, realities that both rely upon and spring from the material bases of their ordering and their articulation, whether these are cellular or celluloid in their substrates. Each in his own way, Bresson, Schrödinger, and Pascal show that how those realities and truths are distinguished from one another and from their worldly contexts depends on how (and whether) we assert distinctions between world and object, part and whole, figure and ground, platform and content.

PLATFORMS ACROSS MEDIA

What can platform studies tell us about cinema? Precisely nothing, according to the narrowest definition of the field. Since its inception, however, the field of platform studies has pushed restlessly at the boundaries of its prescribed range. Steven E. Jones and George K. Thiruvathukal, for instance, write in their study of the Nintendo Wii video game console that "the printing press along with the institutions of print culture can be seen as a kind of platform for producing and disseminating texts in the material form of codex books."[31] Jones and Thiruvathukal here expand the range of the platform to encompass not only noncomputational media but a variety of mechanical devices, social formations, and the coordination among them, all of which form a platform for *the purpose* of making and distributing texts. Jones and Thiruvathukal's extension of the figure of the platform, and thus of the potential range of platform studies as a discipline, illustrates the field's potential to illuminate not only media beyond those that are narrowly defined as computational, but all manner of emergent situations above, around, and beyond media. As noted earlier, when scholars like Gillespie, Benson-Allott, Steinberg, and Altice likewise expand the range of the concept of the platform, they point toward a weakly-emergent, transactional conception of what a platform is, and of what platform studies as a field could be. Doing so facilitates consideration of platforms across media, and of media across platforms.

In her comparative study of exhibition technologies, Benson-Allott draws an analogy between consoles and computer hardware as exhibition sites, on the one hand, and their cinematic equivalents on the other, a comparison that she grounds in the concept of the platform. "In an extended sense," Benson-Allott writes, "movie theaters, DVD players, and operating systems (such as Mac OS X or windows) are all platforms."[32] In discussing extended models of the mind, I have argued that it is more useful to think of extended cognition as extending across a situation than as extending outward into a situation from the mind. Likewise, Benson-Allott's "extended sense" of the platform is especially powerful if we think of it not as a semantic extension outward from the narrow computational definition of the platform but rather as an assertion of the broad extensional range of the quality of being a platform. Benson-Allott exemplifies this extensionality by pushing the concept of the platform further still, pointing out how the language used in (nominally computational) platform studies often suggests qualities that pertain to phenomena beyond computational media and indeed beyond media altogether. Benson-Allott argues that "all matter . . . is generated by natural and cultural forces and is itself generative of natural and cultural forces." For this reason, "thinking about platforms . . . can be a way of thinking about the history of video games as a political, cultural, and deeply material world history."[33] Philosopher of science Karen Barad's characterization of matter as "produced and productive, generated and generative" is especially useful for Benson-Allott in asserting the continuity of platforms with how they are constituted and with what they make possible.[34] In the next chapter of *Media in Mind*, Barad's thinking proves similarly useful in extending the concept of the media interface along transactional lines and in troubling the conceptual boundary between platform and interface.

If, following Benson-Allott's extended sense of media platforms, we eschew the computational requirement and try mapping cinema—its use and its technology— onto Bogost and Montfort's striated levels of analysis, we might then think of "reception/operation" as the metacinematic phenomena that surround the medium, such as analysis and criticism, theory, philosophical engagement, economic effects and investments, fandom, and industry studies. The "interface" of film might be the user-film interaction—without the clear bidirectional causality of a video game but similarly engaged, active, and productive for both "sides." "Form/function," in the case of cinema's formal structure, might be how a film depicts its representational content, how it orders those depictions, how it inflects that ordered depiction through formal devices, and how this all functions together, in a holistic sense, to contribute to the larger-scale agent-environment platforms produced by the exhibition of film for viewers.

Below this level is the code. In the case of classical photographic cinema technologies, this is the compression of a series of images into miniaturized, hypersaturated form on a strip of film. The exhibition platform is the material devices and objects that facilitate the transformation of those images into motion pictures onscreen: the substance of celluloid itself, the reels on which it is wound in strips, the projector with its component mechanisms and electromechanical basis, the rectilinear screen. In the shot from *What Time Is It There?* discussed earlier, this could be any and all of the following: the film on which Truffaut's camera (as well as the processes of development and printing) inscribes images of Jean-Pierre Léaud, the videotape onto which *The 400 Blows'* images of Antoine Doinel are transferred, the film in Tsai's camera, and the digital encoding of images on my DVD of *What Time Is It There?*

Perhaps because they are game designers themselves, Bogost and Montfort focus largely on how designers function in this dynamic and how this dynamic functions in game design. But take the case of someone playing *The Legend of Zelda* (Nintendo R&D4, 1987) on a Nintendo Entertainment System. For this player, does the platform not include the NES, the *Legend of Zelda* cartridge, a CRT television, a source of electrical current, hands, a brain, a body, a room? Doesn't the platform for Hsiao-kang's viewing of *The 400 Blows* include a VCR and a TV, the bodily and spatial conditions of his watching the film, as well as all of the technologies, bodies, and places, extending outward in space and into the past, necessary to deliver images of a boy and an amusement park ride and some sunlight from 1950s Paris to turn-of-the-millenium Taipei?

Turning to Salen and Zimmerman's nuanced account of the code and platform levels in video games, we can observe in cinema a similar blurring of boundaries between physical material and "encoded" information. A five-part breakdown of these levels in the cinematic code and platform might look like this:

images and audio encoded on celluloid
filmstrip and projector
projector settings
mechanical operation of projector
flow of electrical current

The filmstrip and projector are the higher-level material substrate, the objects on a human scale that work together to produce cinematic images. Projector settings correspond to machine language; by making adjustments to variables such as projection speed and frame masking, a projectionist provides the projector with the information it needs in order to perform this operation. Anyone who has been to an improperly masked film can attest to the perceptual distantiation that comes from visible boom microphones at the top of the frame or from characters' heads being cut off by the frame lines. The mechanical operation of the projector, given direction by its settings, is the site of production of patterns of projected light from pigment on celluloid. This level includes the physical functioning of the projector as a mechanical device: the spooling of the reels, the maintenance of a slack loop in the celluloid to prevent tearing, the pacing action of the sprockets, and so on. It also includes the operation of the bulb and the shutter, which restore light and illusory motion to the still images on the celluloid. Underpinning this, below the level at which we might usually look for meaningful insight into the functioning of the cinematic apparatus, is the electrical current through the projector, which powers the gears and shutters and illuminates the bulb filament. In this model, the film is like the software and the projector like the hardware—and, as in the case of video game software and hardware, they function only inasmuch as they intermingle, physically passing through one another. This is less an act of putting them into contact than it is one of blurring the purported boundaries between them.

While there are certainly reasons to want to distinguish computational media from other media forms, it only makes sense to restrict the label "platform" to computational media if you (begging the question) define platforms as computational. On the other hand, if we say that computation is *a* characteristic of *some* platforms, that arranging material and channeling energy in a particular way can produce computational media, then we can at once restore continuity among media and restore continuity between media and other aspects of the natural world. Beyond this, the weakly emergent platform shows itself to be a valuable figure for thinking about the stakes of identifying levels of emergence in a more general sense. The platform provides a way of thinking beyond strong emergence and reductionism as oppositional qualities, toward conceiving of a holism that is neither bottom-up (as in reductive materialism) nor top-down (as in deism) but is instead characterized by what is made possible by particular configurations of matter and energy, observed at any scale.

TRANSACTIONAL PLATFORMS

The field of platform studies is young, and it remains contested. The stakes under contest are both theoretical and disciplinary. As articulated by Bogost and Montfort, the field is dedicated exclusively to the study of computational media technologies and their relationships to the media content that they make possible.[35] Jones and Thiruvathukal suggest that platform studies be extended to noncomputational media technologies, and beyond moving images to technologies like the printing press, and that these platforms should always be thought of as social phenomena.[36] Benson-Allott makes a case for the field's applicability to analog moving-image media, suggesting the term "new video studies" as a way of theorizing, in textual and technological terms, the relationship between motion pictures and video across exhibition platforms, and she argues for the field's potential in conceiving of how, in the case of video games, platforms "are the *thingness* of games that allows us to recognize how our own thingness works with that of a console or operating system and by extension the larger material and political world of which we are all part."[37] The field of platform studies is at a crossroads. It could decisively open itself up to the world, letting the world into the platform and also letting the platform out into the world, or it could commit itself to buttressing the figure of the computational platform against its continuity with other media and with the wider world. To take the latter route, I would suggest, would be to commit to the perpetual work of limiting something that does not want to be limited. As the work of Jones and Thiruvathukal, Benson-Allott, and others shows, the pull of the world is simply too strong.

The platform is for these reasons best conceived as widely as possible. It has enormous potential to revitalize scholarly engagement with media technologies, an engagement that has waned since the heyday of apparatus theory in the 1970s. In particular, platform studies should continue to expand the scope of investigation by more fully engaging with human bodies, feelings, and minds. Conceived thus, the concept of the "platform" is rendered valuable in a way that goes beyond the technological. If a platform is a dynamic relationship among things, then a game console is a platform, and so is a human body. A console and a human body, together, are another platform still, and it becomes difficult to say where one ends and the other begins. This radicalization of platform studies opens the discipline up to contexts— social, material, political—along a transactional model. In its narrower conception, the discipline sacrifices its ability to address the aesthetic, technological, psychological, historical, and sociocultural continuities that computational media share with other media. From a transactional perspective, such a disciplinary model, by way of its insistence on medium specificity, undermines the true specificity of the medium, in that it isolates the medium from the other things—other media, people, minds, cultures, environments—with which it acts.

As we have seen, narrower delineation of the platform as an object of study can clarify one's account of platforms, but this comes at the expense of continuity with the world beyond the platform. This is precisely the problem faced by models of strong emergence that seek to cleanly differentiate things from one another and from the world. In Bogost and Montfort's model, a platform in its purest form is a regulatory conceptual abstraction, a set of preconceived limitations that are then incarnated as physical technologies. "To be used by people and to take part in our culture directly," they write, "a platform must take material form."[38] Abstraction from continuity is intrinsic to this conception of the platform. We might as well call them plat[onic]forms.

The great insight of Bogost and Montfort's program for platform studies is not so much in its delineation of the boundaries of the theoretical figure of the platform as in its demonstration of the ways that scalar, technological, and cultural aspects of using media build upon and feed back into one another. I have argued that even narrower, strongly-emergent, computational conceptions of platform studies (*a*) demonstrate the ways that the demarcation of a discrete "level" of emergence is always a discursive act with particular disciplinary and ideological investments and (*b*) show that even then, in practice, the boundaries among components and levels will necessarily be blurred by the operation of technology and by the operation of theory. When Bogost and Montfort define the platform as "whatever the programmer takes for granted" or the layers "from hardware through operating system and into other software layers," they all but acknowledge that a platform can be whatever is treated as prior to one's own use of, or theoretical intervention in, media technology. It is crucial to take seriously the role that "taking for granted" has in this construction. Platforms are not strongly emergent phenomena; they are functions of discourse, of what is expected and what is understood as given. Strong emergence deals in deducibility, weak emergence in expectedness. Taking for granted has everything to do with expectation.

By thinking relationally about textuality across platforms, and about materiality in and beyond platforms, Benson-Allott enables "a way of thinking carefully about the experience of media specificity diametrically opposed to technological determinism," or a model of platform studies in which the platform, like the text, is not *prior* or abstract but a material thing, the existence of which precedes whatever essence one might ascribe to it.[39] While it restores sociocultural contexts to its model of the constitution of media platforms, such an approach is not a return to apparatus theory. Rather, it suggests an alternative way of thinking about the relationships among politics, technology, psychology, and spectatorship that feels its way around and beyond narrow boundaries of discipline and medium. The weakly emergent conception of the platform that I have proposed in this chapter resonates with the porousness of platform boundaries seen in Benson-Allott's characterization of media technologies. It furthermore provides an opportunity to think of platforms—technological and otherwise—as intertwined, entangled aspects of a continuous whole, which become discernable figures (in perception as in theory) only because their discursive utility differentiates them from the ground.

As the theoretical figure of the platform becomes broader in its boundaries and less rigid in its internal distinctions, the field of platform studies likewise expands in both scope and productivity. The loss of rigidly demarcated disciplinary specificity does not entail a loss of explanatory or descriptive power. On the contrary, a broader conception of the platform still allows for technologically specific studies focused exclusively on computational media, and it in fact underscores these studies' power by allowing them to enter into conversation with other theoretical models and studies of noncomputational digital and analog media rather than by holding the platform apart, like the mysterious inner theater of the mind, within a discrete, distant, and withdrawn realm of its own.

CHAPTER 5

Encounters at the Intraface

If the strongly emergent sense of "platform" denotes a powerful and complete system upon which both media content and media users depend, then the term "interface" commonly designates the channels through which users are assured they can access the operation of a platform. The platform is a consolidation of power, and the interface is that which grants users limited influence upon that power. "Now You're Playing with Power," announced a 1980s advertising campaign for the Nintendo Entertainment System, with television spots that emphasize the system's input elements like handheld controllers and the "Zapper" light gun. Nintendo brings (that is, sells you access to) the power. You bring the play. To paraphrase Pascal, the interface affords media users the dignity of causality, which they claim not by praying but by playing.[1]

"Interface," in this sense, is shorthand for "user interface" or "graphical user interface" (GUI), terms for the controls and visual displays of devices like the computers, phones, tablets, and touchscreens that increasingly permeate the global environment and through which communication, consumption, and navigation are filtered. These interfaces are presented as visualizations of the inner workings of devices, or as translations of the complex computations inside the devices into navigable and manipulable presentations that are legible to the devices' users. As bibliographical scholar Johanna Drucker writes, however, the view of the user interface as a "portal" into the workings of computational media, or as a "representation of computational processes that makes it convenient for us to interact with what is 'really' happening," lends a deceptive impression of transparency to the figure of the interface. On the contrary, Drucker writes, the interface "supports behaviors and tasks . . . But it also disciplines, constrains, and determines what can be done in any digital environment."[2] While the user interface can be understood in part as an opportunity to perceive and interact with what would otherwise be an inscrutable process of abstract computation, it must also be understood as a designed, mediating structure. An interface is not transparent, not a window to the machine's internal world, but an active representational construction in its own right, and it reflects the perspectives and the investments of those who design and employ it. The user interface is more active than it at first seems.

In the tension between active and passive models of the interface, you may notice a parallel to the ways in which perception is often treated as a transparent window outward to the world from the discrete inner realm of the mind, as discussed in chapters 1 through 3. In this analogy, the internal, inaccessible aspect of the platform corresponds to the internal, inaccessible aspect of the mind. The passive interface is used to explain how information, commands, and representations cross the gap between the outside world and the world inside the machine, much as passive perception is used to explain how phenomena in the world can become data for the computational mind. Discreteness and opposition between inner and outer worlds necessitates a window, portal, or channel of some kind that connects them. In erecting theoretical gaps between mind and world and between world and media, one must also propose ways in which mind and media function to bridge those gaps. In these passive models, as illustrated in figure 5.1, perception is how the realm of mental content accesses the external world and how the external world accesses the internal realm of the mind, while the interface is how the world outside the platform accesses the realm of computational content and vice versa.

Just as perception's relationship to (or role in) the mind is more integrative and integral than passive models of perception would have it, so too is the interface less transparent—representationally and interactively—than passive accounts imply. When passive models of the interface and perception are taken for granted, the models themselves become barriers to rethinking the ostensible gaps between mind and world.

This chapter proposes an active, transactional alternative to passive models of the interface. Theoretical work by Drucker, Alexander Galloway, Branden Hookway, and others has expanded the range of the term "interface" to encompass aspects of media users and the contexts and practices of media use. While there

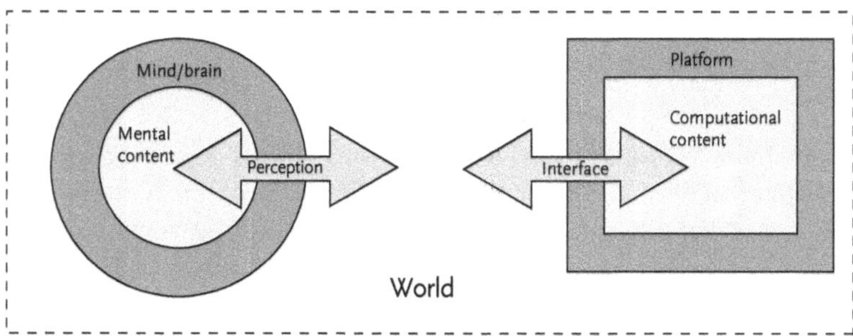

Figure 5.1 The passive model of perception and the passive model of the interface function to "bridge" explanatory gaps caused by dualist, interactional models of the mind (*left*) and media platforms (*right*).

are differences among the approaches that these theorists take and the conclusions that they draw, I will refer to their collective effort as the *expanded interface*. These expanded models, while they trouble the idea of the interface as simply a surface aspect of media, ultimately maintain interactional gaps among media, users, and world. One reason for this is that they remain tethered to the theoretical starting point of the user interface as a surface aspect of media "objects," even as they push the range of what Galloway calls the "interface effect" outward to encompass how media use brings about "transformations in material states."[3]

Seeking a transactional account of the expanded interface, I propose leaving the term "interface" to the user interface/GUI and adopting the term *intraface* to describe the reciprocal and mutually coconstitutive relations that transpire among users and media. Galloway has previously used *intraface* to designate "an interface internal to the interface," or an "internal interface between the edge and the center . . . one that is now entirely subsumed and contained within the image," essentially an interactive mise en abyme "within the aesthetic" of the interface.[4] Galloway's definition of the intraface is invested in internality and containment, and especially in the politically productive tensions that can arise from sustained ambiguity within such containment.

Maintaining this emphasis on productive ambiguity but everting the mechanism so as to restore its material continuity with its worldly context, I draw upon the concept of *intra-action*, developed by Karen Barad to describe how "agents" come into being by way of their dynamic relations with one another, while remaining always fundamentally entangled with one another and with the systems of which they are parts. Much as Barad's theory of the generated generativity of matter facilitates Benson-Allott's opening up of the figure of the platform to new resonances and contexts (see chapter 4), Barad's theory here allows for an account of the continuity of the interface/intraface and its broader spatiotemporal context, without the need for any definitive "cut" that differentiates the intraface from media content or technology, nor from media users' bodies or minds. The intraface, as I use the term, describes a relationship among relationships, a way in which coconstitutive and entangled parts of a larger dynamic (these parts themselves always temporary, contingent, and relational) can be said to "face" one another, to regard one another not across a preexisting gap that separates them but always by way of their spatiotemporal, material, causal continuity. The intraface does not describe only relationships with or within media. It describes relationships with the environment and objects in it, *including* media.

Intraface and (weakly emergent) platform are best understood as complementary ways of conceiving dynamic relationships between users and media. The difference is not one of kind, but of perspective. The intraface is the platform as observed from within. In the previous chapter, I argued that the platform is a productive framework for thinking about weakly emergent structures, not only in media but in life and in mind. Media texts in which characters seek to remake their relationships by way of probing, imaginative, and ludic action in their environments reveal the intraface as a figure not only for transactional participation in media but also for enactive attempts to participate in the seemingly indifferent workings of the wider world. This is illustrated via further discussion of the film *What Time Is It There?*, in which Hsiao-kang grieves for his father by way of his emotional investment in *The 400 Blows*, and analysis of the video game *Don't Look Back* (distractionware, 2009), in which the player-controlled character undertakes an imaginary trip to the underworld in order to recover the ghost of a lost loved one.

That *What Time Is It There?* and *Don't Look Back* share themes of grief and mourning is no coincidence. In each, grieving characters explore the spaces they occupy and the things around them in order to invest themselves anew in those objects and environments. Another "self" is gone and is missed dearly. But, as Douglas Hofstadter writes, a self does not simply disappear at the moment of death, as a self is in fact distributed across space and time, and across multiple people, residing in part in the minds of the people around it. "In the wake of a human being's death," writes Hofstadter, "what survives is a set of afterglows, some brighter and some dimmer, in the collective brains of those dearest to them. There is, in those who remain, a collective corona that still glows."[5] *What Time Is It There?* and *Don't Look Back* remind us that the departed's self persists, too, in the marks that person made in the world, in the objects that she or he used, and in the environments that she or he inhabited. In reacquainting ourselves with the spaces that someone once occupied along with us, in accounting for the ways that the person's absence ripples through our own routines and through the things with which they transacted, we can begin to work our way toward smooth-running functions in a world that is forever changed. To do so is to reclaim one's own continuity with the world—that is, to re-establish one's participation in an intraface.

DIVISION BY INTERFACE

Drucker's description of the user interface focuses on the often-overlooked ways in which the interface is structured, as well as the ways in which it structures user behavior. As she writes, "The structure of an interface *is* information, not merely a means of access to it."[6] In a Foucauldian turn, Drucker writes that an interface "is a space in which a *subject*, not a *user*, is invoked. Interface is an enunciative system."[7] Much like the platform, the user interface is first a discursive structure calibrated to contain and channel the energies of media users—their identities, their conceptual investments, and the labor that they perform in their use of media. This is achieved, in part, by the conceptual separation of platform from interface, in which the platform is that nominally complete and inaccessible thing which creates the conditions for new possibilities to emerge, while the interface is the regulated channel through which users are granted access to the power of the platform. In the passive model of the interface, the split between platform and interface is a site at which the container schema, and thus the idea of discrete internal content, comes into being. The interface is on the outside of the container, while the platform is what lies within it.

This division and containment appears to be built into the very term "interface." The word parses into *inter-* "between/among/amidst" and *face*, which can mean a visage or, more generally, an outward-facing surface. On the one hand, "interface" designates a surface that divides one thing from another; it is that which separates the things on either side of it. But the term is also used to indicate a sense of things coming together. An interface in this sense is whatever it is that allows one "thing" to access another. This definition seems to distinguish the interface as a third term, as separate from both of the things between which it intercedes and between which it facilitates contact. The interface can at the same time be a physical aspect of one of the objects or substances being divided, or of both of them. For instance, when the top layer of a body of water, exposed to air, exhibits surface tension, this constitutes the interface between water and air, the barrier across which evaporation occurs. In media hardware, "interface" can designate a piece of equipment used to connect two others, such as the HDMI (high-definition multimedia interface) cable that might connect your TV to your DVD player, or it can mean a piece of equipment that connects a user to a platform, such as a video game controller or remote control. It can also mean the processes by which media devices communicate with each other, as when Bogost and Montfort write that "the Atari VCS does not automate its interface with the television."[8] The VCS must "talk" to the television in order to tell it what to do, and the functioning of the console and television depends on the smooth functioning of the interface between the two.

The ambiguity of the term is pushed further still when a technological interface is said to incorporate a human being. Friedrich Kittler laments the "general digitization" that "erases differences among individual media," so that "sound and image, voice and text are reduced to surface effects, known to consumers as interface."[9] At the same time, Kittler pushes against this simple GUI model of interface-as-surface. Silent film, he writes, was rarely truly silent because when "media were unable to connect," as in failed attempts to link the gramophone to the film projector, "human interfaces filled the niche" in the form of musicians and vocal performers who would accompany film presentations. Kittler calls these performers "the human interfaces of the silent movie palaces."[10] The roles of these human cinematic interfaces were neither aesthetically nor politically neutral. The arrival of synchronized sound technology in the 1920s was systematically resisted by the musical and vocal performers who accompanied the films, and who saw in sound film a technological usurpation of their bodily labor. For Kittler, the interface of silent film establishes and occupies an aesthetic and economic niche that can be filled by human or machine alike.

Working contrariwise along a similar axis, Lev Manovich sees usurpation of the human interface in technologies that seem to replace or augment human bodily functions. He writes (rather hyperbolically) that software "has become our interface to the world, to others, to our memory and our imagination—a universal language through which the world speaks, and a universal engine on which the world runs."[11] As so often happens around the emergence of new media, here appears a persuasive analogy between media and mind that inflects both how we conceive of media and how we conceive of the mind. The user interface is sometimes called a "user illusion," or a simplification and visual abstraction of what is *really* going on in the underlying software code, machine code, and hardware operation of the platform. Philosopher Daniel Dennett uses the term "user illusion" to characterize consciousness, which he sees as a form of self-narration that provides a legible simplification of the complex and inaccessible processes that occur in the mind. "The evolution of memes," or structures of knowledge, Dennett writes, "provides the conditions for the evolution of a user interface that renders the memes 'visible' to the 'self' which (or who) communicates with others, the self as a *center of narrative gravity*."[12] As with Drucker's take on the structuring function of the user interface, for Dennett the user illusion creates, and constrains, a subject position. Consciousness: Now You're Playing With Power.

THE EXPANDED INTERFACE

Drucker, Galloway, and Hookway have each expanded the scale and the scope of the theoretical construct of the interface, conceiving it as an aspect of media use that supersedes and encompasses the surfaces of media technologies. For Galloway, the interface is best thought of as a higher-level interface effect, which he conceives at once as an effect *of* and an effect *on* media technologies and use practices, both resulting from and affecting its material contexts. For Hookway, the interface is a "form of relating to technology," or a process that transpires via the interaction between two discrete entities: media and user.[13] Drucker identifies the interface in its expanded sense as a performative phenomenon in which the "specific structures and forms, substrates and organizational features, are *probability conditions* for production of an interpretation."[14]

In each of these accounts, the expanded interface becomes a space charged with political potential. To Drucker, "performative materiality," her term for the work that is undertaken at the interface, "suggests that what something *is* has to be understood in terms of what it *does*, how it works within machinic, systemic, and cultural domains."[15] Hookway writes that "if culture is an enacted reconciliation of human beings with the social, biological, material, technological, and other realms, the interface describes a cultural moment" as much as it does a relationship to technology.[16] Galloway suggests that the interface is "above all an allegorical device that will help us gain some perspective on culture in the age of information."[17]

When Galloway writes of what he calls interface effects, he does not refer merely to "interface objects (screens, keyboards)" but rather asserts that interfaces "themselves are effects, in that they bring about transformations in material states. But at the same time interfaces are themselves the effects of other things, and thus tell the story of the larger forces that engender them."[18] For Galloway, the interface is a realm of ideological processes, both a result of and a participant in material and discursive formations. Galloway might alternately have written about the interface *dynamic*, though his choice of "effect" has the utility of establishing an in-out relationship by which interfaces as effects and that which is effected by interfaces are, finally, in interactional relationships with one another. In service of this understanding of interface cause and effect, Galloway establishes a fundamental division at the core of his theory, in which "the interface is a general technique of mediation evident at all levels," and the "social field itself constitutes a grand interface, an interface between subject and world, between surface and source, and between critique and the objects of criticism."[19]

Like Galloway, Hookway conceives of an interface that extends beyond the material surfaces of media technologies. To Hookway, the technological interface originates in material formations but is also an increasingly ubiquitous form of relation, the "gateway through which the reservoir of human agency and experience is situated with respect to all that stands outside it, whether technological, social, economic, or political."[20] It is a two-way conduit through which individual human experience and action flow. Hookway is concerned with how the proliferation of technological devices and networks (external to the individual) has altered the terms of experience and agency (internal to the individual). The interface for Hookway is "a form or relation that obtains between two or more distinct entities, conditions, or states such that it only comes into being as these distinct entities enter into an active relation with one another." It is at once a product of and a constraint upon the entities, conditions, or states that contribute to its existence. In this sense, the interface

> actively maintains, polices, and draws on the separation that renders these entities as distinct at the same time as it selectively allows a transmission or communication of force or information from one entity to the other . . . in the production of a mutualism that may be viewed as an entity in its own right, with its own characteristics and behaviors that cannot be reduced to those of its constituent elements.[21]

By characterizing its product as an irreducible entity, Hookway identifies the interface as a site of emergence. In a sense, he identifies it as *the* site of emergence, as the site at which entities, conditions, or states combine to form something ("a form or relation") that is new and itself distinct both from its underlying parts and from other emergent phenomena at its level. This is to say, in an interactionist understanding of emergence along the lines that Hookway proposes, *every* emergent situation would be constituted by an interface of some kind. To Hookway, the interface "is at every stage of its operation concerned with the liminal . . . [the interface] operates through the seeking out, identification, and development of thresholds of various kinds," so that these bodies seek to define themselves as discrete, then act *as if discrete* in formations that nonetheless "elide" their discreteness.[22] For Hookway, as for Galloway, the power of the interface relies on a seeming contradiction, perhaps on a paradox.

I have been arguing throughout this book that these sorts of apparent paradoxes are unavoidable byproducts of interactionist frameworks. The insights we see in the work of theorists like Münsterberg, when his appreciation of the power of film pulls back the interactionist curtain and allows him to think in prototransactional terms about film perception, but not for perception in general, are illustrative of the difference between thinking in terms of discrete entities acting upon one another and thinking of transactions among constitutionally entangled participants in continuity with an environment. The irony is that these resistant moments of disjunct for Galloway and Hookway emerge precisely at the moments where things seem to be coming together.

THE WORLDLY INTRAFACE

Figure 5.2 presents three images, from two films and a video game, in which one character closely pursues another. In *Sherlock, Jr.* (Buster Keaton, 1924), Buster Keaton tails a robbery suspect at absurd proximity, matching him step for step. Keaton's character, an amateur detective, is presented as naive and feckless. Having read in a book titled *How to Be a Detective* an instruction to "Shadow your man closely," he takes this advice to ridiculous extremes, as when the man discards a cigarette and Keaton catches it out of the air and has a puff, never breaking his stride. Keaton's physical performance is an impressive feat, but rather than conveying virtuosity on the part of his character, the pursuit serves to underscore the character's ineptitude as a detective. He follows badly greatly. Gilberto Perez describes Keaton's onscreen persona as "a bewildered equilibrist whose mind runs counter to the achievements of his body."[23] This is every bit in evidence in this sequence from *Sherlock, Jr.*, with its depiction of intensive bodily investment and deeply engaged perceptual effort in service of a ridiculous endeavor. Keaton's character tries to remake who he is by remaking and extending his intimate connections to the world, and he does so neither through argumentation nor through analysis but through motion in the world, relative to other things in motion.

This classic sight gag is alluded to in a sadder register eight decades later in a scene from *What Time Is It There?* in which a Taiwanese woman, at loose ends on a solo vacation in France, closely follows a Parisian woman down the street. Seemingly desperate for human connection as she drifts through an unfamiliar city, she latches onto the motion of a stranger and matches her stride for stride, her plastic shopping bag a crude simulacrum of the woman's purse. And in the video game *Don't Look Back* (2009), the Orpheus-like player-controlled character is followed by a ghost whom he has recovered from the underworld. As he walks, jumps, and climbs in his journey from right to left across the screen, she stays locked in pursuit. If he turns

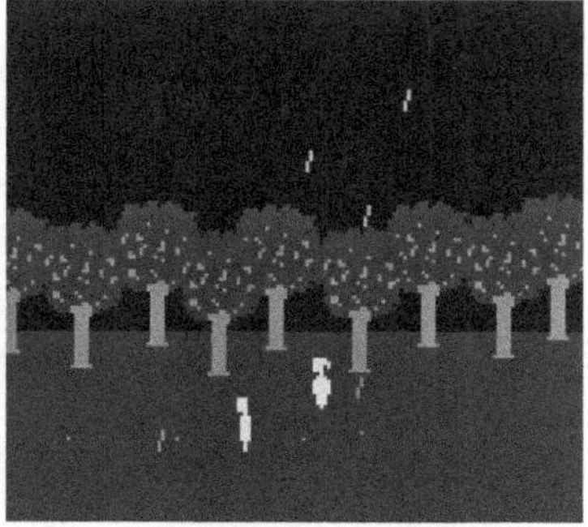

Figure 5.2 Images of close pursuit in the film *Sherlock Jr.* (Buster Keaton, 1924), the video game *Don't Look Back* (distractionware, 2009), and the film *What Time Is It There?*

back to the right—that is, if the player turns him to the right—she disappears like Eurydice.

In each of these cases, the conditions for action are determined by intimate transactions among onscreen bodies as they make their way through space. As one figure moves, so does the other. These relationships are not automatic, nor are they the results of unidirectional action by one thing upon another. In each case, the relevant action is among the bodies in motion, one of which faces away from the other, and the spaces they occupy. To face away from another, however, is not to show them *no* face. The pursuers in each of these images train themselves upon the backs of their targets. Their actions are not determined by those of their targets, nor do the pursuers make their own way through the world independent of those whom they pursue. The action is in the changing relations among the faces that the figures present to one another. It is in what transpires among those faces, inclusive of them. It is in their intraface.

The intraface, as I would like to use the term, is a rethinking of the expanded interface from a transactional perspective. The expanded interface models of Galloway, Hookway, and Drucker all point toward an important aspect of relationships between technology and users, namely that the effects of these relationships cannot be reduced to the material status of one or the other of the "sides" of the event of media use. However, the concept of such distinct sides appears to be built into the very term "interface," a fact that is reflected in the interactional divisions that each of these theorists ultimately retains. Galloway uses the term "intraface" to denote systems of containment and discontinuity internal to media interfaces, which allow for "the presence of the [social] outside within the inside" of the interface.[24] In a transactional perspective, the term is especially useful if everted so that the distinction between inside and outside can be replaced by an understanding of the intraface as continuous with, and not contained by, its material and aesthetic contexts.

Karen Barad uses the term *intra-action* "to signify the mutual constitution of objects and agencies of observation within phenomena (as opposed to "interaction," which assumes the prior existence of distinct entities)."[25] Barad's opposition of intra-action to interaction strongly parallels Dewey and Bentley's opposition of transaction to interaction. Intra-action is a way of acknowledging what Barad calls a "constructed cut between an object and the agencies of observation," whether these agencies are human theorists or devices for imaging or measuring phenomena.[26] More forcefully than do Dewey and Bentley, Barad insists on the power of mutual constitution to disrupt not only structures of knowing but the structures of phenomena themselves. To the degree in which individuals can ever be said to act upon one another, they do so only by way of acting *as if* upon one another. This action constitutes their (contingent) individuality, and that of the objects with which they act, always in the context of their inescapable entanglement and continuity with one another and with their environments. They perform agenthood. Individuality *is* this performance.

The transactional conception of "intraface" acknowledges that objecthood is not a quality inherent to things but is rather a contingent property of how (and to what limited degree) doing constitutes thinghood. Performance is how things distinguish themselves. "Intraface" acknowledges that actions are not undertaken unilaterally by one thing upon another but always reciprocally and in such a way that they constitute the parameters of the things themselves. Experience is never an internal phenomenon, or a quality of a thing, but rather a dynamic that attends the entanglement of things and environments. Recall, from chapter 3, Anthony Chemero's illustration of how conservative embodied cognition (CEC) imposes a consideration of the body into existing representationalist paradigms for understanding the mind, while radical embodied cognition (REC) sees cognition as bodily first— cognition as an aspect of bodily action and not the other way around—and thereby integrates mind, body, and world in a way that is prior to, rather than a function of, representations. Like REC, the intraface reflects a rejection of prior interactional commitments, a wiping clean of the slate of representationalism.

As Drucker, Galloway, and Hookway all argue, the interface is both substance and meaning, both thing and process—it is that which separates things and thus differentiates its constituents. Barad's intra-action takes a crucial step that none of those theorists takes (Hookway gets closest when he writes that the interface "maintain[s] distinction while at the same time eliding it"),[27] reflecting the fact that the two entities constituted by the intraface are never truly discrete but always fundamentally entangled. There has been, and can be, no definitive "cut" distinguishing them entirely from one another or from their environments.

The intraface might be seen as the weakly emergent platform for agenthood. It is a way of describing the material relations necessary to create unexpected possibilities for action and meaning-making, and the constraints on the forms that those actions and meaning-makings can take. The platform is weak emergence as observed from "above," and the intraface is weak emergence as seen from "below" in spatiotemporal and causal scale. The difference between intraface and platform is thus a difference in the positioning (physical and/or theoretical) assumed by an observer, and the distinction between the two reflects only the disciplinary, argumentative, and ideological investments of the parties doing the describing.

Media should not be seen as extensions of their users' intentions, as theorists like Marshall McLuhan would have it, nor should users be seen as conscripted into the technological and social functioning of media devices, as in apparatus theory.[28] As with the images of following in figure 5.2, in which characters with varying investments and intentions lead, follow, are led, and are followed, all at once, media move through their users, and users move through their media. Media and their users move through the world together. Inasmuch as you can say, "There are media" and "Here am I," you still cannot definitively say where the functioning of one begins and the other ends. Media, as used, and you, as media user, are constituted in and by the intraface of yourself and media.

I am playing the video game *Everything* (David OReilly, 2017) on a PlayStation 4. In this game, player control jumps from one object to another and moves up and down in scale, as I guide the motion of objects from the human scale (palomino horses, chairs, fences) to the microscopic (such as oxygen atoms), the macroscopic (galaxies), and the abstract (Planck lengths). As I move up or down from one scale to another, the PlayStation SixAxis controller vibrates pleasantly in my hand. I feel this vibration with my hand and with my arm, with the leg on which my arm rests, with my brain and nervous system, and with my ears as well. The change of scale is initiated by my depressing a button on the controller with my index finger, moving a reticle with the opposing thumb, and releasing the button to select the larger or smaller object that I want to control. I make the movement down in scale; I make the vibration of the controller. But so too do the console, the television, and the game code. As I move upward in spatiotemporal scale, both in *Everything* and in my description of the conditions of gameplay, I find my lower-scale "self," my lower-scale experience, to be a platform, rendered invisible in its stability, for higher-level phenomena. As I move downward, I find those platforms to be constituted by a multitude of intrafaces, by dynamics among things that are entangled and continuous with one another and that assert their contingent agency by way their actions, relative to one another and to the environment. When Germaine Dulac writes that "the very essence of cinema . . . brings Eternity with it since it springs from the very essence of the universe: movement,"[29] she sees how the motion of figures and spaces onscreen, and the motion of cinema itself, are part of and continuous with the motion that characterizes the universe—motion that is continuous and nondecomposable in space or in time.

There is always a balance of power built into this coconstitution. To feel powerless in one's own motion through the world, or in how one constitutes a "self" through transactions with the world, is to be overwhelmed by the conditions that structure and discipline those transactions. The motion of the universe cited by Dulac is irreversible. When we must confront this irreversibility, as we must when someone or something is lost to us forever, then smooth-running functions break down and our intraface in the world becomes suddenly, intolerably apparent. This tension is known as grief.

GRIEF: AN INTOLERABLE INTRAFACE

In order to further feel out the performative nature of the intraface, let us consider two media texts that engage with themes of grief and mourning, the video game *Don't Look Back* and the film *What Time Is It There?* I focus on grief and mourning for three principal reasons. First, they represent universal conditions of human experience. To be alive is to confront death. Grief and mourning are thus "paradigmatic emotions" in the sense used by film theorist Carl Plantinga, both in their ubiquity and in how they can give rise to confusion when they seem to disrupt the emotional flow of life. For Plantinga, paradigmatic emotions "may occur discretely, but . . . often occur in seemingly contradictory or ambiguous combinations."[30] That is, they exert influence on, but also occur within the continuity of, our broader emotional lives (perhaps needless to say, I don't agree with the "discretely" aspect of Plantinga's definition; "states" of experience are continuous in type and time, not discrete from one another). Second, the disappearance of a loved one can focus one's attention on objects, actions, and materiality in new and intensified ways. Representational, interactional conceptions of the mind tend to see such objects and behaviors doing "work" in a psychoanalytic or cognitive vein, helping the griever to overcome symbolic barriers or stagnant thoughts and "move on" with his or her life. A nonrepresentational, transactional conception of the mind is more apt to see actions and environments as material, constitutive parts of subjective experience, as ways of creating and altering one's psychological state by finding new ways of participating in, or of establishing an intraface with, the world. Moving on— literally moving—is how barriers are overcome, and not the other way around. Third, grief is a reaction to the dissolution of what passes for individuality in the object of grieving. When someone is gone, she has in fact gone nowhere at all; the matter and energy that was "she" is redistributed in a way that cannot help but remind us that selfhood (even one's own) is contingent.

In the documentary film *Gates of Heaven* (Errol Morris, 1978), a woman grieving for her dead dog muses, "There's your dog. Your dog's dead. But where's the thing that made it move? It had to be something, didn't it?" For her, this is evidence for the existence of an eternal dog spirit with which she will be united one day. The redirections of attention and engagement that can attend grieving, in which an investment is made in things and behaviors that are *not* the absent physical object of longing, point us in different, non-supernatural (i.e., a naturalist) direction. Your parent (as in *What Time Is It There?*) or your partner (as in *Don't Look Back*) may be gone, but the spaces they occupied and the things with which they engage, and people with whom they engaged, remain. As Hofstadter puts it, in those people, places, and things, is "a collective corona that still glows."[31] To explore places and things in grief is to engage with that mysterious "thing that made it move," as the thing that made it move was in fact the environment and the people and objects entangled within it.

Sometimes this can take the form of an image or other record. In *Camera Lucida*, Roland Barthes reflects on his grief in the wake of his mother's death and the yearning for images that it produces in him. "My grief wanted a just image, an image which would be both justice and accuracy," he writes. Barthes finds such an image in a very old (1898) photograph of his mother as a five-year-old girl. "For once," Barthes writes, "photography gave me a sentiment as certain as remembrance . . . [the photograph] achieved for me, utopically, *the impossible science of the unique being*."[32]

For Eugenie Brinkema, grief is not only a way of being in the world, but a way that the world can be. "Grief," Brinkema writes, "does not limit itself to a model of affect based in and of individual psychology or phenomenological experience. Rather, it inheres in material objects, takes shape in an exteriority and in formal structures bound up intimately with light."[33] This distinguishes grief from mourning, which is often tied up in a sense of self-directed work. An adventure game in genre, *Don't Look Back* by nature entails a kind of ludic work, but, in modulations that it performs on its control scheme, it comes to be about living with, and grieving by way of, its world. *What Time Is It There?*, meanwhile, invites us into a world of objects of grief, of material objects, including the film *The 400 Blows*, a fish tank, and clocks, bound up not only with light but with tactility, intention, and investment. At the intrafaces between *Don't Look Back* and its players, and between *What Time Is It There?* and its viewers, and also between the characters, objects, and worlds depicted by these media, transactions occur that point ever outward to the ceaseless workings of the wider world.

PLAYING THROUGH GRIEF: *DON'T LOOK BACK*

The independently produced video game *Don't Look Back*, designed by Terry Cavanagh, is ascetic in its visual presentation. Its environments and characters are depicted in large pixels and its animation and basic mechanics recall early console games like *Pitfall!* (Activision, 1982), originally released for the Atari 2600 console. *Don't Look Back* retains that game's side-paging action, in which the character moves from one static screen to another in what is implied to be continuous diegetic space, but *Pitfall!*'s bright sprites and chaotic animated setting are replaced by a muted, monochromatic color scheme in shades of maroon and by a simpler and stranger set of character animations. *Pitfall!* pushed the Atari 2600's graphical and processing capacities to their limits, and the game was in fact conceived as a showcase for a realistic walking animation that could be achieved despite the console's limited rendering capacities.[34] Its aesthetic is born of technological constraints. The graphical style of *Don't Look Back* is similarly constrained, but this constraint is self-imposed. Built on the Adobe Flash software platform, the game can be played online or downloaded to a PC. The software and hardware are capable of much more elaborate visual presentations than are those of *Pitfall!*. By adopting a visual and enactive style characteristic of an earlier era in video games and of cinema, *Don't Look Back* defies its own titular entreaty. This is an inherently backward-looking game, an inherently nostalgic one, and it uses this textual nostalgia in service of its themes of loss and grief.

Don't Look Back tells the story of an Orpheus-like man who descends to the underworld in order to retrieve the specter of a woman. (The figures are indistinct, but their genders are coded in their silhouettes and in the myth to which the game alludes.) Generically, it nods to the "damsel in distress" convention employed by many action games, but as it proceeds, *Don't Look Back* thoroughly complicates and problematizes that trope in terms of its surface aesthetics, its narrative structure, and its control scheme. The game opens with the man standing in the rain, regarding a gravestone, at screen left, in front of which the overturned earth is still fresh (figure 5.3). It is night. A jagged, broken tree looms overhead. Everything is depicted in shades of maroon.

At the player's command, the man turns to the right and begins his journey. The game is played via simple keyboard commands. The right and left arrows move the

Figure 5.3 At the grave site in *Don't Look Back*.

character to the right or to the left, while the up arrow makes him jump. If he is climbing a rope, the up and down arrows make him go up or down. A few screens into the game, after being attacked by a snake, the man picks up a pistol, which can be fired by way of the spacebar. During the early screens of the game, these commands are introduced through superimposed titles. The controls are imprecise and loose, especially for a modern game, and it can take considerable trial and error to be able to navigate the game's challenges with the limited control over the character's motion that players are afforded.

In the tradition of classic platforming games, the environment offers a series of increasingly difficult challenges, most of them based on timing and dexterity. A single hit from an enemy or a fall down a deep pit causes the screen to reset, but the player can retry each screen as many times as needed. The character advances from left to right and occasionally from top to bottom, moving first though aboveground space and then into the depths of the underworld. The iterative physical task of controlling the character, often repeating the same challenges again and again, requires physical adaptation to the imprecise keyboard controls of the game. As with *Tetris*, the challenges of *Don't Look Back* cannot be met through observation followed by action; they must be felt through in order to be navigated. Skill-based access to the world of the game requires felt experience and adaptation to its interactive idiosyncrasies.

It is highly ironic that feeling out the world of the game requires the player's character repeatedly to die. The game is very much about the insurmountable death of another, but its action proceeds via the repeated, infinitely reversible death of the self. Death permeates the game thematically, in the figure of the specter whose retrieval represents its goal, but it permeates the gameplay in a different way. At the end of the game, it will become clear that these are imaginary deaths and resurrections, as the game apparently takes place in the imagination of the man standing at the gravesite. He unimagines death both in the quest story that he tells himself and in the ludic form that the telling takes. The gameplay, as it turns out, is an exercise in imagining what it would be like to transcend death. Repeated "lives" are a long-standing convention of adventure games, a convention that *Don't Look Back* critiques and employs in equal measure.

Descending into the underworld, the player soon encounters a series of pitch-black rooms and must navigate them through contextual clues like the motion of enemies, who are still visible, as well as through a sense of groping touch. Barriers to forward motion can only be discovered by bumping into them, and sudden drop-offs can be detected only by falling off of them. While the player's character and his enemies are still visible onscreen, the shape of the environment becomes accessible only through tactility, like the metaphorical blind man's tapping cane to Maurice Merleau-Ponty, Gregory Bateson, Alva Noë, and the others, or like the paint thrown by Monroe in *The Unfinished Swan*. In the dark environments of *Don't Look Back*, a player can, in fact, extend his or her spatial perception a bit by firing the gun and observing the behavior of the bullets to see if they strike an unseen structure ahead.

All of this feeling-through of the game world—both visual and tactile—creates an epistemic framework that loses much of its pragmatic value when, halfway through the game, its rules are suddenly revised.

At the deepest point in the underworld, the player is confronted by a devil figure who serves as the game's primary "boss" character, an overpowered enemy whose defeat would conventionally represent the final challenge of the narrative. However, the protagonist's journey is only halfway over. To defeat the enemy, the player must jump between disappearing platforms and dodge fireballs, bats, and spiders, in order to deliver a series of pistol shots to the adversary's head. After the battle, the man advances along a precipice and finally encounters the spectral woman. He approaches her, then turns back. She follows, gliding along behind him. From here, the game's spatial orientation reverses and the gameplay gains a new enactive twist. The man must now return by moving right to left, followed by the specter, to the gravesite where his journey began, but now he can *only* move to the left. If he turns toward screen right, looking back at his follower, she dissipates into nothingness with a disturbing gasp, at which point the screen resets and the player must make another attempt. This is a significant transformation of the gameplay, but the game does not explicitly alert the player to the new gameplay mechanic. Unlike the initial controls for the game, which are introduced via onscreen text, the new constraint must be discovered through action. It can only be learned, that is, through failure, as the only way to discover the new rule is to break it and thereby to suffer its consequences. After explicitly establishing its control scheme, the game sets its player up to feel through its modulation of that scheme. From a thematic perspective, this represents a new development in the game's thinking about grief. Looking back to the figure of the departed is destructive; navigating the world *with* the reality of the departure is the best one can hope to learn to do. From a gameplay perspective, it can also trigger a sobering moment of realization: not only is the game not over, as one might expect after the conventional boss battle and rescue, but the journey back to the surface will be even more difficult than the game has been thus far.

Don't Look Back is a challenging game in its first half, and it trains its players to make minute positional adjustments and to regularly retreat to reassess spatial relationships and patterns of motion. In its second half, the game all but revokes these capacities. To take a step back from a hazard—even a necessary step away from imminent danger—is to fail. Having just played through the game's first half, turning back can be a difficult physical habit to break. A way of being in the world, of being "intimate participants," in Dewey's terms, that the game has taught its player has been devalued, and a new set of gameplay skills must be developed in response to a new set of enactive constraints.

The trip back is undertaken along a path parallel to the original, and the player is confronted by a series of environmental challenges designed around the new constraint of being able to move in only one direction. For example, the player enters the screen in figure 5.4 at the lower right and must climb and jump between a series

Figure 5.4 *Don't Look Back*: the characters must cross the screen from right to left, climbing the ropes and avoiding the moving obstacles, with no backtracking.

of ropes in order to access the passageway at the top left of the screen. The light-colored shapes make rapid circuits around the F-shaped enclosures to the left and right of the ropes, and then cut across the middle of the screen, killing the character if they touch him. Only the rightmost rope can be reached by jumping from the ground, so the player must time the climbing and jumping perfectly in order to make it across the ropes without being hit. Unlike in the first half of the game, there is no backtracking when such a threat looms. To jump back to a lower rope, because it would require moving to the right, is to reset the screen. What would in the first half of the game be a challenge to one's reactions to an oncoming threat thereby becomes more a task of pure timing and practice, of attempting the room over and again until one either gets the timing of one's gestures down perfectly, or until a player is fortuitous enough to fumble through the situation and move on to the next screen. In either case, getting through the screen, and the many others like it, is a task of feeling, and more specifically a task of refining one's ability to feel by challenging it. This is, in fact, true of the game (and of games) as a whole, but the modulation of the game's control scheme brings it to the forefront in the return journey, making it explicit in a way that prompts reflection on its functioning throughout the rest of the gameplay.

After completing the treacherous journey back to the surface, the character moves leftward toward the grave scene where his journey began. As the character enters the final screen from the right, we also see a double of his figure still standing at the grave. At this point, the game revokes all interactive control. The player's character and the ghost stand frozen on the right side of the screen. After a few seconds, the player-controlled character and his ghostly companion *both* dissipate into thin air, as can be seen in the two frames of figure 5.5.

The game thereby returns to its original state, at which point it can be played again. After a few moments, the game's title card reappears above the character at the gravesite and the player may turn the man again to the right and restart the journey. *Don't Look Back* thematizes the pain and protracted destabilization of grief

Figure 5.5 *Don't Look Back*: returning to the gravesite.

through its visual design, mythic allusions, and ultimate revelation of a recursive narrative structure. Through its changing gameplay parameters, it also embodies emotional tensions and fluctuations distinctive of grief. The game's formal construction, including its modulation of its enactive scheme, is remarkable not for the narrative it facilitates so much as for the refined and intensified forms of experience it enables in the game's players.

Loss, repeated loss—as the player discovers what it happening by turning to the right enough times to recognize the new constraint on the gameplay—thereby becomes a form of epistemic action, of learning something about the world and strategizing about how to negotiate an environment by way of one's actions in it. Recall from chapter 3 that for Kirsh and Maglio's *Tetris* experiment, and for Clark and Chalmers's interpretation of its results, epistemic action is a form of information-gathering, while pragmatic action makes progress toward a goal. I argued that epistemic action is a variety of pragmatic action because knowledge about a situation is itself a form of practical engagement. To lose repeatedly in *Don't Look Back* is also to gain: to gain knowledge about, practice at, and a tactical advantage in the situations that one must negotiate in order to complete the game. "Loss" has many meanings here. Locally, one loses an attempt at navigating a screen and concurrently (identically) loses the woman's ghost. On a wider view, though, the game cannot be lost in a ludic sense, as players are free to attempt any screen as many times as necessary. In this regard, the only way to lose the game is for the player to give up. However, as the end of the game shows, the woman herself *is* permanently lost, and the game reveals itself to be a mere fantasy, albeit one that can be repeated forever.

The game's embodiment of grief trades on a tension between presence and absence, and between finality and perpetuity. It maps the iterative action of life onto the boundless infinite of nonlife, both in its narrative and in its modulation of its control scheme. Focusing on the process rather than on any resolution (which is never forthcoming), *Don't Look Back* depicts the evolving intraface between its grieving protagonist and his world. It concurrently establishes an intraface with its players, encouraging them not only to think about but to feel, and to feel performatively through, the ways that grief destabilizes one's relationship to the material world.

If grieving is an investment in objects and actions in the absence of that for which one grieves, it is a particular, powerful, and pervasive form of intraface. The actions and investments of grieving "point" both to the feeling that they create, that bringing into being of a gradual and painful transition to living with a loved one's loss, and to the fundamental absence, always an absence, of the one who is lost. If the player's character in *Don't Look Back* grieves though his negotiation (in the navigational sense) of the underworld—or, more properly, though what appears to be his fantasy of negotiating the underworld—and thus his negotiation (in the sense of bargaining) with the permanence of grief, he does so by establishing new transactional relationships with the changing structures and challenges of his environment. A player of the game must do the same, and in the intraface between player and game, *Don't Look Back* provokes not grieving itself but opportunities to feel through, and thereby to feel out the structures of, the game's spatialization of its character's grief.

Don't Look Back reminds us that physical reality, the reality of the body and of the world, is also the reality of the mind. Experience is the body's fundamental entanglement with its environment. When we make the trip to the underworld, negotiating its perils and adjusting to its modulating challenges, we do so not only to enact an impossible fantasy of retrieval but also to engage with an enactive challenge. If we play the game again, we are aware of the journey's final revelation. The game does not change at all when we repeat it. We can only become more skillful, or more efficient, at enacting what will always be a fantasy, for our character and for ourselves.

Video games, like other media, present fictional worlds that have their own relational systems of space, time, and causality. But media also participate in the making of the wider world in which they are embedded along with their users. Just as the mind can never be independent of the body and the world, neither can fictional worlds be independent of the media through which they are instantiated or of the environments in which those media are situated. The question becomes how our use of media "remakes the world" or, in Dewey's pragmatic phrasing, how it "is valuable in the degree in which it is effective."[35] When *Don't Look Back* strips its character of the ability to move, or even to look, in one direction—the direction that has signified *progress* for the entire game until that point—and ultimately strips the player of *all* enactive capacity, it asks us to revise our understanding of the game and to rethink the implications of what we have been doing all along. The phrase "don't look back" is as much an appeal to the character at the gravestone as it is a description of the sudden twist in the gameplay. To begin the journey, the character must turn away from the grave—he must look back. The ensuing fantasy of retrieving a loved one from the dead is futile, but it is not unproductive. *Don't Look Back* returns time and again (and, potentially, always again) to the unity of the mental and the physical. Each time we play, we come closer to understanding that it is time to stop playing. The game is over when we are done with it.

GRIEVING THROUGH FEELING: *WHAT TIME IS IT THERE?*

Throughout his career, Taiwan-based director Tsai Ming-liang has made films particularly sensitive to their characters' bodily relationships with objects and their environments. Tsai's cinema, much like *L'Argent* and Robert Bresson's other films, is especially attentive to transactions among characters and their worlds, and to the relationships between films, viewers, and the material reality that films record, represent, and occupy. Among Tsai's films, *What Time Is It There?* in particular is concerned with characters' intrafaces with media. In chapter 4, I pointed to a scene from *What Time Is It There?* that, from one perspective, is constituted by a matrix of interrelated and inseparable platforms, in order to trouble the discursive naturalness, and the boundedness, of the theoretical figure of the platform. Earlier in this chapter, I pointed to another moment in the film, in which a woman named Shiang-chyi closely pursues another woman down the streets of Paris, as an exemplar of the coconstitutive intimacy that characterizes the intraface. I have argued that, on a transactional model, the platform and the intraface are two sides of the same coin, that they are alternative ways of describing weakly emergent dynamics, either from "above" or from "below" in terms of the spatiotemporal scale from which they are observed. Like the character in *Don't Look Back*, two of the primary characters in *What Time Is It There?* are grieving the loss of a loved one. Also like the character in *Don't Look Back*, they embark on new relationships with the physical environment and the objects in it as a way of feeling through their loss. Their transactions with things around them—media and technology, but also personal effects and ephemera—are intrafaces if we think about *how they are*, and they are platforms (in my broader conception of the term) if we think about *what they make possible*. But how they are and what they make possible, in the end, are inseparable, in space, in time, and in meaning. As it is in *Tetris*, so it is in life: the epistemic is pragmatic.

The film opens with a stationary long take in which a man in late middle age paces slowly around a working-class Taipei apartment, preparing a plate of food and smoking a cigarette. The camera lingers for minutes as the man moves about the frame, the unhurried feeling of the shot underscoring the deliberateness of his movements. He is at ease, and we understand that he is doing things he has done countless times before, occupying familiar space and touching familiar things. As the camera holds on the room, duration and continuity emerge as deeply felt qualities of the shot. We perceive diegetic space and time, but we also feel the way that the film channels and constrains our perspective on its space while maintaining the continuity of its time. If the stationary single take of *How It Feels to Be Run Over* initiates thinking about the fixative power of cinematic technology in its ability to confront us with the unavoidable threat of its oncoming car, the opening of *What*

Time Is It There? demonstrates how film's ability to fix its viewers in relation to diegetic space is also a capacity to modulate their relationships to diegetic time. Time, we are soon reminded, is a fleeting resource. The man walks into the depth of the shot, out onto the apartment's enclosed balcony. Cut to the second shot of the film, and the man is dead. His son, Hsiao-kang, sits in the back of a car, carrying the urn that contains his father's cremated remains. Hsiao-kang deposits the urn in a columbarium. We see neither the urn nor the father again until the closing moments of the film, when the father makes a mysterious reappearance in Paris, near a pond in the Jardin du Luxembourg.

Leaving the columbarium, Hsiao-kang returns to work as a street vendor selling watches on a Taipei skywalk. About to leave for Paris, Shiang-chyi visits his shop, and he reluctantly agrees to sell her the watch off his own wrist. Throughout the remainder of the film, we will follow Hsiao-kang and Shiang-chyi in parallel, him in Taipei and her in Paris. Although he does not know Shiang-chyi, Hsiao-kang longs for her once she is gone, and after a visit to a video store he becomes fascinated with the Paris-set film *The 400 Blows*. He begins compulsively to set every clock he sees to Paris time, seven hours earlier than the time in Taipei. Meanwhile, his mother, also grieving, preoccupies herself with intimate details around the family apartment: evaporating water, the behavior of a pet fish, the (from her perspective) mysteriously changing times on the clocks. Through her alienated observations of these phenomena, she becomes convinced that the apartment is haunted by the ghost of her husband. The space that he once occupied remains charged for her by his presence. This space and these things were part of his transactionally constituted self, and they remain even as he is gone. As illustrated in the first shot of the film, these are the "thing that made him move," and his corona, in Hofstadter's term, lingers on in them.

Both mother and son seek solace in closely monitoring and altering their immediate surroundings. The son changes his environment by ritually watching *The 400 Blows* and by resetting the clocks, while the mother is more inclined to interpret her surroundings in new and obsessive ways. In each case, the characters refashion their relationships to their environments so that those environments might serve as aides-memoires, facilitating thought about and remembrance of how they felt in the presence of someone who is now absent. We might take this a step further and say that these objects do more than aid, flesh out, or trigger memories and feelings. Through their intrafaces with the people who use them, they constitute those phenomena. The objects are inextricable parts of the feelings, as they were inextricable parts of the father. Changes in objects correspond to changes in feelings. The act of changing an object is also an act of changing how one feels.

This form of meaning-making transaction is most readily apparent in Hsiao-kang's rewatching of *The 400 Blows*, in that we are somewhat accustomed to thinking of cinema as directly affecting perception, concept formation, and emotions. Münsterberg posited as much, and theorists across a broad range of ideological and theoretical persuasions have articulated similar positions, each with different nuances and to different ends. Likewise, our bodily states, cultural contexts, and viewing situations can profoundly affect our feelings about a film during and after a particular viewing. In this view of media-user transactions, meaning is thoroughly contingent even as fundamental aspects of the intraface remain relatively stable. Our own experience is continuous from one viewing to the next, and our bodies remain intact, one hopes, across viewings, though they are never unchanged. Continuity is not the opposite of difference, however. Among viewings, our moods may change, we may be intoxicated or sleepy or agitated, or our frameworks for assessing a film may shift according to our recent experiences or to the situation of exhibition (such as where, how, and why the film is being shown, or with whom we are watching it). The media objects with which we transact might be different, due to degradation, differences among versions of films or games, screening situations, and so on, but these differences are made meaningful by the continuity that is their context. As Barad might say, they are performative. This is why repetition and ritual are possible. This is why *Don't Look Back* rewards repeated attempts at a given screen and repeated play of the entire game, and why for Hsiao-kang *The 400 Blows* rewards repeated viewing.

In the case of Hsiao-kang's private cinematic ritual, his tape of *The 400 Blows* furthermore facilitates a felt connection to an imaginary Paris and an imagined connection to Shiang-chyi. The physical distance between Taipei and Paris is unsurmountable for Hsiao-kang, but he can feel something of the city, of its space and of life there, by way of the film. John Berger calls this cinema's ability to transport. "The cinema, because its images are moving, takes us *away* from where we are to the *scene of action*," he writes. "The cinema . . . transports its audience individually, singly, *out* of the theater towards the unknown."[36] Stanley Cavell identifies this effect as having its origins in the photographic referentiality of the film medium. A photograph, writes Cavell, is "*of* reality or nature." It "does not present us with 'likenesses' of things; it presents us, we want to say, with the things themselves."[37] Put into motion, such images, in Berger's account, extract us from daily life and allow us to transcend the world as we know it. If we are thinking transactionally, in terms of the intraface, it is not enough to say that films "transport us." Rather, we, along with films, produce an intraface that points to something however spatiotemporally remote and however remotely potential, whether far-off Paris or the depths of the underworld, whether a departed loved one or a teenage actor like Jean-Pierre Léaud in *The 400 Blows*, recorded by a camera, half a century in the past.

By changing the times on clocks and by repeatedly watching *The 400 Blows*, Hsiao-kang reorganizes his environment, bringing it, in limited ways, into accord with how it might be to be in Paris. Something as simple as the time of day has profound implications for what one can and cannot do at a particular moment. To live on Paris time in Taipei is to imagine oneself to be profoundly elsewhere. Likewise, to return to the same Paris-set, location-shot film in a ritual fashion is to make Parisian "things themselves," in Cavell's terms, part of daily experience. However, these environmental adjustments do not, and could never, overcome the fact that Hsiao-kang remains an embodied being, in Taipei and on Taipei time, nor the fact that Hsiao-Kang's father is permanently out of time in a bodily sense. Hsiao-kang's efforts result not in the romantic "transportation" of Berger's cinemagoer, but rather in new forms of intraface in a physical environment populated, if not by Parisian things themselves, then at least by the presence in Taipei of photographic images that are, as Cavell puts it, ontologically of Paris in the late 1950s and, as such, are able to provide Hsiao-kang with a variety of presence to that city across time and spaces. In his room in Taipei, his face is illuminated by a beam of light from Paris.

Tsai's film contrasts the 1959 Paris of *The 400 Blows* with both the Taipei and the Paris of around 2001, as *What Time Is It There?* follows Shiang-chyi on her journey to France. The temporal distance between 1959 and the present is underscored by a scene in which Jean-Pierre Léaud, who was a teenager when he played the lead role in *The 400 Blows*, appears in *What Time Is It There?*, apparently playing himself, more than forty years older. There Léaud is, cinematically present to us, as both a teenager and a man in his fifties. That some of the images are decades older than the others makes them no less present. As *The 400 Blows* grants Hsiao-kang time and space to expand and explore his grief, *What Time Is It There?* facilitates our own thought and feeling through its organization and representation of the events it depicts, both in Hsiao-kang's time and in Antoine Doinel's. Hsiao-kang's viewing of *The 400 Blows* always points elsewhere, to an absence, and so too does *What Time Is It There?* function in its own viewers' lives, bringing a new intraface into being each time we encounter it.

Echoing the self-imposed constraint of *Don't Look Back*'s visual asceticism, *What Time Is It There?* presents Hsiao-kang's experiences through an edifice of formal rigor, chiefly in its commitment to long takes and a stationary camera. There are no camera movements at all in the shots original to the film. The only times the camera moves are in shots excerpted from *The 400 Blows* that occasionally take over the screen. This textural contrast emphasizes the functioning of *The 400 Blows* in Hsiao-kang's longing for different, more fluid conditions in his own life. In its side-paging action, *Don't Look Back* is likewise presented as a series of stationary "shots" between which the player's character moves. At the end of that game, when we learn that the character has in fact never moved, the game's static shots come to underscore the contrast between the man's paralyzing grief and his fantasy of mobility. *What Time Is It There?* similarly foregrounds the contrast between its stationary camera and semistatic compositions and the relative visual dynamism of *The 400 Blows*. In the long takes, the stasis of Tsai's camera elicits a feeling of patient anticipation, bordering at times on impatience or boredom. Looking back on the opening shot of the father in the context of his subsequent death, though, we can appreciate its duration in other ways. This is the only time we will be allowed to spend with the father while he is alive, and we spend it with him in real time. The sequence is unbroken, both temporally and spatially. It is framed as a long shot, allowing us to take in the depth of the apartment space and the father's movement through it. After he is dead he will, in a sense, be contained by the urn that holds his ashes. But that urn does not contain what was him, and not because his spirit has left his body. In looking for what contains what was him, we can look to Hsiao-kang and to his mother, and to the spaces and objects that surround them and that likewise surrounded him. We can look, too, to Tsai's lingering shot of the father that opens the film. All of these things contained him and continue to do so, but only inasmuch as they also contain one another, and inasmuch as he contained them. "The one the other can contain," as Emily Dickinson writes. To answer the question "Where's the thing that made it move," we need only look around.

The final sequence of *What Time Is It There?* further emphasizes the continuity of self and world. A lonesome Shiang-chyi lies asleep in Paris's Jardin de Luxembourg. While she sleeps, mischievous children throw her suitcase into a pond. The suitcase floats slowly by, and then a well-dressed man hooks it with the handle of his umbrella and sets it safely on dry ground. Shiang-chyi remains asleep. As he turns to walk away, we see that the man is Hsiao-kang's father. The film cuts to its final shot, centered on a Ferris wheel in the middle distance. The father, seen in medium-long shot, lights a cigarette, then turns toward the camera for a moment before walking off into the distance. The end of *What Time Is It There?* echoes the film's beginning, in which the father also smoked a cigarette and moved into the depth of the shot. It also resonates with the end (which is also the beginning) of *Don't Look Back*. In that game's final moments, a specter disappears, while in the final moments of *What Time is It There?* a specter of sorts appears, although nobody seems to see it except for us. The father's miraculous reappearance—and the performative agency that it establishes in the film's final moments—is, for all of its unrealism, the image of the intraface.

THE CONTEMPORARY INTRAFACE

In *What Time Is It There?*, longing for distant, absent figures—and a desire to bridge distances of space and time—is expressed, given form, and explored diegetically through characters' use of media and their restructuring of their environments. By way of its formal construction, the film pushes its viewers to experience new modes of presence and to feel out new modes of understanding of the possibilities afforded by grieving. It does not—nor does any media object—present an ontologically discrete aesthetic experience. Rather, it facilitates contextually specific embodied experience, aesthetic experience that is continuous with the rest of one's own life. It is a local dynamic, an intraface, within the broader spatiotemporal context of one's life in the world. To borrow an analogy from Dewey, media use is in our lives as events are in history.[38]

When thinking about the relationships among media, mind, life, and world, we would do well to always be mindful both of Dewey's *in* and of Barad's *intra-*. A hundred years after Münsterberg, philosophy of mind remains largely divided between structuralist and functionalist models of mental activity. Cognitive science and neuroscience still tend strongly toward structuralism in their models of the mind and in their understanding of the relationship between mind and brain. It is becoming increasingly clear, though, that models of the mind that differentiate modes of experience from one another, that break up the flow of life into discrete kinds of experience, and that treat experience as fundamentally separate from the "external" world, thereby impoverish themselves. In this context, aesthetic experience must be theoretically incorporated into an account of the flow of the rest of our experience, not elevated above or set aside from it.

Aesthetic experience occupies a central role not only in our interpretation and appreciation of art but also in our beliefs, reasoning, and action. Our previous experiences, our perception of our surroundings, the physical structures of our bodies, and the social contexts in which we live all contribute to how we sense, and how we make sense of, events in our lives, whether these are pressing challenges, quotidian tasks, or encounters with media. They provide the background that we have at our disposal in our skill-based access to media forms. Münsterberg saw that media have profound effects on the functioning of our minds that go well beyond the presentation of narrative events. Although the events in a film are not happening in front of us, in "real life," a film is happening in front of us, in our real lives.

Living with and using a medium entails a particular mode of being. If the media that we use partly constitute our minds, then minds can be different things in the era of contemporary media than they could be before the appearance of cinema in the late nineteenth century. Not only are new forms of consciousness made possible by the representational and depictive capacities of media, but being in the world itself has necessarily been impacted by the proliferation of contemporary media. This is not because these media stimulate the formerly internal mind to work in new ways, but because they participate in new ways in what has always been a transactional process, neither external nor internal, characterized by the intrafaces among agents, objects, and environments. What is "the" contemporary mind? I would argue that every mind is contemporary, in that it is characterized and made possible by its very contemporaneity. This is not to say that this contemporaneity takes the same form from one mind to the next. However, we share our environments with others. We are, in fact, parts of one another's environments and, as Hofstadter and others show, parts of one another's selves. This overlap between the physical and historical contexts of our being and (on a more local scale) the structuring of the depictions that media make possible means that multiple minds can be partly constituted by the same objects. We share them.

The expanded interfaces proposed by Drucker, Galloway, and Hookway, and the transactionist model of the intraface that I have proposed in this chapter, point toward the continuity of mind, media, and world, and thus to the underlying movement that Dulac calls the "essence of the universe." Media do not move only in the images that they present—they also move together with their users through the world. As the following chapter shows, nowhere is this more apparent than when media devices become portable. In the development of such devices, as exemplified by the case of the Nintendo Game Boy portable video game console, designers articulate conceptions of human bodies and the intrafaces that will develop among these bodies and the devices that they encounter.

CHAPTER 6

Designing a Game Boy

The cover of the November–December 1989 issue of Nintendo's official fan magazine, *Nintendo Power*, both touts the release of *Tetris* for the Nintendo Entertainment System (NES) home console and promises an "Update And More!" on the company's recently launched Game Boy portable console (figure 6.1). In the cover text, Nintendo encourages its users to "Get 'Tetrisized,'" a proposal visualized via an image of a game player (young, white, male, presented as a proxy for hypothetical readers of the magazine) holding the "NES Max" console controller, an optional add-on to the NES home console, walking into what appears to be a "Tetrisized" world made of the game's distinctive block patterns, and transforming, stepwise, into Tetris blocks himself. In these details and in its strange mixture of other imagery, the *Nintendo Power* cover image exemplifies how Nintendo, the corporation, imagines its users—their desires, their minds, their bodies, and their culture—by way of imagining its video game hardware and software.

Having descended into the ostensible internal depths of the mind (perception, representation), and having then crossed over into the equivalent depths of media technologies (interface, platform), we now find ourselves re-emerging into the "external" world. Challenging the conceptual gaps that we have encountered along the way, we have endeavored always to a leveling action—leveling not in the sense of reducing everything to the same level by separating object from object and unit from world, but leveling in the sense of elevating everything to the same level, acknowledging the continuity, entanglement, and coconstitution of body, perception, mind, platform, interface/intraface, and media. To borrow a term from video games, we have been "leveling up."

Returning to the external world, we have arrived the other side of the initial conceptual gap that divides media from their users. All of the gaps that we have encountered on this journey, between things and their "content," or between wholes and their parts (and the parts of those parts), have followed from a first ontological opposition between things and other things: "The medium is over there,

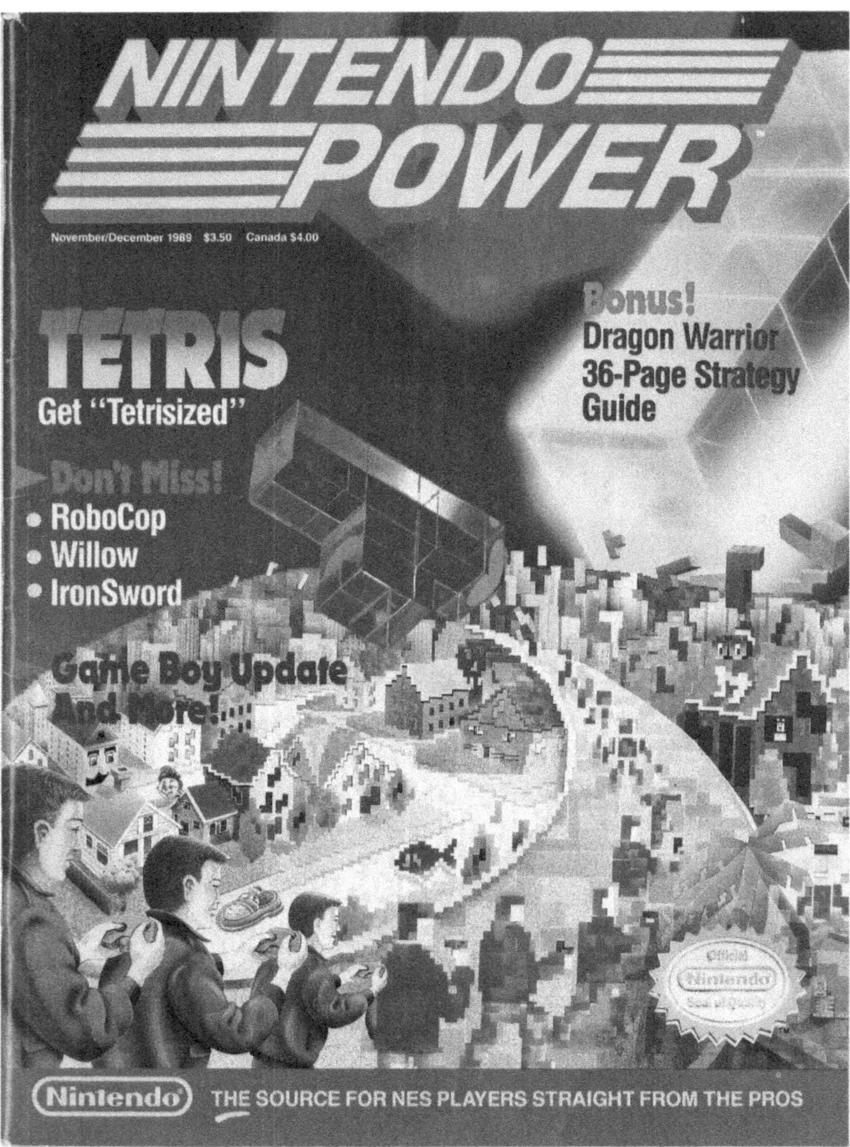

Figure 6.1 *Nintendo Power* magazine cover, November–December 1989. Design by Griffes Advertising, photography by Darrell Peterson, illustration by Dan McGowan.

and I am over here." Transactionism as a way of knowing, and as a way of conceiving of knowing, tells us that this opposition is only a conceptual contrivance, and that when we draw these contingent conceptual boundaries, there will always follow constraints on how we can conceive of media and how we can conceive of minds. Media users *feel* their bodily (and thus their mindful) relationships to media. The designers of media texts and media technologies, likewise, are obliged to conceive of the bodies and minds of media users, and to build into their creations an attitude or orientation toward those hypothetical bodies and minds. This chapter takes the development and release of the Game Boy as a case study in the articulation of media technology as a mode of transactional thinking, tracing how the design of the Game Boy functioned both in the development of Nintendo's conception of the minds and bodies of its users and in the development of Nintendo's own branding as a developer of games and consoles.

Nintendo is both a software company and a hardware manufacturer. Like Apple, Nintendo presents its products as integrated experiences in which platform and software harmonize smoothly with one another. Also like Apple, Nintendo maintains close control over its corporate branding, including in its development of a Disney-style stable of characters who appear time and again across home and portable console games, arcade machines, and other media, including film, television, and comic books. (I'd say that Nintendo is where Apple meets Disney, but that is already Pixar.) Nintendo's consoles have waxed and waned in popularity over the decades since the blockbuster release of the NES in 1985, but during that period other console companies such as Sega (maker of the Sega Master System, Genesis, Saturn, and Dreamcast), SNK (maker of the Neo•Geo), and NEC (maker of the TurboGrafx-16) have withdrawn entirely from the console market. Nintendo now stands alongside relative newcomers Sony, whose PlayStation line debuted in 1994–95, and Microsoft, whose original Xbox appeared in 2001, as one of the three dominant console manufacturers. With each passing console generation, Microsoft and Sony have sought to increase the power of their devices and to refine their interactive schemes, favoring incremental change over radical revision of their consoles and controllers. As David Parisi points out, Sony's DualShock 4 controller, released in 2013, "does not feel or look significantly different from the DS1 Sony first sold in 1997."[1] Nintendo, on the other hand, has experimented relentlessly with console formats, control devices, and display technologies. What has remained consistent for Nintendo has been a commitment to probing the ways that players incorporate gameplay into their lives and worlds, and to doing so by exploring how technological components can be articulated relative to the bodies and minds of video game players. This has been a key aspect of Nintendo's corporate philosophy and, increasingly, a prominent element of its brand identity.

In the *Nintendo Power* cover, we can see a number of themes that are central to Nintendo's corporate identity, both in its attitude toward hardware and software development and in the image of itself that it presents to its consumers. The cover depicts the transubstantiation of the player and the environment into the blocky substrate of the game, and the game at the same time surging forth into three-dimensional space to meet the player, visualized most dramatically in giant, prismatic *Tetris* blocks that float menacingly in the sky above the player's path, the most prominent of which seems to announce, via its "T" shape, that *Tetris* looms over the boy's future, not as a threat but as a transformative opportunity. The block-based aesthetic of *Tetris* lends itself to a cubist mapping of the player's diachronic transformation over time onto the synchronic space of the image (call it "Nerd Descending a Staircase"). It serves as a visualization of the "*Tetris* effect," discussed in chapter 3, in which video game play affects players' perceptual relationships to their environments. It promises mobility rather than the static bodily experience players might associate with console video game play. The boy is depicted holding a home console controller, but he is using it as one would use a Game Boy. The cover promotes the NES release of *Tetris*; the Game Boy version had launched with the Game Boy earlier that year. In its sales pitch for the home console edition of the game, Nintendo seems to want to draw here not only on the popularity of *Tetris*, but on the feeling of playing *Tetris* specifically on the Game Boy.

The magazine cover furnishes a highly specific image of the game's imagined player. He appears to be styled after James Dean's appearance in *Rebel Without a Cause* (Nicholas Ray, 1955): red jacket with upturned collar, blue jeans, hair pomaded up away from his face (though this being 1989, it is probably mousse and not pomade). He is a young white male with money to burn, but, thanks to the association with Dean, he is presented as a possible iconoclast as well, at least in the secure context of the American-looking suburb he occupies. He is coded as safe and is safe in code. He can move through the suburban streets without needing to look around himself for safety, and he can play the world as if it is a game. He does not need to worry about what city block he is on, but only about what *Tetris* block he is on. He is able-bodied and takes his ability to walk for granted. The yellow-block road that he travels carries him toward a city on the horizon, not a fantastical Emerald City but a cityscape composed of tetrominoes poised to fall into place just for him. As he himself mutates into *Tetris* bricks, their red and blue contrast mirroring the bold coloring of his jacket and jeans, he is transformed from one type of icon to another. Nintendo will take this experiential transformation to be emblematic of what it offers to its consumers. In this imaging of the extended gaming self, Nintendo assures us, one can be both privileged and revolutionary. But first one must be willing to show up and accept the challenge. Nintendo's imaginary player is in every respect a game boy.

A COMPACT

The Game Boy portable console was released in the United States and Japan in 1989. In its various iterations before its replacement by the Game Boy Advance in 2001 and then the Nintendo DS in 2005, the Game Boy would sell nearly 120 million hardware units.[2] Beyond its market success, the Game Boy represented a turning point in how Nintendo conceived of its corporate and brand identity, its users, and the intimate relationship between bodies and technologies that characterizes video game play.

The Game Boy's packaging artwork (figure 6.2) depicts a pair of black-and-neon-blue hands holding a similarly stylized Game Boy in front of a wireframe

Figure 6.2 The box art for the Nintendo Game Boy portable console.

background. Like the *Nintendo Power* cover, this image draws on a contrast between two-dimensional and three-dimensional perspectives. The hands are drawn in linear perspective, while the Game Boy appears to be a flat surface. The depth of the wireframe background is exaggerated, as if space is telescoping around the player. Luminous projectiles hurtle forth from it. The vanishing point of the background is occluded by the Game Boy. On the unit's screen, a game of *Tetris* (Game Boy version by Bullet-Proof Software and Nintendo, 1989) is in progress, its player poised to complete a successful "tetris." The box art is in first-person POV, seemingly designed to make you imagine yourself holding the Game Boy. The effect of physical and perceptual transformation resonates with imagery in the relatively recent film *Tron* (Steven Lisberger, 1982), in which game designer Flynn is transported into the internal world of a computer. Upon his arrival in computer space, Flynn immediately examines his own hands, depicted in a POV shot from his perspective (figure 6.3). The most pressing question, having been digitized or Tetrisized, seems to be: *Can I still use my hands?* Nintendo answers: Yes, but only if we can use them too.

The Game Boy box image summarizes a pivotal moment in the development of Nintendo's corporate identity as a video game publisher and console manufacturer. From the 1950s onward, Nintendo had sought to become a global corporation with a stable of transmedia properties, taking its initial cues from the Walt Disney Company (the producer and distributor of *Tron*, incidentally).[3] Building

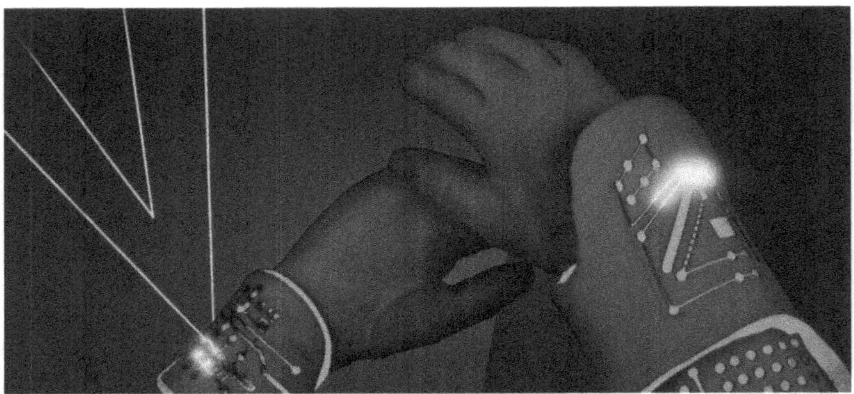

Figure 6.3 *Tron* (Steven Lisberger, 1982): Flynn's hands as he arrives in the computer space.

upon Disney's focus on iconic characters and consistent themes, style, and tone, Nintendo strove also toward an ecosystem of readily identifiable and distinctive configurations of interactive media technology.

Nintendo's is an embodied brand. The bodily ways that users feel themselves present to, and present in, Nintendo's games are as important for Nintendo as the recurring cast of characters and environments in their games and the often minimal and repetitive stories that the games tell. In the terms of embodied cognition, this bodily engagement is necessarily extended engagement, in that it incorporates not only the mind and the body, but also the devices and the game structures with which players interact. While Nintendo, especially in the case of the Game Boy, exemplifies a particular kind of corporate intuition about the evocative power of this relationship, the relationship itself pertains to all video game play and indeed to experience beyond games and media. Gameplay and other media use, as I have been arguing throughout *Media in Mind*, represent just one way in which an environment can be structured, a structuring that *necessarily* affects the behavior (mind and body) of those agents who act within it. As Anthony Chemero writes, agent and environment "form a unified, nondecomposable system."[4] This is why Andy Clark's concept of "coupling" between objects or between agents and environments should be used with caution: we are never uncoupled, never decoupled from our material contexts.

The experience of gameplay does not occur in the mind or on the screen, but across the dynamic among body, hardware, and game. The embodied mind must always be understood as extended across and embedded in its environment.[5] As illustrated in chapter 3, the mind, understood in this way, is nonrepresentational in that it functions by way of action in the world rather than by internal abstractions. This perspective troubles the idea that our relationships with video games are based on cognitive modeling or imaginative projection of ourselves into game world.[6] Cognitive modeling effectively renders the mind virtual to the world and the world (including games) virtual to the mind. Each becomes "content" for the other. The relationships between media and users are better understood as what Alva Noë calls varieties of presence. "Presence," writes Noë, "is availability. . . . To differences in varieties of access, there correspond differences in varieties of presence."[7] In the Game Boy—its hardware, its games, and its branding—we find Nintendo thinking its way toward a new corporate conception of gameplay as a mode of embodied and extended being in the world, distinguished in part by the ubiquity of access granted by a self-contained, portable game device. In this sense, the Game Boy anticipates later Nintendo products like its Wii console, which foregrounds "the kinesthetic dimension of all gaming"[8] as well as "the physical space . . . between the player and the display,"[9] as Steven E. Jones and George K. Thiruvathukal put it, by way of its use of motion detection hardware that encourages players to stand while they play and to pantomime the actions that they wish their avatars to undertake onscreen.

The *Nintendo Power* cover and the image on the Game Boy's packaging imply technological immersion, as the world of the game becomes the world of the player, and simultaneous perfectible bodily extension, as the intentions of the player become identical with his or her ability to act on (and thus to act *as within*) the world of the game. This image of melding promises a spatial and kinesthetic relationship to games that Gordon Calleja has called incorporation.[10] Incorporation, for Calleja, can only occur once players have learned how to navigate a game, at which point they can explore freely without being overly conscious of their mode of engagement with the game's world. Rune Klevjer proposes the alternative concept of "prosthetic telepresence," in which a player's self-awareness is projected into the world of third-person games via control both of the player character and of the game's virtual camera.[11] These theories of immersion are predicated on an interactionist gap between player and game world that must be overcome in order for the special perceptual relationship called immersion to occur. Whether or not this interactionist perspective captures the true nature of immersion (or whether immersion simply *is* the task of overcoming such a divide), the Game Boy's packaging presents the device both as a tool for bodily and perceptual experience and as a way to transform one's relationship to the wider world, outside of the game. The immersion that it implies is not so much the penetration of a virtual world of perception and action, as in Calleja and Klevjer's accounts, as it is a mutualistic constitution of experience, a transaction shared between player and technology.

As does any media device, the Game Boy came into being at a nexus of preexisting technologies, corporate history and culture, market pressures, and the particularities of human bodies. Nintendo's negotiation of this complex of constraints is instructive in understanding the emergence of media technologies in terms of their cultural, industrial, and physiological contexts. The packaging of the Game Boy foregrounds the connections between bodies and media devices; a study of the Game Boy's case is also a case study in Nintendo's canny marketing of the intraface. It sells its customers not only on the device within the box, but on what it can do for the hands (and the body, and the mind) outside the box.

The box, in this sense, disavows itself. Holding it, one's hands partially occlude the images of hands on the box. It looks almost as if one has the Game Boy in his or her own hands. It is up to you, the potential customer, to make the system complete. Gameplay on the Game Boy requires both a body and a console, so it is reasonable to say that the Game Boy is an incomplete platform without those hands and the body that they belong to. But the platform will in practice be completed by particular hands and particular bodies, not by idealized abstractions like those on the Game Boy box or the *Nintendo Power* cover.

LATERAL THINKING

While most portable gaming devices prior to the Game Boy's release were self-contained units capable of running only one game apiece, the Game Boy plays games stored on interchangeable read-only memory (ROM) cartridges. To switch to a new game, a player need only change out the cartridge and reset the unit. The device draws on design lessons that Nintendo learned in the development of its NES home console and in the development of its Game & Watch series of single-game handhelds, as well as in its earlier incarnation as a toy and playing card company. The release of the Game Boy anticipated the smartphone-driven "casual games" movement by two decades, and the constraints imposed by the unit's relatively low processing power and low-resolution grayscale LCD display led to innovations in game design that reverberate to the present day.

The console is also a reminder that innovation, whether it seems incremental or radical, is always characterized by technological, cultural, and industrial continuity. The Game Boy's lead developer, Gunpei Yokoi, had decades of experience with video game and analog game technology, as well as a deep understanding of Nintendo's corporate culture and a hard-won intuition for the relationships among technological platforms, media content, and human bodies. Yokoi developed a design philosophy usually translated as "lateral thinking of withered technology," which espouses the use of older technological components in new, creative articulations.[12] As Lara Crigger puts it, Yokoi's philosophy encourages the use of

> mature technology in novel or radical applications. At the time of the invention of the Game & Watch, LCD technology was everywhere . . . because prices for individual components had dropped so much, integrating LCD into a product was relatively inexpensive. Some people wanted to use fancier technology in the Game & Watch . . . but Yokoi insisted that affordability was key and that the player cared more about fun gameplay over fancy technology.[13]

Yokoi's "lateral thinking" is at once driven by a conception of the market for devices (and by a strategy toward the market for components) and also shaped by the convictions that (1) existing technological components can be rearticulated to create novel and compelling possibilities and (2) players will prefer a "fun" felt relationship to games over ownership of pure processing power. In other words, Yokoi's philosophy is against technological objects being treated as if they exist in isolation. In their origins, they are continuous with what has come before; in their use, they are defined not by their processing power but by the power they and players achieve together, in transaction. Nintendo's slogan throughout the late 1980s, "Now You're Playing with Power," was appended for the Game Boy's release to "Now You're Playing with Portable Power."

Yokoi's philosophy guided the development of the Game Boy, and it continues to inform Nintendo's later-generation products such the Wii U home console and the handheld 3DS, more than two decades after Yokoi's death in 1997. The Japanese phrasing for Yokoi's philosophy can also be read as "withered technology's lateral thinking," a reading that underscores a key aspect of the relationship between media platforms and their designers. Technologies such as game consoles or film projectors participate in complex relationships between media content, media technology, and human bodies. Thinking about technology does not occur merely within the human "thinker," whether an individual, a design team, or a corporation, but in the dynamic relationships among technologists and technologies. Likewise, video game players think not only with their brains, but also, as Torben Grodal writes, with their eyes, ears, and muscles,[14] not to mention with the consoles and the games themselves.

As argued in chapter 4, we should not think of the "platform" as a prior or as, in Bogost and Montfort's terms, something to take for granted.[15] This strongly emergent conception of the platform obscures the continuity of technologies, bodies, and world. Nor does it do justice to the spatiotemporal continuity of technological development. As a review of Nintendo's patent filings surrounding the development of the Game Boy shows, Nintendo thinks its way through technological possibilities by thinking *through* (that is with, or by means of) the material articulation of technology itself, and always in consideration of the ways in which the gameplay platform might be constituted—the different cartridges that might be introduced the system, and the different bodies with which it might transact.

Technological innovation is by nature exploratory and contingent. As Gilles Deleuze writes, artists, scientists, and philosophers are all inventors by nature. To Deleuze, filmmakers "have ideas in cinema," creating filmic blocks of movement and duration through their use of cinematic technology.[16] Engineers like those at Nintendo, I would argue, are similarly engaged in the creation of new functions. Pursuing Yokoi's "lateral thinking," they have ideas in the technology itself. They create and alter the structure of the technology *as* an idea. It is clear that early video game developers worked at the nexus between media forms and technologies, as their games were hardwired into the machinery, not stored on removable media. For consoles such as the Magnavox Odyssey, released in 1972, the hardware engineers were also the game designers. The roles were indistinguishable; to change the game was to change the physical constitution of the console. Hardware developer Ralph

Baer, who developed the prototype that would become the Odyssey, classes a hockey game not as a sports game but as a "'de/dt' (the derivative of voltage vs. time) game, because the puck's velocity was the derivative of the voltage generated by the joystick controlling the hockey puck's motion."[17] From the designer's perspective, the game's genre is defined in terms of the electrical operation of the console rather than the depictive content of the game itself.

Media technologies function by way of their relationships with the bodies of their users, and the configurations of media technologies are shaped by how technologists conceive of those bodies. Much as Nintendo thinks with "withered technology" in its development of new consoles, anybody who picks up a Game Boy thinks via transactions with the technology and thereby enters into a matrix of technological, cultural, and cognitive relations. If the Game Boy was designed for its theoretical players' hands, eyes, ears, and minds, each of these was necessarily an abstraction, an idealization of structure and process. But no body is an abstraction.

MEDIA, AND BODIES, IN THE WORLD

As embodied beings, we negotiate an environment characterized by perceptual structures and variations, opportunities and challenges, affordances and constraints. Whether in a forest or an urban environment, we constantly perceive, assess, predict, and plan for the contingencies of the world around us. As James J. Gibson writes, "Animals seem not only to recognize constant objects, but to orient themselves to a constant environment . . . territorial behavior also suggests that [they] can respond . . . to the habitat as a whole; and exploratory behavior suggests a kind of striving to extend the boundaries of this whole."[18] This exploratory behavior is achieved not only with our brains but with our whole bodies, in ongoing use of the affordances of our surroundings. We merge in meaningful ways with the tools that we employ in order to do work, whether we are using a hand tool to manipulate physical material or easing our mental work or "cognitive load" by "[leaving] information in the world," as Clark puts it.[19] Tools merge, too, with the work to which we put them, as in Dewey's concept of smooth-running functions, or in what Martin Heidegger calls getting lost in the world of tools.[20] What is the boy on the *Nintendo Power* cover doing? I would argue that, tool in hand, he is precisely "striving to expand the boundaries" of his "habitat as a whole," visualized in the cover image of him striding forth into the world on his elevated golden path, to explore the world before him but also to play with it, and to remake it according to his desires. The boundaries of our environments are not just in what we "recognize" but in the range of our effective action.

Media technologies, especially computational platforms that facilitate algorithmic responses to input from an "external" world that is causally intertwined with the internal workings of the device, participate in this relationship not transparently but, as Johanna Drucker makes clear in her analysis of the interface, always in ways structured by their industrial and sociocultural contexts. As Deleuze writes, "The limit common to [invention] is space-time."[21] In other words, the limit is material constraint. Countless technological, financial, and legal constraints bear on what console designers bring to market. As tools, these technologies are also constrained by the particularities of the human bodies that use them. The illustration at left in figure 6.4, a schematic from a US patent for the Game Boy, idealizes the relationship between the handheld and the hands and thumbs of a hypothetical user—Vitruvian thumbs, one might say, whose size and range of motion align perfectly with the configuration of the device.[22] For the ancient architect Vitruvius, the human body was designed by nature "so that its members are duly proportional to the frame as a whole," and it is important that built structures maintain similar principles of symmetry and proportion.[23] Leonardo da Vinci modeled his iconic *Vitruvian Man* (c. 1490) study on Vitruvius's description of anatomic proportion (figure 6.4, right side). The Game Boy patent illustration conceives of the hands of the player in perfect harmony with the dimensions of the Game Boy unit, echoing both da Vinci's drawing and the image from the Game Boy's packaging. If the Game Boy box seems to say, "Yours are the hands for which this device was designed," the patent reveals an inverse logic at work. This is the device for which these hands were designed, the ground against which they can move.

In the patent illustration, as in the box art, Game Boy and hands are depicted as in harmony, tool and user as one. The relationship is one of due proportionality, and also of normative functionality. The hands implied by the Game Boy have thumbs and fingers that are able to grasp and reach, attached to arms that are able to lift the device toward eyes that see. Thus constructed, the imagined embodied player is, like the boy on the *Nintendo Power* cover, empowered to feel through the intraface.

Video game play is a reflexive variety of tool use. Among its challenges is divining the structures, dynamics, and rules of the tool itself. This might be achieved through exploration of game space, experimentation with control schemes, probing of a game's narrative possibilities, or, as we saw in the example from *The Unfinished Swan*

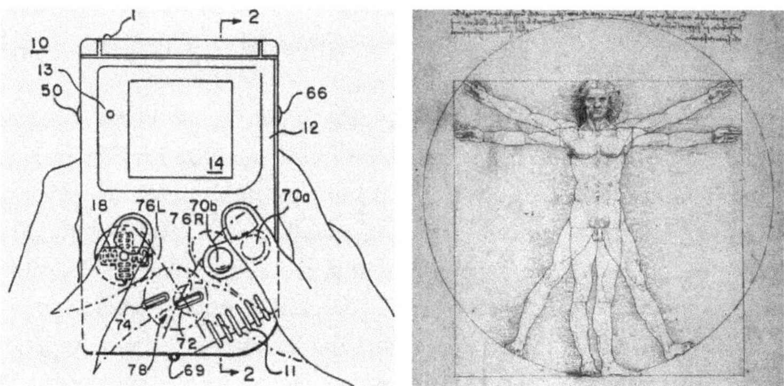

Figure 6.4 Vitruvian thumbs in a patent for the Game Boy (*left*) Leonardo DaVinci's *Vitruvian Man* (*right*).

from chapter 1, merely from discovering *how to perceive* in a new context. A similar challenge confronts game designers when they develop games for a device like the Game Boy. During the lifecycle of a console, its idiosyncrasies become increasingly clear, so that games developed later in the cycle achieve effects that seemed impossible earlier in the life of the device. Montfort and Bogost point out that the Atari Video Computer System (VCS), introduced in the late 1970s, was a remarkably flexible platform for game design because "the few things it could do well . . . could be put together in a wide variety of ways to achieve surprising results."[24] The longevity of a platform relies on designers' ability to exploit its idiosyncrasies. This ability requires a kind of aesthetic-technological research into the representational and expressive contours of the systems. Again, the limit is space-time. "By the early 1980s," write Montfort and Bogost, "VCS programmers had . . . grown more fluent in the platform, and they began to push it in new ways with their growing expertise."[25]

There are further constraints particular to handheld consoles. If such a device is too heavy or too large, or if its dimensions are awkward, it will be difficult to carry or to hold in one's hands for an extended time. A home console has the relative luxury of outputting its video and audio signals to a TV, and of outsourcing its input to a controller and its power supply to an electrical outlet. A handheld console must incorporate all of these components, as well as a microprocessor and any necessary memory units, within a self-contained and durable chassis that can withstand being carried around in bags, stuffed into pockets, and occasionally, tragically, dropped. Furthermore, this chassis must make ergonomic sense as something to be held, looked at, and manipulated. These constraints are evident in concessions that designers inevitably make in the computational and display capacities of the hardware, which in turn become visible in the textures and details of the games that the consoles run.

As a result of such considerations, the Game Boy imposes a range of qualities on the games that can be designed for it. Their graphics must be legible on a four-tone grayscale display. They must employ, at most, four channels of sound. They must be navigable via an eight-direction joypad and four-button input scheme. They must do all of this in a way that is comprehensible and accessible to their users, or at least to the users that they imagine they will have.

While it is a quality that all media share, the entanglement of user, technology, and media is especially evident when a player holds an entire gaming device, from power supply to processor to software to display, in the palms of his or her hands. For this reason, handheld consoles like the Game Boy are helpful in thinking about how game consoles work for their players, and, more importantly, what media, in a more general sense, do for users. In media use, I have argued, media and user are constituted by the dynamic between them. The intraface is by nature pragmatic, continuous, and transitive. In developing subsequent consoles such as the Wii U, the 3DS, and the Switch, Nintendo has pursued a brand identity as a producer of devices rhetorically tied into the embodied intentions of their users. With their emphases on motion control, multimodal input, binocular 3D vision, and blurring the distinction between home and portable consoles, these more recent devices point up the fact that people using media technologies are always blended, in body and in mind, with the structures of those technologies, a fact that Nintendo recognized, and exploited, from early in the modern console era.

Much as people strive to make practical use of their surroundings in order to complete tasks, Nintendo, under the continued influence of Yokoi's philosophy of "lateral thinking," often seeks to marshal its financial and technological resources to prioritize using already-available components in novel articulations. The design of the Game Boy reflects over a decade of technological experimentation. Its image and sound technology were oriented toward their potential in future development and experimentation, even as Nintendo's patent history lays bare the Game Boy's continuity with the technological past.

TECHNOLOGICAL ARTICULATIONS

Weighing around 400 grams and measuring nearly 15 centimeters in length, the Game Boy is only marginally portable by today's standards, but for its time it was a highly efficient use of material resources that managed to encapsulate essential characteristics of a home video game console. As originally released in the United States, the device consists of a four-shade LCD screen with a resolution of 160 by 144 pixels and a refresh rate of approximately 60 frames per second, a mono audio speaker and stereo headphone jack, an 8-bit processor running at 4.19 MHz with 8k of internal RAM and 8k of dedicated video RAM, and a four-button controller with an eight-direction joypad, housed in a hard, plastic shell and powered by four AA batteries or an optional A/C adapter. It features analog dial-controlled contrast and volume levels, a hard on-off switch, and an "ext. connector" port through which it can be connected to up to three other Game Boys for competitive or collaborative gameplay.

No component of the Game Boy was particularly new or innovative. The unit as a whole, however, articulates its components in a way that embodies Yokoi's philosophy of lateral thinking. The resulting system is robust and versatile. In the twelve years before its replacement by the Game Boy Advance, the Game Boy saw a number of hardware expansions and enhancements, and its programmers found creative ways of working with and within its affordances and constraints. All of this serves to illustrate the productivity of the intraface. Components in connection with one another do not merely output to, or "speak" to, one another across the divide that separates them or through the channel that connects them. They constitute one another, and thereby work together, by way of their mutual entanglement.

The Game Boy's central processing unit, the Sharp LR35902, is derived from the Intel 8080 and Zilog Z80 microprocessors.[26] The Z80 first went to market in 1976, a full thirteen years before the Game Boy's release. Among its many commercial and industrial applications, it was used in the *Pac-Man* (Namco, 1980) arcade cabinet.[27] In video game cabinets and consoles, the Z80 was used alongside other chips and dedicated ROM modules to create the complex multicolor graphics familiar from eye-catching arcade games like *Pac-Man*. When paired with the Game Boy's less-demanding LCD screen, the LR35902 can smoothly handle complex relationships between multiple moving objects and environmental structures. This can be observed in games available at the system's launch such as *Super Mario Land* (Nintendo R&D1, 1989) and in more elaborate form in later games like *Donkey Kong Land* (Rare, 1995).

The Game Boy's LCD screen has a slight green tint. Lighter pixels appear barely colored, while darker pixels take on an olive hue, an effect similar to color toning of black-and-white film. This coloration is at once distinctive to the Game Boy and effectively transparent in any particular game, as it is shared by all games on the system. The display area of 160 by 144 pixels is a relatively small portion of a 256 by 256 screen buffer that facilitates a smoothly scrolling onscreen background by loading off-screen objects into the system's visual memory before they are displayed onscreen.[28] With the RAM at their disposal, Game Boy programmers have the capacity to compose vibrant and complex game worlds.

The screen's low contrast can make fine visual details difficult to perceive in low or high lighting conditions. The contrast dial provides some adaptability, as players can darken or lighten the image to suit the ambient light, but the unit's promise of portable play is undercut by the system's lack of internal illumination. When playing in motion, say while on a bus or while walking (the latter is not recommended unless you want to end up like the runner in *QWOP*), changes in ambient lighting conditions can introduce an extradiegetic element to the challenge of gameplay. The system's very portability entails new challenges for players and designers alike, as the contingencies of the environment enter into the gameplay.

The plastic body of the Game Boy is the same light gray color as the NES console casing. Its controller is modeled on the NES controller, with its readily recognizable red B and A buttons, "Start" and "Select" buttons, and a black, eight-direction joypad in the shape of a cross. The visual association with the Nintendo hardware brand is complemented by the system's in-game use of iconic Nintendo characters such as Mario and Luigi, Link and Zelda, Donkey Kong, and Samus. Game Boy titles such as *The Legend of Zelda: Link's Awakening* (Nintendo EAD, 1993) and *Metroid II: Return of Samus* (Nintendo R&D1, 1991) are canonical entries in their respective ongoing transmedia franchises. By playing similarly branded games through a similar control interface, Game Boy players participate in corporate branding on multiple levels. Despite the limitations of the screen, and despite the constraints of the portable format, players both see and feel that they are transacting with a Nintendo product. Through their intraface with the Game Boy, players coconstitute the working of the device, and the device coconstitutes the working of the players. It positions them to *be* the Vitruvian thumbs of the Game Boy patent and packaging artwork, or to be the boy on the *Nintendo Power* cover, striding as he does into a word remade by his entanglement with the device in his hands.

A BRAND, A PROTECTORATE

The promise of portable game technology is also a promise of ubiquitous, embodied brand identification. The technological innovation reflected in Nintendo's patent activity in the decades around the Game Boy's release reveals a company thinking though possible relationships between bodies and technologies, a preoccupation with the roles that interactivity could have in the lives of users.

The Game Boy is protected by a US patent describing it as a "Compact hand-held video game system,"[29] and by complementary patents such as "Electronic gaming device with pseudo-stereophonic sound generating capabilities."[30] The Game Boy is distinguished from Nintendo's Game & Watch handhelds, a series of devices that ran from 1980 to 1991, by the possibility of switching out one game for another in a single hardware unit. While the Game Boy was the first widely successful cartridge-based handheld, it was beaten to market by over a decade by the Milton Bradley Microvision, developed by Smith Engineering. The 1978 patent for that device asserts an ontological difference between cartridge-based systems and self-contained units, the representational capacities of which are tailored to single games:

> [In single-game handhelds, the] driver circuitry transmits signals to the display which are subjectively determined by a player within the preset confines of the game. . . . Characteristic of each of these games is the fact that a predetermined movable and moving symbol, as for example a ball or a racing car appears on the display unit and undergoes a predetermined path of motion which can be altered by a player by manipulating the control elements.[31]

This description classes prior handhelds, with their predetermined symbols and paths of motion, with physical manipulation games in which material objects are moved through a path, devices such as Nintendo's "Ten Billion Barrel," designed by Yokoi and released in 1980. The "Ten Billion Barrel" is a derivative of the Rubik's Cube in which players move "rotary indicators" and "shunting bodies" in order to organize the balls within by color.[32] Single-game handhelds, in Smith's description, are in many respects closer to physical manipulation toys than to modern handhelds. Nintendo cannily drew upon this association by bundling *Tetris* (Game Boy version, Bullet-Proof Software and Nintendo, 1989) with the Game Boy for its US release. For its Japanese release, Nintendo packaged the Game Boy with the Mario title *Super Mario Land,* but for the US release, Nintendo eschewed its established character-driven branding and opted for the more toylike *Tetris* as a flagship title.

Smith's patent for a replaceable-cartridge handheld is careful to class the new unit with existing replaceable-cartridge home consoles. At the time, the Atari VCS was the best known of these, and the NES was still seven years from release in the United States. Atari had come to dominate the home console market with the VCS, which offers more versatility than game-specific consoles like the Magnavox Odyssey, Atari's own Home Pong (released in 1974), and Nintendo's Japan-only Color TV-Game (1977). Those systems allow players to choose among only a few hardwired gameplay variables. Smith, however, sought to realign handheld gaming with the cartridge console market. "For the present," the patent filing reads, "handheld electronic game devices are capable of playing only one game. Only large console devices that need to be connected to television sets have the capability of providing at least a limited selection of games to the user."[33]

While opening a unit up to exchangeable cartridges increases its versatility, it also divides the gaming hardware. As the game information is contained on ROM cartridges, the console is in a sense incomplete without a cartridge inserted. While most contemporary consoles read game information from optical media like disks or from internal hard drives, or stream game data over the internet, a cartridge-based console can be seen as *most* of a game machine, with some of the hardware left out. Neither an NES nor a Game Boy will boot without a cartridge inserted.

In Gunpei Yokoi's first digital media patent in the United States, the Game & Watch mechanism is described as a "Timepiece apparatus having a game function."[34] Figure 6.5 illustrates the graphical possibilities of *Ball* (Nintendo, 1980), the first of the Game & Watch series, in an image that echoes both da Vinci's *Vitruvian Man* and the cubism of the *Nintendo Power* cover. [35] A range of diachronic possibilities, suited to the demands of a situation, are mapped onto synchronic space.

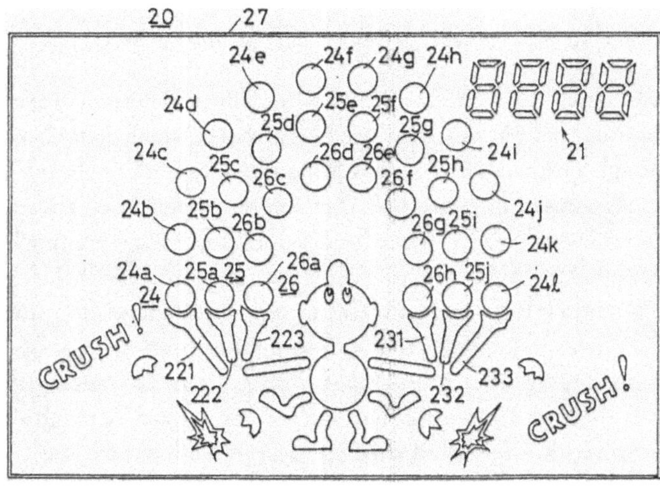

Figure 6.5 "Predetermined paths of motion" in the Game & Watch game *Ball* (Nintendo, 1980).

Since the launch of the NES, Nintendo has steadfastly protected both its technological innovations and its brand identity, often devising innovative ways to do both at once. The NES features the 10NES chip, a "lock device" that required game publishers to license a "key device" from Nintendo for inclusion on their cartridges.[36] This compels publishers and developers to clear potential NES games with Nintendo or to be locked out of developing for the system. The chip also functions as a form of brand protection, allowing Nintendo to act as a gate-keeper and regulate the tone and narratives of games developed by third parties.[37] Patent protection of the console technology is thus conflated with protection of Nintendo's family-friendly brand.

This relationship is tighter still in the Game Boy, which features a novel initiation device that requires games to display the Nintendo logo as a condition of the system booting. The Nintendo logo is encoded on the Game Boy's internal memory and the device is directed to look for a corresponding logo in the ROM cartridge memory. If the two images match precisely, the unit boots, displays the Nintendo logo, and runs the game. However, "If the . . . character data are not coincident with each other, the LCD panel is wholly turned on or off or flashed, whereby the operator or user is notified that the external ROM cartridge . . . is not an author-ized one."[38] Bootleggers who circumvent this authorization check by encoding the Nintendo logo in their ROM cartridge memories thereby expose themselves not only to claims of patent infringement, but also to claims of trademark infringement for using the Nintendo logo without permission. Through this elegant mechanism, Nintendo's logo, its technological protection of its brand, and its control over the third-party software developed for its devices become one and the same.

TETRIS, AGAIN

The Game Boy version of *Tetris* (figure 6.6) is a port of the then-five-year-old game designed by Russian computer engineer Alexey Pajitnov. As detailed in chapter 3,

Figure 6.6 *Tetris* on the Nintendo Game Boy (Bullet-Proof Software, 1989).

Tetris is one of the most popular games of all time and one that has lent itself to all manner of study from computer-science and psychological perspectives. Nintendo's selection of *Tetris* proved to be a wise move, and one sensitive to the particularities of playing games on a portable device. Relative to the representational worlds of Zelda and Mario games, *Tetris* is set in a more abstract and minimal space. The complexity of its gameplay arises from variations on simple spatial manipulations rather than on narrative developments or complex spectacles.

Though it debuted as a game for personal computers, *Tetris* proved particularly suited to portable play. Games can be long or short, and they always start from the same point, so there is less pressure on a player to continue with a given game session. The repetitiveness of the gameplay promotes practice and expertise in a simple task rather than the tracking of a complex narrative or the memorization of the environmentally specific challenges and obstacles of a large game world. At the same time, the game does not require expertise. It can be picked up and played at any time, and players are free to play it for as long as they can, or for as long as they want to. In this way, *Tetris* anticipates the "casual revolution" in videogames that arrived decades later, a surge in gameplay driven by games easy to pick up on desktops and mobile devices.[39] Indeed, Nintendo hoped from the beginning that the Game Boy would make gameplay ubiquitous. The company sought to

> make [it] a mainstream addiction, doing for games and puzzles what the Sony Walkman did for music.... "The guy out fishing, the businessman on the airplane, the kid on the schoolbus, we think they'll all like it," said Peter Main, vice president for marketing at Nintendo. "We think the handhelds have broad appeal."[40]

The casual feel of games like *Tetris* complements the (also felt) portability of the hardware. Such games are accessible to, and can be appealing to, both casual and more hardcore players, in ways that more complex games cannot. As Jesper Juul writes,

> Where a casual game is flexible toward different types of players and uses, a hardcore game makes inflexible and unconditional demands on the skill and commitment of a player ... a casual game is sufficiently flexible to be played with a hardcore time commitment, but a hardcore game is too inflexible to be played with a casual time commitment.[41]

The selection of *Tetris* for inclusion with the original Game Boy release encourages players to identify the console itself with this kind of pick-up-and-play attitude toward gaming, in which it is possible for anyone to play just a little, or a lot, of a game.

Furthermore, *Tetris* suits the Game Boy in that the formal properties of the game are especially appropriate to the control apparatus, screen, and processor of the Game Boy unit. The game's five basic commands move the current block to the left or right, accelerate its fall, and rotate it either clockwise or counterclockwise. These actions map geometrically onto the game's plus-shaped joypad, with its right-angle lines, and onto its two control buttons, which rotate the block in either direction. The control scheme achieves a kind gestural indexicality. Rather than abstracting actions like running, jumping, or shooting onto buttons, *Tetris* requires players to undertake actions physiologically similar to those that would produce corresponding in-game effects, should they find themselves physically nudging and rotating falling blocks in a vertical corridor.

The gesture-like control of in-game objects can make *Tetris* on the Game Boy feel more physical than virtual, an object to be directly manipulated rather than a media device depicting a fictional world. In this way, it recalls physical manipulation games like the Ten Billion Barrel, as well as the single-game handheld, such as Game & Watch games, with which many players in the late 1980s would be familiar. The importance of this effect for the Game Boy's popularity cannot not be overstated. The Game Boy, and *Tetris* in particular, appeals to the worldly, embodied knowledge of its users, opening gaming up to potential players who might have been put off by learning seemingly arbitrary control schemes. To hold a Game Boy in one's hands, to feel its weight, is engage in an intraface in a more immediately intimate way than that which a user establishes with a home console attached to a TV, in which the weight of the controller is perceptibly distant from the console hardware and the screen.

Graphically, the game is so well suited to the particularities of the Game Boy's LCD screen it might be read as an allegory of the tasks that the Game Boy performs as a computational and display device. The game space is a tall rectangle, with right angles that line up to the right angles of the display screen. The action of the game takes place in two-dimensional space, and its main challenges are in actively tracking and manipulating spatial and directional relationships between moving collections of squares. The LCD screen of the Game Boy unit is itself composed of smaller squares, the pixels that the unit's processor activates and deactivates, and the relationships between which it continually monitors, tracking their coordinates and determining when they collide or overlap. In the confluence among the player's actions, the device display, and the processor's tasks, *Tetris* becomes a kind of graphical, processing, and bodily tech demo, which, rather than showcasing the most complex or impressive things that the Game Boy can do, rather lays bare the fundamental operations of the device. *Tetris* looks and feels great on the Game Boy because the Game Boy is especially well suited for handling the processes that underlie *Tetris*.

It is little wonder that Nintendo promoted the NES version of *Tetris* not on the strength of the game alone but by allusion to the experience of playing *Tetris* on the Game Boy. With a hit console and game on its (metaphorical) hands, Nintendo recognized that the appeal of the Game Boy was not just in making the home console experience mobile, but also in imagining what mobility could *feel* like as an aspect of gaming. Acknowledging the ways that gameplay extends across transactions among bodies, technologies, and environments, Nintendo cannily drew on this insight, first in its promotion of the NES version of *Tetris* and later in its subsequent home and portable consoles, which sought to explore further the confluence of "withered technologies" and bodies in motion.

The year 2017 saw the release of the Nintendo Switch, a hybrid home/portable video game console. When the device is disconnected from a television, a built-in screen displays the game, which can now be played on the go. The Switch is, in many ways, a realization of the premise of the *Nintendo Power* cover from twenty-eight years prior. That cover depicts a boy whose experience of, and access to, the world is augmented by a home console controller that he wields as if it were a portable device. Owing to the constraints inherent to mobile console design, the Switch had to be underpowered as compared to contemporaneous home-only consoles like the PlayStation 4 and Xbox One. This was a sacrifice that Nintendo was more than willing to make in service of its ongoing construction of an ideal, mobile user for its devices. The flagship software title for the Switch at launch was *The Legend of Zelda: Breath of the Wild* (Nintendo, 2017), an open-world exploration game in which protagonist (and perpetual young boy) Link's ability to act in the diegetic world is augmented by his "Sheikah Slate," a magical device that he carries with him everywhere he goes, that extends his physical abilities and alters his enactive relationship to space and time, and that looks like nothing so much as . . . a Nintendo Switch.

INCOMPLETENESS

Just as the selves of media users are partly constituted by media, so too are media partly constituted by their users. It is impossible to draw a definitive line dividing one from the other. The fundamental incompleteness of the Game Boy is a testament to the fundamental incompleteness of theories of media apparatuses that do not take into consideration the roles of the users of those apparatuses. As the technologists at Nintendo illustrate through the form of the Game Boy hardware, technological experimentation is a form of embodied and extended thinking. Technology does not change instantaneously, but incrementally, just as do evolving bodies and evolving ideas. Technology evolves in continuity with the bodies with which it shares its environments. Still, bodies tend to be imagined for their uniformity rather than their variation. The Vitruvian thumb persists, even as no such actual thumb will ever exist.

When we think of video game technologies as platforms, we would do well to think not only of their affordances and the constraints that they impose upon games and users, but also of the idealized bodies that they imply, as well as the transactional relationships among game technologies and the *actual* bodies of the people who use them. Platforms are not prior, nor are bodies, and when we think of the human mind, we should think of it not as an interior, discrete realm of abstraction, but as the product of physical action in the world, of a relationship between parts that include a body, an environment, and objects—some of which are game consoles—working in concert with one another. If we do so, we can see that, when we think of the mind, we think of a platform.

Conclusion

The Continuity

At the beginning of *Media in Mind*, I asked you to imagine yourself using media—watching a film, playing a video game, or reading a book—and then to demarcate where the one began and the other ended, tracing lines at the edge of "you" and at the edge of "it." While the locations of these lines may have at first seemed intuitive, I have argued throughout this book the very concept of such lines is misleading. The appearance of new media technologies and forms often prompts theoretical reconsideration of where those lines lie. I have argued that this is not because the lines move when new media appear, but rather because the lines do not exist in the first place. They are conceptual conveniences that allow us to speak of "I" and "it," to use the language of containment and interactionism and to treat the world as if it were composed of discrete things. It is the *language* used to describe the lines that changes with new media and new theories. The lines themselves do not move or change, as they were only ever conceptual to begin with.

From the starting point of bodies in the world encountering media, *Media in Mind* has moved to consideration of how interactional media theories partition perception, mental representation, media platforms, and media interfaces from one another, creating conceptual gaps among them. By creating these gaps, theory obligates itself to explain how they are "crossed" by media and by the mind. These gaps spin out from an initial alienation, a conceptual division between self and world in which the self, as contained by the body or the brain or the mind, acts *upon* the world rather than acting within it, as an aspect of it.

The gaps appear in what, in a disciplinary taxonomy of media studies, appear to be far-flung branches of the family tree, subdisciplines such as psychoanalytic film theory, platform studies, cognitivism, and apparatus theory. These subdisciplines are more closely related, conceptually and historically, than they may at first appear to be. That these subdisciplines often define themselves in opposition to one another is telling; they must do this work in order to differentiate themselves because they occupy a more similar disciplinary domain than they might be inclined to admit.

Transactionism is an argument for continuity in space, time, and causality: continuity among media technologies, media "content," media users, and media use, and also continuity between media use and the action of the world at large. In its structure, this book has traced a trajectory across the domain of interactionist theories of media. Chapters 2 and 3 moved progressively into the ostensible depths of the mind of the media user. We then crossed over into the depths of media platforms and in chapters 4 and 5 moved back upward (and outward) toward the external world. In so doing, *Media in Mind* has run two risks that must be acknowledged. First, the trajectory of the book has been "down, across, and up" through a conceptual domain that, in a transactionist perspective, would have no up or down, and in which "across" would mean something profoundly different from the gap-crossing that we have had to do to traverse the domain of interactionist media studies. A transactional "across" is extensional and encompassing, neither a leap nor a reach. Moving though foreign disciplinary territory, one runs the risk of defining one's terms negatively rather than positively—that is, of defining them primarily via their opposition to the dominant terms that one wishes to critique.

While some such contrast is necessary and appropriate, I have throughout *Media in Mind* sought to define a transactional perspective on media use positively rather than negatively, in terms of what it is rather than what it is not. I have sought to nudge theories of perception and representation, and of platforms and interfaces, beyond their interactionist commitments while holding onto their valuable insights about media technology, media use, and the minds of media users. I have tried to remain positive in another sense as well, as I see a transactional model for media use as both promising in addressing long-standing interactionist theoretical dilemmas, and hopeful in that it seeks to celebrate the power and possibility of media use in the context of the rest of our lives and the rest of the world. Along with that power and promise, of course, comes considerable risk. In illustrating the power of media *in* mind, rather than its power on or over minds, transactionism calls attention to the foundational roles that media can have in how people see themselves in terms of personal, social, and political identity, not to mention the developmental effects of media use in people who, as Louise Barrett puts it, are "learning to live in [their] bodies."[1] This means young people, but it also means everybody else. We never stop learning how to live in our bodies, and our bodies never stop changing. Nor do media.

Media in Mind has mostly been restricted to the domain of these mind-body-world gaps. This has been a necessary focus, but is has come at the expense of further consideration of issues of identity and development that take into account broader sociocultural and economic contexts. While such topics have lain mostly outside of the scope of *Media in Mind*, they are, as a transactionist framework tells us, continuous with the topic of this book. A transactional perspective that more fully engages those topics will illuminate that continuity, as well as continuities within those topics themselves. John Dewey's own career is a testament to this; complementary to his philosophy of mind, he is a highly influential figure in twentieth-century educational theory, and he was throughout his life deeply engaged in politics, political theory, and activism. More recently, Karen Barad's theory of agential realism and her concept of intra-action likewise illustrate the political potency of naturalist thinking.

This brings us to a second risk built into the structure of this book. Tracing a path around the theoretical domain of dualist media studies, one risks creating a container of one's own by closing off the resulting circle and treating its content as separate from the rest of the world. The transactionally continuous figure of media in mind (and mind in media) that I have been describing is no more a discrete unit than are media and mind themselves. In focusing on transactions among bodies and media, I have sought to acknowledge the continuity of those bodies and those media with the world around them—sociocultural continuity and technological continuity, to be sure, but also spatiotemporal and causal continuity. While the scope of this book has been localized around the coconstitution of media and mind, transactionism is ultimately an ethos grounded in a holist conception of the cosmos. To understand the cosmos in a transactional way is to see life and mind as nondiscrete, localized behaviors of the universe. While types of language and tools used for describing large-scale mechanisms can be incapable of characterizing more local phenomena, any account of localized transactions like media use must be made with the tacit understanding that there are always larger- and smaller-scale systems at work, systems that not only provide context for media use, but that also pervade and encompass it. It is not a closed loop, not a container, but a disciplinary wrinkle, a stretching of the continuous substance of transactionism over the gap-riddled domain of interactionist media theory. It remains open to, and continuous with, the wider disciplinary domain and the wider world.

There is no such thing as a closed system. Like a straight line or a perfect circle, a closed system is a theoretical abstraction, a descriptive convenience. Straight lines and perfect circles are fictions, little diegeses, only uniform and only complete inasmuch as we determine to treat them as such, and meaningful not in their own right but only in the ways in which they are employed. A system is always embedded in a broader spatiotemporal and causal context that cannot help but affect the system and our observations of it. Nor can our observations help but affect the system, as they are always ultimately actions undertaken from within the system itself. This has largely been accepted in fields like physics, but not so much in cognitive science, nor in media studies. The dominant approaches to the embodied mind in conservative embodied cognition and in media studies have maintained these gaps when they have introduced consideration of "the body" to already-dualist models of the mind and of media use.

My argument throughout *Media in Mind* has been for material continuity and for models of knowing that conceive of the world as continuous, conceive of themselves as continuous with the world, and understand themselves as continuous with other ways of knowing. *Media in Mind*, in other words, is a call for transdisciplinarity, for thinking not merely between the traditional disciplines, as in interdisciplinary research, but rather for thinking across and among the disciplines, for thinking not just about what they could show and tell one another but about what they can say in their polyphonous, entangled collectivity. Neuroscience can certainly tell an important part of the story of the brain, with specificity and granularity that no other field can achieve, but its self-imposed limits, like those of cognitive science in telling us about the mind, are erected to protect it as a discipline, and they tend to contract defensively just when they ought to expand. Likewise, media systems—analog, digital, mechanical, computational—are never closed systems. They are not platforms in the strongly emergent sense, not in their physical technologies nor in the spaces they depict, the stories they tell, nor the feelings and concepts expressed through their use.

Media, in their myriad forms, will always structure our ways of imagining and pursuing possible futures for ourselves, our communities, and our local and planetary ecosystems. A transactional perspective is deeply ecological, in that it sees humans as participatory constituents in the ecology, not as occupants of it nor as stewards of it. In a disciplinary sense, transactional theory suggests that, as "natural" as the divisions between some academic disciplines may seem, they are all in the end grappling with the same fundamental problems, feeling out the contours of a barely perceptible world. Humanistic understanding of media technologies and media forms will for these reasons be crucial to our ability to think about what (in the world) a mind is, and will furthermore be crucial to the future of empirical scientific study of the mind, which gravitates toward abstraction and discreteness when it ought to do just the opposite.

DECENTERINGS

Recent centuries have seen a series of decenterings of the human figure in the perceived order of the cosmos. The Copernican revolution decentered the earth in the heavens, and thus the human world in creation. Darwinism decentered humans among the living things on earth by dissolving the conceptual gap that set them apart from other terrestrial life. Sciences that frame their subject matter at large and small scales, such as molecular biology and statistics, decentered human-scale perception as *the* perspective on the world, revealing in the process the contingency of "single" human lives. "In space, there is no center," sings David Berman. "We're always off to the side."[2] Beyond this, space itself is felt to be decentered: "Space is neither in the subject nor is the world in space," writes Heidegger. "Rather, space is 'in' the world since the being-in-the-world constitutive for [the living subject] has disclosed space."[3] Space is no longer a given context for, but rather a product of, being in the world, a product that itself has no relationship to any consensus center.

Each of these developments has been received, in some quarters, as an affront, as an existential threat to the privilege of discreteness. "Major scientific theories rebuff common sense," as Gillian Beer writes. "They call on evidence beyond the reach of our senses and overturn the observable world. They disturb assumed relationships and shift what has been substantial into metaphor."[4] These decenterings of the human continue to produce existential, theological, moral, political, and ecological crises. They represent moves away from the privileges of discreteness and toward continuity. Privilege responds with retrenchment, whether theological, political, philosophical, or theoretical.

The decentering of the mind concurrently decenters identity or the "self," which is not a unique, discrete unit of being but rather a distributed, temporary, and ever-changing constellation of matter and energy. As Douglas Hofstadter puts it, the self, while produced in part by the living body, is spread across space, across multiple people, and across time, even preceding and following the body's existence, in the minds of the people around it, in the "set of afterglows" that remain, the "collective corona that still glows."[5] André Bazin writes of the photograph being the "object itself"; perhaps we can extend this notion by taking it to mean not just the object's material presence but a persistence of the object's "self" in Hofstadter's sense: something of the field of meanings, influences, and materials that constitute its presence in the world, as "freed from the conditions of time and space that govern it," as Bazin puts it.[6]

FEELING A WAY TOGETHER THROUGH THE COSMOS

Katamari Damacy (Namco, 2004) is a landmark of mainstream surrealist video game design. The slovenly and temperamental "King of All Cosmos," on an overnight bender, drunkenly knocks all of the stars and planets from the sky. After sobering up, he bullies his diminutive son, the Prince, into going to Earth and rolling terrestrial objects up into giant balls that he can use as raw material for rebuilding the cosmos he has destroyed, one constellation at a time (The Japanese *katamari damashii* translates roughly to "clump spirit"). Meanwhile, the children of a Japanese astronaut detect something off-kilter in the heavens, though their parents—even the astronaut—seem blissfully unaware that anything is amiss. The daughter, Michiru Hoshino, is especially sensitive to the disturbance in the cosmic order. As the King reconstructs the constellations with the material that the Prince provides, Michiru feels order being restored both in the cosmos and in her own body (figure C.1). "Oh! I feel it. I feel the cosmos," exclaims Michiru, as the crab constellation retakes its place in the heavens. "Cancer came scuttling back." As she speaks, Michiru turns to face us, extends her arms outward, and recedes into a diagram of the constellation Cancer, an image that (once again) recalls da Vinci's Vitruvian Man.

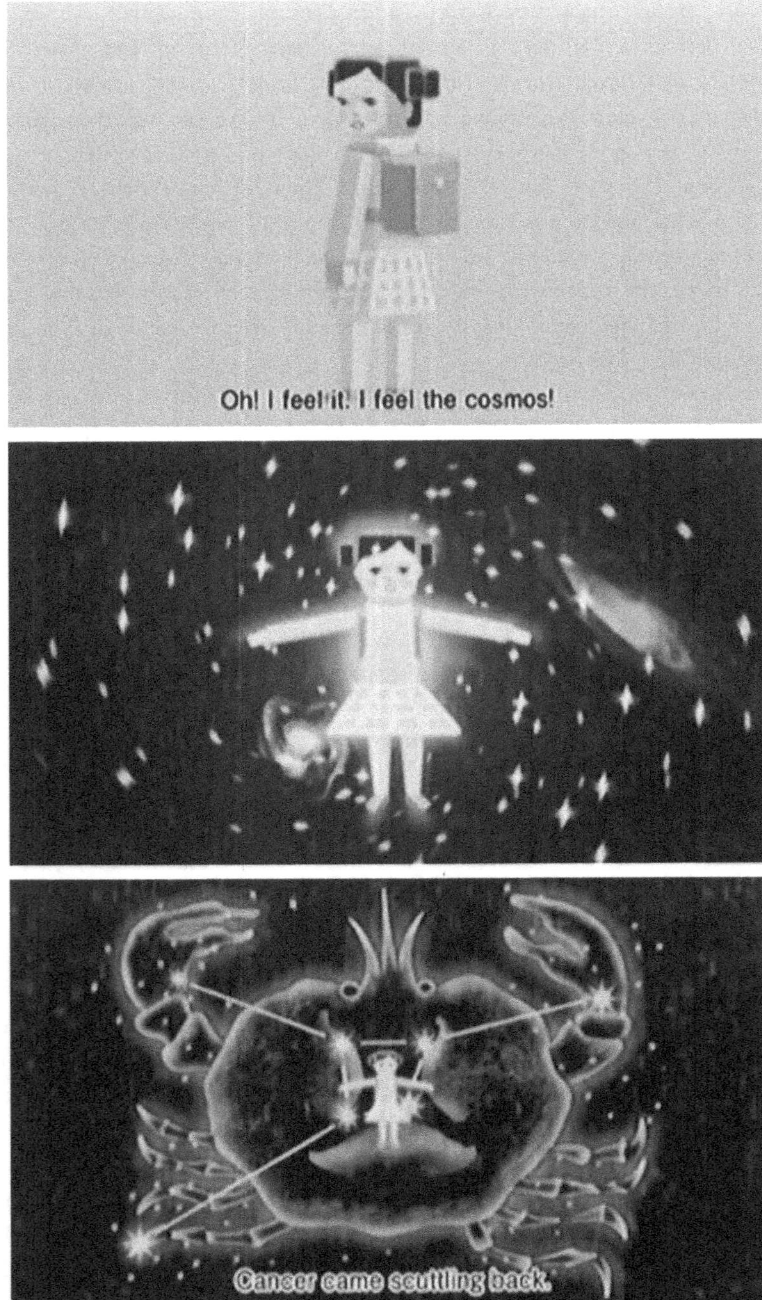

Figure C.1 In *Katamari Damacy* (Namco, 2004), Michiru Hoshino feels order being restored to the cosmos.

Each level of *Katamari Damacy* begins with the King demanding that his son roll up a ball of a particular circumference, a clump of objects of various scales found in and around the cities of Earth. Although the game only (visibly) allows for physical objects to be picked up, in his spoken dialogue the King makes no distinction between these and subjective phenomena. "Sending things to Earth," bellows the King as he sets up a level for his son, "trees . . . elephants . . . hopes . . . dreams." This list could go on forever, and the game plays as a kind of cosmic mania, an effort to establish an order by participating in *the* order. "The fear of being able to say everything," writes Umberto Eco, "seizes us not only when we are faced with an infinity of names but also with an infinity of things."[7] *Katamari Damacy*, a supremely tactile game with a straightforward play mechanic and responsive, exceedingly simple controls, allows us to feel our way through its alternative cosmogony and thereby to think about if, and how, we can participate in and understand a cosmic order characterized largely by our insignificance within it—as tiny things, as young things, and as laboring things. But, first, as feeling things.

The ball-rolling mechanic of *Katamari Damacy* could have been implemented in any number of other narratives. But it is fitting that *Katamari Damacy*, like *The Unfinished Swan*, is the story of a child laboring to make sense of the material world. As Mark Johnson writes, we are "big babies."[8] Gropingly, graspingly, we feel our way through life, through the cosmos and the local ecology, and through the cultural, political, economic, and physical structures that constitute and constrain us. In doing so, we feel our way toward one another. Like Alva Noë's tap-tapping blind man, we trace the contours of our realities by navigating them, whether we ourselves happen to be sighted or not. Like Gregor von Rezzori's drunk man, we sometimes (or often) find ourselves locked into perceptual "rails," allowing ourselves to be led along by our biases about what is and what could be, whether we ourselves happen to be sober or drunk. Theory and philosophy are practices of detaching oneself from the perceptual and narrational rails of routine experience and feeling out new enactive, perceptual, and intuitive possibilities. So, too, are practices of making, perceiving, and interpreting media, which can allow for newly emancipated and speculative understandings of time, causality, contingency, and identity.

If minds worked by way of consistent, abstracted logic, by internal symbolic representations, we might hope to bridge the divisions between ourselves and other people by learning about the visual abstractions in which their minds dealt. But if we are in the first instance creatures of feeling rather than creatures of logic, then we need to find other grounds upon which to base our ways of understanding the people with whom we share our world. Thinking back to the fMRI study in chapter 3—the one that was portrayed in many accounts as reconstructing internal mental images of films that its subjects were watching—we will see that, though it did not in fact do that, the study achieved something equally promising and equally profound by demonstrating material and perceptual commonalities among film viewers. The experiment was able to reconstruct somewhat accurate estimations of the original screen images from activation patterns in the visual cortices of viewers, indicating a physical similarity in the relationship, across subjects, between media users' bodily states and the media they used. That the experiment was successful in this respect is in fact a testament to what we have in common as perceiving, embodied, materially embedded beings. And this points to a way that media routinely bridge distances among people.

You can be on the other side of the world from other people and still see what they see, still hear what they hear, or still play what they play. In different contexts, as different bodies, you enter into transactions with substantially identical objects. You and this distant person remain different people, in different places, with different bodies and different histories, and your experiences may produce radically different reactions or interpretations. For a time, though, your living, perceiving, feeling, extended selves become partly identical in their very constitutions. In your continuity with media, you enact your continuity with the world and with one another.

If we want to better understand one another's minds—to think across both the distances and the entanglements among ourselves and other selves—it does indeed help to look at the physical structures and functional activation patterns of one another's brains. But it is equally important that we go to the movies, and that we play video games, and that we read books and watch shows, alone and together, and also that we talk about them: how they are made, what they are made of, and what we make of them.

Media constitute the largest and most nuanced material record of human mental activity in the world. Media are not merely an archive of images and sounds, nor of stories, but a history of human transaction. But they are *not* a storage medium for meaning. Rather, they are there for us to feel through, both in the sense of feeling our way through them and in the sense of forming our feelings by way of using them. We need to think seriously about how to use media, and to use the range of methodologies we have developed for interpreting media, in service of better understanding ourselves as physical, biological, socially and ecologically embedded, transactional beings. This will require a willingness to think scientifically about media form and function. It will also require that the humanities be permitted— and that they be pushed—to play central roles in the future of our philosophical and scientific understanding of perception, cognition, and consciousness. While this will inevitably present methodological and disciplinary challenges, I expect that these will be easier to resolve than they might at first seem, so long as we remain willing to think transactionally. What we do in the sciences is more experiential than we often acknowledge, and what we do in the humanities is more experimental than we often realize.

NOTES

INTRODUCTION

1. Edward Branigan, "Sound, Epistemology, Film," in *Film Theory and Philosophy*, ed. Richard Allen and Murray Smith (Oxford: Clarendon Press, 1997), 99.

2. Matthew B. Crawford, *The World Beyond Your Head* (New York: Farrar, Straus, and Giroux, 2015), 223.

3. Ed Yong, *I Contain Multitudes: The Microbes Within Us and a Grander View of Life* (New York: HarperCollins, 2016), 11.

4. Plato, *Phaedo*, trans. David Gallop (Oxford: Clarendon Press, 2008), 64.

5. Sean Carroll, *The Big Picture* (New York: Dutton, 2016), 20.

6. Daniel D. Hutto and Patrick McGivern, "How Embodied Is Cognition?," *Philosophers' Magazine* 68 (2015): 77.

7. See Hugo Münsterberg, "The Photoplay: A Psychological Study," in *Hugo Münsterberg on Film*, ed. Allan Langdale (New York: Routledge, 2002), 45–162, and Rudolf Arnheim, *Film as Art* (Berkeley: University of California Press, 1967).

8. Terrence W. Deacon, *Incomplete Nature: How Mind Emerged from Matter* (New York: Norton, 2011), 544.

9. See W. Teed Rockwell, *Neither Brain nor Ghost: A Nondualist Alternative to the Mind-Brain Identity Theory* (Cambridge, MA: MIT Press, 2005).

10. Christian Metz, *Film Language: A Semiotics of the Cinema*, trans. Michael Taylor (Oxford: Oxford University Press, 1974), 10.

11. Metz, *Film Language*, 11–12.

12. Louise Barrett, *Beyond the Brain* (Princeton: Princeton University Press, 2011); George Lakoff and Mark Johnson, *Philosophy in the Flesh* (New York: Basic Books, 1999); and Maxine Sheets-Johnstone, *The Primacy of Movement* (Philadelphia: John Benjamins, 2011), especially chapter 10, "Why a Mind Is Not a Brain and a Brain Is Not a Body."

13. James J. Gibson, *The Ecological Approach to Visual Perception* (Boston: Houghton Mifflin, 1979); Andy Clark and David J. Chalmers, "The Extended Mind," *Analysis* 58, no. 1 (1998): 7–19; and Alva Noë, *Out of Our Heads* (New York: Hill and Wang, 2009).

14. Michael S. Gazzaniga, *Who's in Charge? Free Will and the Science of the Brain* (New York: HarperCollins, 2011), especially chapters 5, "The Social Mind," and 6, "We Are the Law."

15. Michael Spivey, *The Continuity of Mind* (Oxford: Oxford University Press, 2006).

16. Andy Clark, *Surfing Uncertainty* (Oxford: Oxford University Press, 2015).

17. Eva Jablonka and Marion J. Lamb, *Evolution in Four Dimensions: Genetic, Epigenetic, Behavioral, and Symbolic Variation in the History of Life* (Cambridge, MA: MIT Press, 2006).

18. Louis Menand, *The Metaphysical Club: A Story of Ideas in America* (New York: Farrar, Straus and Giroux, 2001), 439–442.

19. Eugenie Brinkema, *The Forms of the Affects* (Durham: Duke University Press, 2014), xii.

20. André Breton, *Manifestoes of Surrealism* (Ann Arbor: University of Michigan Press, 1969), 14.

21. Antonin Artaud, *Selected Writings*, ed. Susan Sontag (Berkeley: University of California Press, 1988), 150.

22. Germaine Dulac, "The Aesthetics. The Obstacles. Integral *Cinégraphie*," trans. Stuart Liebman, in *Framework: The Journal of Cinema and Media* 19 (1982): 6.

23. Dulac, "The Aesthetics," 9.

24. André Bazin, "The Ontology of the Photographic Image," in *What Is Cinema?* vol. 1, trans. and ed. Hugh Gray (Berkeley: University of California Press, 1968), 9–16.

25. Jean Epstein, *The Intelligence of a Machine*, trans. Christophe Wall-Romana (Minneapolis: University of Minnesota Press, 2014), 15.

26. Maurice Merleau-Ponty, *Sense and Non-sense*, trans. Hubert L. Dreyfus and Patricia Allen Dreyfus (Chicago: Northwestern University Press, 1964), 58.

27. Merleau-Ponty, *Sense and Non-sense*, 54.

28. Merleau-Ponty, *Sense and Non-sense*, 59.

29. Gilles Deleuze, "Having an Idea in Cinema (on the Cinema of Straub-Huillet)," trans. Eleanor Kaufman, in *Deleuze & Guattari*, ed. Eleanor Kaufman and Kevin Jon Heller (Minneapolis: University of Minnesota Press, 1998), 14.

30. Deleuze, "Having an Idea," 19.

31. Gilles Deleuze, *The Fold: Leibniz and the Baroque*, trans. Robert Hurley (Minneapolis: University of Minnesota Press, 1993), 19.

32. Mark B. N. Hansen, *New Philosophy for New Media* (Cambridge, MA: MIT Press, 2004), 6.

33. Vivian Sobchack, *The Address of the Eye: A Phenomenology of Film Experience* (Princeton: Princeton University Press, 1992), 23.

34. Laura U. Marks, *The Skin of the Film: Intercultural Cinema, Embodiment, and the Senses* (Durham: Duke University Press, 2000); and *Touch: Sensuous Theory and Multisensory Media* (Minneapolis: University of Minnesota Press, 2002).

35. Jennifer Barker, *The Tactile Eye* (Berkeley: University of California Press, 2009), 2.

36. Barker, *The Tactile Eye*, 109.

37. Marks, *Touch*, 20.

38. Scott Richmond, *Cinema's Bodily Illusions: Flying, Floating, and Hallucinating* (Minneapolis: University of Minnesota Press, 2016), 73.

39. Richmond, *Cinema's Bodily Illusions*, 15.

40. Hansen, *New Philosophy*, and D. N. Rodowick, *Reading the Figural, or, Philosophy after the New Media* (Durham: Duke University Press, 2001).

41. N. Katherine Hayles, *How We Think: Digital Media and Contemporary Technogenesis* (Chicago: University of Chicago Press, 2012), 1.

42. Ray Carney, *The Films of John Cassavetes: Pragmatism, Modernism, and the Movies* (Cambridge: Cambridge University Press, 1994), 285 n. 13.

43. Mark B. N. Hansen, *Feed-Forward* (Chicago: University of Chicago Press, 2015), 240.

44. John Dewey, *Art as Experience* (New York: Perigee Books, 2005), 2.

45. Phillip Seng, "Dewey and Movies: A Missed Opportunity?" conference paper, Annual Meeting of the Society for the Advancement of American Philosophy, 2007, accessed August 1, 2017, http://www.philosophy.uncc.edu/mleldrid/SAAP/USC/TP32.html.

46. Dewey, *Art as Experience*, 4.

47. David I. Waddington, "Dewey and Video Games: From Education through Occupations to Education through Simulations," *Educational Theory* 65, no. 1 (February 2015): 1–20;

Tad Bratkowski, "Applying Dewey's Aesthetics to Video Games: An Experience of 'Rock Band,'" *Soundings: An Interdisciplinary Journal* 93, nos. 1–2 (2010): 83–93; and Phillip D. Deen, "Interactivity, Inhabitation and Pragmatist Aesthetics," *Game Studies* 11, no. 2 (2011).

48. John Dewey and Arthur F. Bentley, *Knowing and the Known* (Boston: Beacon Hill Press, 1949), 67–69.

49. Carroll, *The Big Picture*, 230.

50. Karen Barad, *Meeting the Universe Halfway* (Durham: Duke University Press, 2007), 33.

51. Alexander Galloway, *The Interface Effect* (Cambridge: Polity, 2012), 40–42.

52. Gunpei Yokoi and Makino Takefumi, *Gunpei Yokoi Game House* (Tokyo: ASCII Media Works, 1997), 77.

53. George Saunders, *Lincoln in the Bardo* (New York: Random House, 2017), 335.

CHAPTER 1

1. Michael Polyani, *The Tacit Dimension* (Chicago: University of Chicago Press, 2009), 29.

2. Barrett, *Beyond the Brain*, 177.

3. Marshall McLuhan, *Understanding Media: The Extensions of Man* (Cambridge, MA: MIT Press, 1994), 132.

4. See Joseph D. Anderson, *The Reality of Illusion* (Carbondale: Southern Illinois University Press, 1996).

5. Susan Sontag, *Against Interpretation* (New York: Picador, 1966), 10.

6. Dewey and Bentley, *Knowing and the Known*.

7. John Dewey, "The Metaphysical Assumptions of Materialism," *Journal of Speculative Philosophy* 16, no. 2 (1882): 208–213, and "On Philosophical Synthesis," *Philosophy East and West* 1, no. 1 (1951): 3–5.

8. See Mark Johnson, *The Meaning of the Body: Aesthetics of Human Understanding* (Chicago: University of Chicago Press, 2007); and Alva Noë, *Varieties of Presence* (Cambridge, MA: Harvard University Press, 2012).

9. Dewey, *Art as Experience*, 3.

10. Dewey, *The Later Works of John Dewey, 1925–1953*, ed. Jo Ann Boydson, vol. 1, *1925, Experience and Nature* (Carbondale: Southern Illinois University Press, 1981), 224.

11. See Dewey and Bentley, *Knowing and the Known*, especially 67–69, 104, and 270.

12. Dewey and Bentley, *Knowing and the Known*, 68–69. "Subjectmatter" is spelled this way in the original, a typographical embodiment of the unity that it describes.

13. Dewey and Bentley, *Knowing and the Known*, 71.

14. Johnson, *Meaning of the Body*, 212.

15. Alva Noë, *Action in Perception* (Cambridge, MA: MIT Press, 2004), 1.

16. Johnson, *Meaning of the Body*, 25.

17. Nicholas J. Wade and Benjamin W. Tatler, *The Moving Tablet of the Eye* (Oxford: Oxford University Press, 2004). See especially chapter 4, "Saccades and Fixations."

18. David Bordwell, "A Case for Cognitivism," *Iris* 9 (Spring 1989): 17; Christian Metz, "The Fiction Film and Its Spectator: A Metapsychological Study," trans. Alfred Guzzetti, *New Literary History* 8, no. 1 (1976): 75–105, 95, 89; Münsterberg, "The Photoplay," 90.

19. Jay Bolter, *Turing's Man: Western Culture in the Computer Age* (Chapel Hill: University of North Carolina Press, 1984), 10–11.

20. James Paul Gee, "Video Games and Embodiment," *Games and Culture* 3, nos. 3–4 (2008): 253–263, 254.

21. Henri Bergson, *Creative Evolution*, trans. Arthur Mitchell (Mineola: Dover, 1998), 306.

22. Metz, "Fiction Film," 95.

23. Dziga Vertov, *Kino-Eye: The Writings of Dziga Vertov*, ed. Annette Michelson, trans. Kevin O'Brien (Berkeley: University of California Press, 1984), 63.

24. Münsterberg, "The Photoplay," 73.

25. Bordwell, "A Case for Cognitivism," 27.

26. Rodowick, *Reading the Figural*, 44.

27. Hansen, *New Philosophy*, 22.

28. Hansen, *New Philosophy*, 124.

29. Steven Shaviro, *The Universe of Things: On Speculative Realism* (Minneapolis: University of Minnesota Press, 2014), 114.

30. Hansen, *Feed-Forward*, 5.

31. John Dewey, "The Changing Intellectual Climate," in *The Later Works of John Dewey, 1925–1953*, ed. Jo Ann Boydson, vol. 2, *1925–1927, Essays, The Public and Its Problems* (Carbondale: Southern Illinois University Press, 2008), 223.

32. Alfred North Whitehead, *Process and Reality* (New York: Free Press, 1978), 31.

33. John Dewey, "An Organic Universe: The Philosophy of Alfred N. Whitehead," in *The Later Works of John Dewey, 1925–1953*, ed. Jo Ann Boydson, vol. 5, *1929–1930, Essays, The Sources of a Science Education, Individualism, Old and New, and Construction and Criticism* (Carbondale: Southern Illinois University Press, 2008), 281.

34. Alfred North Whitehead, *Adventures of Ideas* (Cambridge: Cambridge University Press, 1961), 208.

35. Hansen, *Feed-Forward*, 6.

36. Hansen, *Feed-Forward*, 83–84.

37. Hansen, *Feed-Forward*, 171–174.

38. Shaviro, *The Universe of Things*, 61.

39. Mark Johnson, *The Body in the Mind* (Chicago: University of Chicago Press, 1987), 21.

40. George Lakoff and Mark Johnson, *Metaphors We Live By* (Chicago: University of Chicago Press, 2003), 214.

41. Réné Descartes, *Discourse on the Method and the Meditations*, trans. John Veitch (New York: Cosimo, 2008), 115. Brackets in the original.

42. Plato, *Phaedo*, 28 (79c).

43. Emily Dickinson, "The Brain is wider than the sky," in *The Poems of Emily Dickinson: Reading Edition*, ed. Ralph W. Franklin (Cambridge, MA: Belknap Press of Harvard University Press, 1999).

44. Christian Metz, "The Imaginary Signifier [Excerpts]," in *Narrative, Apparatus, Ideology*, ed. Philip Rosen (New York: Columbia University Press, 1986), 254.

45. Plato, *Theaetetus*, trans. John Henry McDowell (Oxford: Clarendon Press, 1996), 78 (191c–d).

46. Barker, *The Tactile Eye*, 86.

47. Metz, "Imaginary Signifier," 261.

48. Robert Bresson, *Notes on the Cinematographer*, trans. Jonathan Griffin (Copenhagen: Green Integer Books, 1997), 76.

49. Maurice Merleau-Ponty, *Phenomenology of Perception*, trans. Colin Smith (London: Routledge Classics, 2003), 165–166.

50. Gregor von Rezzori, *An Ermine in Czernopol*, trans. Phillip Boehm (New York: NYRB Classics, 2012), 5.

51. Gregory Bateson, *Steps toward an Ecology of Mind* (Chicago: University of Chicago Press, 2000), 318.

52. Noë, *Action in Perception*, 1.

53. Lambros Malafouris, *How Things Shape the Mind* (Cambridge, MA: MIT Press, 2013), 5.

54. Noë, *Action in Perception*, 1.

55. Daniel C. Dennett, *Consciousness Explained* (Boston: Back Bay Books, 1991), 39.

56. Bresson, *Notes on the Cinematographer*, 33.

57. Bresson, *Notes on the Cinematographer*, 12.

58. Bresson, *Notes on the Cinematographer*, 93.

59. Brian Price, *Neither God nor Master: Robert Bresson and Radical Politics* (Minneapolis: University of Minnesota Press, 2011), 187.

60. Merleau-Ponty, *Phenomenology of Perception*, 474.

61. Emily Dickinson, "We grow accustomed to the dark," in *Poems of Emily Dickinson*.

CHAPTER 2

1. Barrett, *Beyond the Brain*, 177–181.

2. Johnson, *Meaning of the Body*, 33.

3. Arnheim, *Film as Art*, 9.

4. Ian Bogost, *Play Anything* (New York: Basic Books, 2016), x.

5. Mihaly Csikszentmihalyi, *Flow: The Psychology of Optimal Experience* (New York: Harper & Row, 1990).

6. See, for example, Rebecca Solnit, *River of Shadows* (New York: Penguin, 2004).

7. Tom Gunning, "The Cinema of Attraction[s]: Early Film, Its Spectator, and the Avant-Garde," in *The Cinema of Attractions Reloaded*, ed. Wanda Strauven (Amsterdam: Amsterdam University Press, 2007), 385.

8. David S. Landes, *The Unbound Prometheus* (Cambridge: Cambridge University Press, 1969), 235.

9. Vaclav Smil, *Creating the Twentieth Century* (Oxford: Oxford University Press, 2005), 19, 3.

10. James Leo Cahill, "How it Feels to Be Run Over: Early Film Accidents," *Discourse* 30, no. 3 (Fall 2008): 298.

11. Karen Beckman, *Crash: Cinema and the Politics of Speed and Stasis* (Durham: Duke University Press, 2010), 29.

12. Jean-Louis Comolli, "Machines of the Visible," in *The Cinematic Apparatus*, ed. Stephen Heath and Teresa de Lauretis (New York: St. Martin's Press, 1980), 123.

13. Vivian Sobchack, *Carnal Thoughts* (Berkeley: University of California Press, 2004), 60.

14. For an in-depth discussion of the relationship between *How It Feels to Be Run Over* and *Arrival of a Train at La Ciotat*, and between early automobile films and early train films more generally, see Beckman, *Crash*, 30–36.

15. Tom Gunning, "'Primitive' Cinema: A Frame-Up? Or the Trick's on Us," *Cinema Journal* 28, no. 2 (1989): 9.

16. Simon Brown, *Cecil Hepworth and the Rise of the British Film Industry, 1899–1911* (Exeter: University of Exeter Press, 2016), 27.

17. See David Bordwell, *Narration in the Fiction Film* (Madison: University of Wisconsin Press, 2015), especially chapter 3, "The Viewer's Activity."

18. Noël Burch, *Theory of Film Practice*, trans. Helen R. Lane (Princeton: Princeton University Press, 1981), 110.

19. Charles Darwin, *The Descent of Man, and Selection in Relation to Sex* (New York: D. Appleton Press, 1972), 101.

20. See Susanne Langer, *Mind: An Essay on Human Feeling*, 3 vols. (Baltimore: Johns Hopkins University Press, 1967–1982); Gregory Bateson, *Mind and Nature: A Necessary Unity* (Cresskill, NJ: Hampton Press, 2002); Gibson, *Ecological Approach*.

21. Noë, *Varieties of Presence*, 2.

22. Jesper Juul, *The Art of Failure: An Essay on the Pain of Playing Video Games* (Cambridge, MA: MIT Press, 2013), 123.

23. Csikszentmihalyi, *Flow*, 49–67.

24. Martin Heidegger, *Being and Time*, trans. Joan Stambaugh (Albany: State University of New York Press, 2010), 354.

25. Katie Salen and Eric Zimmerman, *Rules of Play* (Cambridge, MA: MIT Press, 2004), 326.

26. Jesper Juul, *Half-Real* (Cambridge, MA: MIT Press, 2005), 112–113.

27. Salen and Zimmerman, *Rules of Play*, 339.

28. Raymond Williams, *Television: Technology and Cultural Form* (London: Routledge, 2003), 86.

29. Williams, *Television*, 91.

30. Williams, *Television*, 113.

31. See John Caldwell, *Televisuality: Style, Crisis and Authority in American Television* (New Brunswick, NJ: Rutgers University Press, 1995), and Mimi White, "Reconsidering Television Program Flows, or Whose Flow Is It Anyway?," *Electronic Journal of Communication / La Revue Electronique de Communication* 5, nos. 2–3 (July 1995), accessed June 15, 2017, http://www.cios.org/EJCPUBLIC/005/2/00527.html.

32. John Dewey, *Democracy and Education* (New York: Macmillan, 1916), 195.

33. Noë, *Varieties of Presence*, 2.

CHAPTER 3

1. Immanuel Kant, *Kant's Kritik of Judgement*, trans. J. H. Bernard (London: Macmillan, 1892), 69.

2. Classic Tetris World Championship rules, accessed July 10, 2017. http://thectwc.com/rules.

3. Robert Stickgold et al., "Replaying the Game: Hypnagogic Images in Normals and Amnesics," *Science* 290, no. 5490 (13 October 2000).

4. Ella L. James et al., "Computer Game Play Reduces Intrusive Memories of Experimental Trauma via Reconsolidation-Update Mechanisms," *Psychological Science* 26, no. 8 (2015).

5. Emily A. Holmes et al., "Can Playing the Computer Game 'Tetris' Reduce the Build-Up of Flashbacks for Trauma? A Proposal from Cognitive Science," *PLoS One* 4, no. 1 (January 2009), accessed June 15, 2017. https://doi.org/10.1371/journal.pone.0004153.

6. See Davide Baccherini and Donatella Merlini, "Combinatorial Analysis of Tetris-Like games," *Discrete Mathematics* 308 (2008), among many others.

7. Jessica Skorka-Brown et al., "Playing Tetris decreases drug and other world cravings in real-world settings," *Addictive Behaviors* 51 (2015).

8. David Kirsh and Paul Maglio, "On Distinguishing Epistemic from Pragmatic Action," *Cognitive Science* 18 (1994).

9. Kirsh and Maglio, "On Distinguishing," 513. Emphasis mine.

10. Paul P. Maglio, Michael J. Wenger, and Angelina M. Copeland, "Evidence for the Role of Self-Priming in Epistemic Action: Expertise and the Effective Use of Memory," *Acta Psychologica* 127 (2008): 87.

11. Daniel D. Hutto and Erik Myin, *Radicalizing Enactivism* (Cambridge, MA: MIT Press, 2013), 10–11.

12. Hutto and Myin, *Radicalizing Enactivism*, 11.

13. Example drawn from Andy Clark, *Natural Born Cyborgs* (Oxford: Oxford University Press, 2003), 6–7.

14. Clark and Chalmers, "The Extended Mind," 8.

15. Andy Clark, *Being There: Putting Brain, Body, and World Together Again* (Cambridge, MA: MIT Press, 1998), 47.

16. Eugene Jolas, *Cinema: Poems* (New York: Adelphi Company, 1926), 15.

17. Paul Churchland, *Plato's Camera* (Cambridge, MA: MIT Press, 2012), vii.

18. Aristotle, *De Anima*, trans. R. D. Hicks (New York: Cosimo, 2008), 90–91.

19. See Aristotle, *Prior Analytics* Book II, trans. Gisela Striker (Oxford: Oxford University Press, 2009), Chapter 5.

20. Thomas Hobbes, *Elements of philosophy of the first section, concerning body* (London: R.&W. Leybourn, 1656), 3.

21. Bordwell, "A Case for Cognitivism," 17.

22. Richard L. Gregory, *Seeing through Illusions* (Oxford: Oxford University Press, 2009), 6–7.

23. See Jerry Fodor, *The Elm and the Expert: Mentalese and its Semantics* (Cambridge, MA: MIT Press, 1995).

24. Churchland, *Plato's Camera*, vii.

25. Münsterberg, "The Photoplay," 90.

26. Germaine Dulac, "The Essence of Cinema," in *The Avant-Garde Film*, ed. P. Adams Sitney (New York: New York University Press, 1978), 41.

27. Comolli, "Machines of the Visible," 123.

28. Rockwell, *Neither Brain nor Ghost*, xi.

29. See Anthony Chemero, *Radical Embodied Cognitive Science* (Cambridge, MA: MIT Press, 2011), 18–33.

30. Anderson, *The Reality of Illusion*, 30.

31. Richmond, *Cinema's Bodily Illusions*, 8.

32. Kristin Thompson, *Breaking the Glass Armor* (Princeton: Princeton University Press, 1988), 36.

33. Chemero, *Radical Embodied Cognitive Science*, 18.

34. Hugo Münsterberg, *Grundzüge der psychologie* (Leipzig: Verlag von Johann Ambrosius Barth, 1900), dedication page. Translation mine.

35. Allan Langdale, "S(t)imulation of Mind," in *Hugo Münsterberg on Film*, 4–5.

36. Frank Landy, "Hugo Münsterberg: Victim or Visionary?," *Journal of Applied Psychology* 77, no. 6 (1992): 794.

37. Langdale, "S(t)imulation of Mind," 6.

38. "Drops Dead at His Class," *Boston Sunday Post* December 17, 1916.

39. Münsterberg, "The Photoplay," 73.

40. Münsterberg, "The Photoplay," 88.

41. Lev Vygotsky, *Mind in Society* (Cambridge, MA: Harvard University Press, 1978), 39–40.

42. Vygotsky, *Mind in Society*, 40.

43. Lev Vygotsky, *The Psychology of Art* (Cambridge, MA: MIT Press, 1971), 211.

44. Münsterberg, "The Photoplay," 220.

45. Karla Oeler, *A Grammar of Murder* (Chicago: University of Chicago Press, 2009), 26.

46. See Joseph Dumit, *Picturing Personhood: Brain Scans and Biomedical Identity* (Princeton: Princeton University Press, 2004), especially chapter 5, "Traveling Images, Popularizing Brains."

47. Shinji Nishimoto, An T. Vu, Thomas Naserlaris, Yuval Benjamani, Bin Yu, and Jack L. Gallant, "Reconstructing Visual Experiences from Brain Activity Evoked by Natural Movies," *Current Biology* 21, no. 19 (22 September 2011).

48. Clips from the reconstructed films can be viewed on the Jack Gallant YouTube Page, accessed May 15, 2018, https://www.youtube.com/watch?v=nsjDnYxJ0bo.

49. Gallant Lab, "Reconstructing visual experiences from brain activity evoked by natural movies," press release, accessed May 15, 2018, http://gallantlab.org/index.php/publications/nishimoto-et-al-2011/.

50. Yasmin Anwar, "Scientists Use Brain Imaging to Reveal the Movies in Our Mind," *UC Berkeley News Center*, September 22, 2011, accessed December 14, 2015, http://newscenter.berkeley.edu/2011/09/22/brain-movies.

51. Katie Moisse, "UC Berkeley Scientists 'See' Movies in the Mind," *ABC News*, September 22, 2011, accessed December 14, 2015, http://abcnews.go.com/Health/MindMoodNews/scientists-youtube-videos-mind/story?id=14573442#.T5G9ve3dOnA.

52. Martin Hägglund, *Radical Atheism: Derrida and the Time of Life* (Palo Alto: Stanford University Press, 2002), 82.

53. Mark Fisher, "What Is Hauntology?" *Film Quarterly* 66, no. 1 (Fall 2012): 19.

54. Carolyn Marvin, *When Old Technologies Were New* (Oxford: Oxford University Press, 1988), 192.

55. Andy Clark, *Supersizing the Mind: Embodiment, Action, and Cognitive Extension* (Oxford: Oxford University Press, 2008), 15.

CHAPTER 4

1. Geoffrey G. Parker, Marshall W. Van Alstyne, and Sangeet Paul Choudary, *The Age of the Platform* (New York: Norton, 2016), 5.

2. David J. Chalmers, "Strong and Weak Emergence," in *The Re-emergence of Emergence*, ed. Philip Clayton and Paul Davies (Oxford: Oxford University Press, 2006), 244. Italics in original.

3. Chalmers, "Strong and Weak Emergence," 246.

4. "Platform," in *The Barnhart Concise Dictionary of Etymology*, ed. Robert K. Barnhart (New York: H.W. Wilson, 1995), 575. See Caetlin Benson-Allott, "Platform" in *Debugging Game History: A Critical Lexicon*, eds. Henry Lowood and Raiford Guins (Cambridge, MA: MIT Press, 2016), for an in-depth critical discussion of the term's etymological history.

5. Ian Bogost and Nick Montfort, *Racing the Beam* (Cambridge, MA: MIT Press, 2009), 2.

6. Johannes Burge, Charles C. Fowkes, and Martin S. Banks, "Natural-Scene Statistics Predict How the Figure–Ground Cue of Convexity Affects Human Depth Perception," *Journal of Neuroscience* 30, no. 21 (May 26, 2010): 7277.

7. John D. Sutter and Doug Gross, "Apple Unveils the 'Magical' iPad." *CNN.com*, January 28, 2010, accessed June 6, 2017, http://www.cnn.com/2010/TECH/01/27/apple.tablet.

8. Ruth Krauss, *A Hole Is to Dig*, pictures by Maurice Sendak (New York: HarperCollins, 1989), unnumbered pages.

9. John Berger, *Ways of Seeing* (New York: Penguin, 1990), 16.

10. Jean-Louis Baudry, "The Apparatus: Metapsychological Approaches to the Impression of Reality in Cinema," *Camera Obscura* 1, no. 11 (1976): 104–126.

11. Constance Penley, *The Future of an Illusion* (Minneapolis: University of Minnesota Press, 1989), 80.

12. Marc Steinberg, "A Genesis of the Platform Concept: i-mode and Platform Theory in Japan," *Asiascape: Digital Asia* 4 (2017); Tarleton Gillespie, "The politics of 'platforms,'" *New Media and Society* 12, no. 3 (2010); Benson-Allott, "Platform," 345.

13. Nathan Altice, *I Am Error: The Nintendo Family Computer / Entertainment System Platform* (Cambridge, MA: MIT Press, 2015), 193.

14. Vivian Sobchack, "The Active Eye" (Revisited): Toward a Phenomenology of Cinematic Movement," *Studia Phaenomenolgica* 16 (2016): 63–90, 68–69.

15. Bogost and Montfort, *Racing the Beam*, 2.

16. Bogost and Montfort, *Racing the Beam*, 144–147.

17. Salen and Zimmerman, *Rules of Play*, 146.

18. Paul N. Edwards, *The Closed World* (Cambridge, MA: MIT Press, 1997), 244.

19. Bogost and Montfort, *Racing the Beam*, 3.

20. Blaise Pascal, *Thoughts*, trans. W. F. Trotter (New York: P.F. Collier, 1910), 49.

21. Schrödinger, *What is Life?*, 91–92.

22. Bresson, *Notes on the Cinematographer*, 80–81.

23. R. B. Laughlin et al., "The Middle Way," *Proceedings of the National Academy of Sciences* 97, no. 1 (January 4, 2000): 32.

24. Douglas Hofstadter, *I Am a Strange Loop* (New York: Basic Books, 2008), 102.

25. Deacon, *Incomplete Nature*, 315–318.

26. Pascal, *Thoughts*, 167.

27. Hugo Münsterberg, "Why We Go to the Movies," in *Hugo Münsterberg on Film*, 177.

28. Epstein, *Intelligence of a Machine*, 61.

29. Epstein, *Intelligence of a Machine*, 66–67.

30. Bazin, *What Is Cinema?*, 14.

31. Steven E. Jones and George K. Thiruvathukal, *Codename Revolution: The Nintendo Wii Platform* (Cambridge, MA: MIT Press, 2012), 10.

32. Caetlin Benson-Allott, "The Algorithmic Spectator," *Film Quarterly* 64, no. 3 (2011): 55.

33. Benson-Allott, "Platform," 346.

34. Barad, *Meeting the Universe Halfway*, 137.

35. Bogost and Montfort, *Racing the Beam*, 2–3.

36. Jones and Thiruvathukal, *Codename Revolution* 5.

37. Caetlin Benson-Allott, *Killer Tapes and Shattered Screens* (Berkeley: University of California Press, 2013), 10–13; Benson-Allott, "Platform," 347.

38. Bogost and Montfort, *Racing the Beam*, 2.

39. Benson-Allott, *Killer Tapes*, 90.

CHAPTER 5

1. Pascal, *Thoughts*, 167.

2. Johanna Drucker, *Graphesis: Visual Forms of Knowledge Production* (Cambridge, MA: Harvard University Press, 2014), 138–139.

3. Galloway, *The Interface Effect*, vii.

4. Galloway, *The Interface Effect*, 40–41.

5. Hofstadter, *Strange Loop*, 258.

6. Hofstadter, *Strange Loop*, 143.

7. Johanna Drucker, "Performative Materiality and Theoretical Approaches to the Interface," *DHQ: Digital Humanities Quarterly* 7, no. 1 (2013), paragraph 33, accessed September 17, 2015, http://www.digitalhumanities.org/dhq/vol/7/1/000143/000143.html.

8. Bogost and Montfort, *Racing the Beam*, 153.

9. Friedrich Kittler, *Gramophone, Film, Typewriter* (Palo Alto: Stanford University Press, 1999), 1.

10. Kittler, *Gramophone, Film, Typewriter*, 171–172.

11. Lev Manovich, *Software Takes Command* (New York: Bloomsbury, 2013), 2.

12. Daniel C. Dennett, *From Bacteria to Bach and Back: The Evolution of Minds* (New York: Norton, 2017), 338.

13. Branden Hookway, *Interface* (Cambridge, MA: MIT Press, 2014), 1.

14. Drucker, "Performative Materiality," paragraph 17.

15. Drucker, "Performative Materiality," paragraph 4.

16. Hookway, *Interface*, 15–16.

17. Galloway, *The Interface Effect*, 54.

18. Galloway, *The Interface Effect*, vii.

19. Galloway, *The Interface Effect*, 54.

20. Hookway, *Interface*, 1.

21. Hookway, *Interface*, 4.

22. Hookway, *Interface*, 5–6.

23. Gilberto Perez, *The Material Ghost* (Baltimore: Johns Hopkins University Press, 1998), 121.
24. Galloway, *The Interface Effect*, 42.
25. Barad, *Meeting the Universe Halfway*, 197.
26. Barad, *Meeting the Universe Halfway*, 196.
27. Hookway, *Interface*, 4.
28. See McLuhan, *Understanding Media*, in which McLuhan defines "electric media" as "the technological extension of our central nervous system" (352), and Metz, *Film Language*, especially chapter 1, "On the Impression of Reality in the Cinema."
29. Dulac, "The Aesthetics," 9.
30. Carl Plantinga, *Moving Viewers* (Berkeley: University of California Press, 2009), 60.
31. Hofstadter, *Strange Loop*, 258.
32. Roland Barthes, *Camera Lucida*, trans. Richard Howard (New York: Hill and Wang, 1980), 70–71.
33. Brinkema, *Forms of the Affects*, 76–77.
34. See Bogost and Montfort, *Racing the Beam*, 107–109.
35. Dewey, *Democracy and Education*, 393.
36. John Berger, *Keeping a Rendezvous* (New York: Vintage, 1992), 14.
37. Stanley Cavell, *The World Viewed* (Cambridge, MA: Harvard University Press, 1979), 16–17.
38. See Dewey, *Later Works, 1925–1953*, vol. 1, 224.

CHAPTER 6

1. David Parisi, "A Counterrevolution in the Hands: The Console Controller as Ergonomic Branding Mechanism," *Journal of Games Criticism* 2, no. 1 (2015).
2. Nintendo Co., Ltd., "Consolidated Sales Transition by Region," accessed June 1, 2015, http://www.nintendo.co.jp.
3. Jeff Ryan, *Super Mario* (London: Portfolio, 2012), 12.
4. Chemero, *Radical Embodied Cognitive Science*, 31.
5. See Hutto and McGivern, "How Embodied Is Cognition?"
6. See Gee, "Video Games and Embodiment."
7. Noë, *Varieties of Presence*, 32.
8. Bart Simon, "Wii Are Out of Control: Bodies, Game Screens, and the Production of Gestural Excess," *Loading* 3, no. 4 (2009): 12.
9. Jones and Thiruvathukal, *Codename Revolution*, 91.
10. Gordon Calleja, *In-Game: From Immersion to Incorporation* (Cambridge, MA: MIT Press, 2011), 167ff.
11. Rune Klevjer, "Enter the Avatar: The Phenomenology of Prosthetic Telepresence in Computer Games," in *The Philosophy of Computer Games*, ed. John Richard Sageng, Hallvard J. Fossheim, and Tarsei Mandt Larsen (London: Springer, 2012), 17–38.
12. Gunpei Yokoi and Makino Takefumi, *Gunpei Yokoi Game House* (Tokyo: ASCII Media Works, 1977).
13. "Retroinspection: Game & Watch," *Retro Gamer* 55 (2008): 46.
14. Torben Grodal, *Embodied Visions: Evolution, Emotion, Culture, and Film* (Oxford: Oxford University Press, 2009), chapter 7.
15. Bogost and Montfort, *Racing the Beam*, 2.
16. Deleuze, "Having an Idea."

17. Ralph H. Baer, "Setting Things Straight," in *Before the Crash: Early Videogame History*, ed. Mark J. P. Wolf (Detroit: Wayne State University Press, 2012), 229.

18. James J. Gibson, "Visually Controlled Locomotion and Visual Orientation in Animals," *British Journal of Psychology* 100 (2009): 268–269.

19. Clark, *Supersizing the Mind*, 69.

20. See Dewey, *Democracy and Education*, and Heidegger, *Being and Time*, 354.

21. Deleuze, "Having an Idea," 16.

22. Satoru Okada and Shin Kojo, Compact hand-held video game system, US Patent US 5184830 A, filed June 15, 1992, and issued February 9, 1993.

23. Vitruvius, *The Ten Books on Architecture*, trans. Morris Hickey Morgan (Cambridge, MA: Harvard University Press, 1914), 73.

24. Bogost and Montfort, *Racing the Beam*, 15.

25. Bogost and Montfort, *Racing the Beam*, 104.

26. Marat Fayzullin, Pascal Febler, Paul Robson, and Martin Korth, "Everything You Always Wanted to Know about GAMEBOY," accessed July 22, 2016, http://www.devrs.com/gb/files/gbspec.txt.

27. *Midway's Pac-Man: Parts and Operating Manual* (Franklin Park, IL: Midway Manufacturing Company, 1980), 35–37.

28. DP, *Game Boy CPU Manual*, 22, accessed June 15, 2014, http://marc.rawer.de/Gameboy/Docs/GBCPUman.pdf.

29. Okada and Kojo, Compact hand-held video game system.

30. Satoru Okada and Hirokazu Tanaka, Electronic gaming device with pseudo-stereophonic sound generating capabilities, US Patent 5095798 A, filed January 8, 1990, and issued March 17, 1992.

31. Jay Smith III, Gerald S. Karr, and Lawrence T. Jones, Hand-held electronic game playing device with replaceable cartridges, US Patent 4359222 A, filed October 30, 1978, and issued November 16, 1982.

32. Gunpei Yokoi, Rotary puzzle device, US Patent 4376537 A, filed December 30, 1980, and issued March 15, 1983.

33. Smith, Karr, and Jones, Hand-held electronic.

34. Gunpei Yokoi and Satoru Okada, Timepiece apparatus having a game function, US Patent 4424967 A, filed February 3, 1984, and issued April 15, 1986.

35. From Gunpei Yokoi and Satoru Okada, Electronic toy having a game function, US Patent 4582322 A, filed December 12, 1983, and issued January 10, 1984.

36. Katsuya Nakagawa, System for determining authenticity of an external memory used in an information processing apparatus, US Patent 4799635 A, filed December 23, 1985, and issued January 24, 1989.

37. Douglas C. McGill, "A Nintendo Labyrinth Filled with Lawyers, Not Dragons," *New York Times*, March 9, 1989.

38. Okada and Tanaka, Electronic gaming device.

39. See Jesper Juul, *A Casual Revolution* (Cambridge, MA: MIT Press, 2010).

40. Douglas C. McGill, "Now, Video Game Players Can Take Show on the Road," *New York Times*, June 5, 1989.

41. Juul, *A Casual Revolution*, 10.

CONCLUSION

1. Barrett, *Beyond the Brain*, 176.

2. From the Silver Jews song "The Ballad of Reverend War Character," written by David Berman, on the album *The Natural Bridge* (Chicago: Drag City, 1996).

3. Heidegger, *Being and Time*, 112.

4. Gillian Beer, *Darwin's Plots* (London: Routledge & Kegan Paul, 1983), 1.

5. Hofstadter, *Strange Loop*, 258.

6. Bazin, *What is Cinema?*, 14.

7. Umberto Eco, *The Infinity of Lists*, trans. Alastair McEwen (New York: Rizzoli, 2009), 67.

8. Johnson, *Meaning of the Body*, 33.

BIBLIOGRAPHY

Altice, Nathan. *I Am Error: The Nintendo Family Computer/Entertainment System Platform.* Cambridge, MA: MIT Press, 2015.

Anderson, Joseph D. *The Reality of Illusion.* Carbondale: Southern Illinois University Press, 1996.

Anwar, Yasmin. "Scientists Use Brain Imaging to Reveal the Movies in Our Mind." *UC Berkeley News Center,* September 22, 2011. Accessed December 14, 2015. http://newscenter.berkeley.edu/2011/09/22/brain-movies.

Aristotle. *De Anima.* Translated by R. D. Hicks. New York: Cosimo, 2008.

Aristotle. *Prior Analytics.* Book II. Translated by Gisela Striker. Oxford: Oxford University Press, 2009.

Arnheim, Rudolf. *Film as Art.* Berkeley: University of California Press, 1967.

Artaud, Antonin. *Selected Writings.* Edited by Susan Sontag. Berkeley: University of California Press, 1988.

Baccherini, Davide, and Donatella Merlini. "Combinatorial Analysis of Tetris-Like Games." *Discrete Mathematics* 308 (2008): 4165–4176.

Baer, Ralph H. "Video Game History: Setting Things Straight." In *Before the Crash: Early Videogame History,* edited by Mark J. P. Wolf, 225–233. Detroit: Wayne State University Press, 2012.

Barad, Karen. *Meeting the Universe Halfway.* Durham: Duke University Press, 2007.

Barker, Jennifer. *The Tactile Eye: Touch and the Cinematic Experience.* Berkeley: University of California Press, 2009.

Barrett, Louise. *Beyond the Brain.* Princeton: Princeton University Press, 2011.

Barthes, Roland. *Camera Lucida.* Translated by Richard Howard. New York: Hill and Wang, 1980.

Bateson, Gregory. *Mind and Nature: A Necessary Unity.* Cresskill, NJ: Hampton Press, 2002.

Bateson, Gregory. *Steps toward an Ecology of Mind.* Chicago: University of Chicago Press, 2000.

Baudry, Jean-Louis. "The Apparatus: Metapsychological Approaches to the Impression of Reality in Cinema." *Camera Obscura* 1, no. 11 (1976): 104–126.

Bazin, André. "The Ontology of the Photographic Image." In *What is Cinema?,* vol. 1, translated and edited by Hugh Gray, 9–16. Berkeley: University of California Press, 1968.

Beckman, Karen. *Crash: Cinema and the Politics of Speed and Stasis.* Durham: Duke University Press, 2010.

Beer, Gillian. *Darwin's Plots.* London: Routledge & Kegan Paul, 1983.

Benson-Allott, Caetlin. "The Algorithmic Spectator." *Film Quarterly* 64, no. 3 (2011): 55–58.

Benson-Allott, Caetlin. *Killer Tapes and Shattered Screens.* Berkeley: University of California Press, 2013.

Benson-Allott, Caetlin. "Platform." In *Debugging Game History: A Critical Lexicon,* edited by Henry Lowood and Raiford Guins, 343–349. Cambridge, MA: MIT Press, 2016.

Berger, John. *Keeping a Rendezvous*. New York: Vintage, 1992.

Berger, John. *Ways of Seeing*. New York: Penguin, 1990.

Bergson, Henri. *Creative Evolution*. Translated by Arthur Mitchell. Mineola: Dover, 1998.

Berman, David. "The Ballad of Reverend War Character." On the album *The Natural Bridge*. Drag City, 1996.

Bolter, Jay. *Turing's Man: Western Culture in the Computer Age*. Chapel Hill: University of North Carolina Press, 1984.

Bogost, Ian. *Alien Phenomenology*. Minneapolis: University of Minnesota Press, 2012.

Bogost, Ian. *Play Anything*. New York: Basic Books, 2016.

Bogost, Ian, and Nick Montfort. *Racing the Beam*. Cambridge, MA: MIT Press, 2009.

Bordwell, David. "A Case for Cognitivism." *Iris* 9 (Spring 1989): 11–40.

Bordwell, David. *Narration in the Fiction Film*. Madison: University of Wisconsin Press, 2015.

Branigan, Edward. "Sound, Epistemology, Film." In *Film Theory and Philosophy*, edited by Richard Allen and Murray Smith, 95–125. Oxford: Clarendon Press, 1997.

Bratkowski, Tad. "Applying Dewey's Aesthetics to Video Games: An Experience of 'Rock Band.'" *Soundings: An Interdisciplinary Journal* 93, nos. 1–2 (2010): 83–93.

Bresson, Robert. *Notes on the Cinematographer*. Translated by Jonathan Griffin. Copenhagen: Green Integer Books, 1997.

Breton, André. *Manifestoes of Surrealism*. Ann Arbor: University of Michigan Press, 1969.

Brinkema, Eugenie. *The Forms of the Affects*. Durham: Duke University Press, 2014.

Brown, Simon. *Cecil Hepworth and the Rise of the British Film Industry, 1899–1911*. Exeter: University of Exeter Press, 2016.

Burch, Noël. *Theory of Film Practice*. Translated by Helen R. Lane. Princeton: Princeton University Press, 1981.

Burge, Johannes, Charles C. Fowkes, and Martin S. Banks. "Natural-Scene Statistics Predict How the Figure-Ground Cue of Convexity Affects Human Depth Perception." *Journal of Neuroscience* 30, no. 21 (May 26, 2010): 7269–7280.

Cahill, James Leo. "How it Feels to Be Run Over: Early Film Accidents." *Discourse* 30, no.2 (Fall 2008): 289–316.

Caldwell, John. *Televisuality: Style, Crisis and Authority in American Television*. New Brunswick, NJ: Rutgers University Press, 1995.

Calleja, Gordon. *In-Game: From Immersion to Incorporation*. Cambridge, MA: MIT Press, 2011.

Carney, Ray. *The Films of John Cassavetes: Pragmatism, Modernism, and the Movies*. Cambridge: Cambridge University Press, 1994.

Carroll, Sean. *The Big Picture*. New York: Dutton, 2016.

Cavell, Stanley. *The World Viewed*. Cambridge, MA: Harvard University Press, 1979.

Chalmers, David J. "Strong and Weak Emergence." In *The Re-emergence of Emergence*, edited by Philip Clayton and Paul Davies, 244–254. Oxford: Oxford University Press, 2006.

Chemero, Anthony. *Radical Embodied Cognitive Science*. Cambridge, MA: MIT Press, 2011.

Churchland, Paul. *Plato's Camera*. Cambridge, MA: MIT Press, 2012.

Clark, Andy. *Being There: Putting Brain, Body, and World Together Again*. Cambridge, MA: MIT Press, 1998.

Clark, Andy. *Natural Born Cyborgs*. Oxford: Oxford University Press, 2003.

Clark, Andy. *Supersizing the Mind: Embodiment, Action, and Cognitive Extension*. Oxford: Oxford University Press, 2008.

Clark, Andy. *Surfing Uncertainty*. Oxford: Oxford University Press, 2015.

Clark, Andy, and David J. Chalmers. "The Extended Mind." *Analysis* 58, no. 1 (1998): 7–19.

Classic Tetris World Championship rules. Accessed July 10, 2017. http://thectwc.com/rules.

Comolli, Jean-Louis. "Machines of the Visible." In *The Cinematic Apparatus*, edited by Stephen Heath and Teresa de Lauretis, 121–142. New York: St. Martin's Press, 1980.

Crawford, Matthew B. *The World beyond Your Head.* New York: Farrar, Straus and Giroux, 2015.

Csikszentmihalyi, Mihaly. *Flow: The Psychology of Optimal Experience.* New York: Harper & Row, 1990.

Darwin, Charles. *The Descent of Man, and Selection in Relation to Sex.* New York: D. Appleton Press, 1972.

Deacon, Terrence W. *Incomplete Nature: How Mind Emerged from Matter.* New York: Norton, 2011.

Deen, Phillip D. "Interactivity, Inhabitation and Pragmatist Aesthetics." *Game Studies* 11, no. 2 (May 2011).

Deleuze, Gilles. *The Fold: Leibniz and the Baroque.* Translated by Robert Hurley. Minneapolis: University of Minnesota Press, 1993.

Deleuze, Gilles. "Having an Idea in Cinema (on the Cinema of Straub-Huillet)." Translated by Eleanor Kaufman. In *Deleuze & Guattari: New Mappings in Politics, Philosophy, and Culture,* edited by Eleanor Kaufman and Kevin Jon Heller, 14–19. Minneapolis: University of Minnesota Press, 1998.

Dennett, Daniel C. *Consciousness Explained.* Boston: Back Bay Books, 1991.

Dennett, Daniel C. *From Bacteria to Bach and Back: The Evolution of Minds.* New York: Norton, 2017.

Descartes, Réné. *Discourse on the Method and the Meditations.* Translated by John Veitch. New York: Cosimo, 2008.

Dewey, John. *Art as Experience.* New York: Perigee Books, 2005.

Dewey, John. "Body and Mind." *Bulletin of the New York Academy of Medicine* 4, no. 1 (1928): 3–19.

Dewey, John. "The Changing Intellectual Climate." In *The Later Works of John Dewey,* edited by Jo Ann Boydson, vol. 2, *1925–1927, Essays, The Public and Its Problems,* 221–225. Carbondale: Southern Illinois University Press, 2008.

Dewey, John. *Democracy and Education.* New York: Macmillan, 1916.

Dewey, John. *The Later Works of John Dewey, 1925–1953.* Edited by Jo Ann Boydson. Vol. 1, *1925: Experience and Nature.* Carbondale: Southern Illinois University Press, 1981.

Dewey, John. "The Metaphysical Assumptions of Materialism." *Journal of Speculative Philosophy* 16, no. 2 (1882): 208–213.

Dewey, John. "On Philosophical Synthesis." *Philosophy East and West* 1, no. 1 (1951): 3–5.

Dewey, John. "An Organic Universe: The Philosophy of Alfred N. Whitehead." In *The Later Works of John Dewey, 1925–1953,* edited by Jo Ann Boydson, vol. 5, *1929–1930, Essays, The Sources of a Science Education, Individualism, Old and New, and Construction and Criticism,* 375–381. Carbondale: Southern Illinois University Press, 2008.

Dewey, John, and Arthur F. Bentley. *Knowing and the Known.* Boston: Beacon Hill Press, 1949.

Dickinson, Emily. *The Poems of Emily Dickinson: Reading Edition.* Edited by Ralph W. Franklin. Cambridge, MA: Belknap Press of Harvard University Press, 1999.

DP. *Game Boy CPU Manual,* 22. Accessed June 15, 2014. http://marc.rawer.de/Gameboy/Docs/GBCPUman.pdf.

"Drops Dead at His Class." *Boston Sunday Post,* December 17, 1916.

Drucker, Johanna. *Graphesis: Visual Forms of Knowledge Production.* Cambridge, MA: Harvard University Press, 2014.

Drucker, Johanna. "Performative Materiality and Theoretical Approaches to the Interface." *DHQ: Digital Humanities Quarterly* 7, no. 1 (2013). Accessed September 17, 2015. http://www.digitalhumanities.org/dhq/vol/7/1/000143/000143.html.

Dulac, Germaine. "The Aesthetics. The Obstacles. Integral *Cinégraphie.*" Translated by Stuart Liebman. *Framework* 19 (1982): 6–9.

Dulac, Germaine. "The Essence of Cinema." In *The Avant-Garde Film,* edited by P. Adams Sitney, 36–42. New York: New York University Press, 1978.

Dumit, Joseph. *Picturing Personhood: Brain Scans and Biomedical Identity*. Princeton: Princeton University Press, 2004.

Eco, Umberto. *The Infinity of Lists*. Translated by Alastair McEwen. New York: Rizzoli, 2009.

Edwards, Paul N. *The Closed World*. Cambridge, MA: MIT Press, 1997.

Epstein, Jean. *The Intelligence of a Machine*. Translated by Christophe Wall-Romana. Minneapolis: University of Minnesota Press, 2014.

Fayzullin, Marat Pascal Febler, Paul Robson, and Martin Korth. "Everything You Always Wanted to Know about Gameboy." Accessed July 22, 2016. http://www.devrs.com/gb/files/gbspec.txt.

Fisher, Mark. "What Is Hauntology?" *Film Quarterly* 66, no. 1 (2012): 16–24.

Fodor, Jerry. *The Elm and the Expert: Mentalese and Its Semantics*. Cambridge, MA: MIT Press, 1995.

Gallant Lab. "Reconstructing Visual Experiences from Brain Activity Evoked by Natural Movies." Press release. Accessed December 14, 2015. http://sites.google.com/site/gallantlabucb/publications/nishimoto-et-al-2011.

Galloway, Alexander R. *The Interface Effect*. Cambridge: Polity, 2012.

Gazzaniga, Michael S. *Who's in Charge? Free Will and the Science of the Brain*. New York: HarperCollins, 2011.

Gee, James Paul. "Video Games and Embodiment." *Games and Culture* 3, nos. 3–4 (2008): 253–263.

Gibson, James J. *The Ecological Approach to Visual Perception*. Boston: Houghton Mifflin, 1979.

Gibson, James J. "Visually Controlled Locomotion and Visual Orientation in Animals." *British Journal of Psychology* 100 (2009): 259–271.

Gillespie, Tarleton. "The Politics of 'Platforms.'" *New Media and Society* 12, no. 3 (2010): 347–364.

Gregory, Richard L. *Seeing through Illusions*. Oxford: Oxford University Press, 2009.

Grodal, Torben. *Embodied Visions: Evolution, Emotion, Culture, and Film*. Oxford: Oxford University Press, 2009.

Gunning, Tom. "The Cinema of Attraction[s]: Early Film, Its Spectator, and the Avant-Garde." In *The Cinema of Attractions Reloaded*, edited by Wanda Strauven, 381–388. Amsterdam: Amsterdam University Press, 2007.

Gunning, Tom. "'Primitive' Cinema: A Frame-Up? Or the Trick's on Us." *Cinema Journal* 28, no. 2 (1989): 3–12.

Hägglund, Martin. *Radical Atheism: Derrida and the Time of Life*. Palo Alto: Stanford University Press, 2002.

Hansen, Mark B. N. *Feed-Forward*. Chicago: University of Chicago Press, 2015.

Hansen, Mark B. N. *New Philosophy for New Media*. Cambridge, MA: MIT Press, 2004.

Hayles, N. Katherine. *How We Think: Digital Media and Contemporary Technogenesis*. Chicago: University of Chicago Press, 2012.

Heidegger, Martin. *Being and Time*. Translated by Joan Stambaugh. Albany: State University of New York Press, 2010.

Hobbes, Thomas. *Elements of Philosophy of the First Section, concerning Body*. London: R.&W. Leybourn, 1656.

Hofstadter, Douglas. *I Am a Strange Loop*. New York: Basic Books, 2008.

Holmes, Emily A., et al. "Can Playing the Computer Game 'Tetris' Reduce the Build-Up of Flashbacks for Trauma? A Proposal from Cognitive Science." *PLoS One* 4, no. 1 (January 2009). Accessed June 15, 2017. https://doi.org/10.1371/journal.pone.0004153.

Hookway, Branden. *Interface*. Cambridge, MA: MIT Press, 2014.

Hutto, Daniel D., and Patrick McGivern. "How Embodied is Cognition?" *Philosopher's Magazine* 68 (2015): 77–83.

Hutto, Daniel D., and Erik Myin. *Radicalizing Enactivism*. Cambridge, MA: MIT Press, 2013.

Jablonka, Eva, and Marion J. Lamb. *Evolution in Four Dimensions: Genetic, Epigenetic, Behavioral, and Symbolic Variation in the History of Life.* Cambridge, MA: MIT Press, 2006.

James, Ella L., et al. "Computer Game Play Reduces Intrusive Memories of Experimental Trauma via Reconsolidation-Update Mechanisms." *Psychological Science* 26, no. 8 (2015): 1201–1215.

Johnson, Mark. *The Body in the Mind.* Chicago: University of Chicago Press, 1987.

Johnson, Mark. *The Meaning of the Body: Aesthetics of Human Understanding.* Chicago: University of Chicago Press, 2007.

Jolas, Eugene. *Cinema: Poems.* New York: Adelphi Company, 1926.

Jones, Steven E., and George K. Thiruvathukal. *Codename Revolution: The Nintendo Wii Platform.* Cambridge, MA: MIT Press, 2012.

Juul, Jesper. *The Art of Failure: An Essay on the Pain of Playing Video Games.* Cambridge, MA: MIT Press, 2013.

Juul, Jesper. *A Casual Revolution.* Cambridge, MA: MIT Press, 2010.

Juul, Jesper. *Half-Real.* Cambridge, MA: MIT Press, 2005.

Kant, Immanuel. *Kant's Kritik of Judgement.* Translated by J. H. Bernard. London: Macmillan, 1892.

Kirsh, David, and Paul Maglio, "On Distinguishing Epistemic from Pragmatic Action." *Cognitive Science* 18 (1994): 513–549.

Kittler, Friedrich. *Gramophone, Film, Typewriter.* Palo Alto: Stanford University Press, 1999.

Klevjer, Rune. "Enter the Avatar: The Phenomenology of Prosthetic Telepresence in Computer Games." In *The Philosophy of Computer Games,* edited by John Richard Sageng, Hallvard J. Fossheim, and Tarsei Mandt Larsen, 17–38. London: Springer, 2012.

Krauss, Ruth. *A Hole Is to Dig.* Pictures by Maurice Sendak. New York: HarperCollins, 1989.

Lakoff, George, and Mark Johnson, *Metaphors We Live By.* Chicago: University of Chicago Press, 2003.

Lakoff, George, and Mark Johnson. *Philosophy in the Flesh.* New York: Basic Books, 1999.

Landes, David S. *The Unbound Prometheus.* Cambridge: Cambridge University Press, 1969.

Landy, Frank. "Hugo Münsterberg: Victim or Visionary?" *Journal of Applied Psychology* 77, no. 6 (1992): 787–802.

Langdale, Allan. "S(t)imulation of Mind." In *Hugo Münsterberg on Film,* edited by Allan Langdale, 1–41. New York: Routledge, 2002.

Langer, Susanne. *Mind: An Essay on Human Feeling.* 3 vols. Baltimore: Johns Hopkins University Press, 1967–1982.

Laughlin, R. B., et al. "The Middle Way." *Proceedings of the National Academy of Sciences* 97, no. 1 (January 4, 2000): 32–37.

Maglio, Paul P., Michael J. Wenger, and Angelina M. Copeland. "Evidence for the Role of Self-Priming in Epistemic Action: Expertise and the Effective Use of Memory." *Acta Psychologica* 127 (2008): 72–88.

Malafouris, Lambros. *How Things Shape the Mind.* Cambridge, MA: MIT Press, 2013.

Manovich, Lev. *Software Takes Command.* New York: Bloomsbury, 2013.

Marks, Laura U. *The Skin of the Film: Intercultural Cinema, Embodiment, and the Senses.* Durham: Duke University Press, 2000.

Marks, Laura U. *Touch: Sensuous Theory and Multisensory Media.* Minneapolis: University of Minnesota Press, 2002.

Marvin, Carolyn. *When Old Technologies Were New.* Oxford: Oxford University Press, 1988.

McGill, Douglas C. "A Nintendo Labyrinth Filled with Lawyers, Not Dragons." *New York Times,* March 9, 1989.

McGill, Douglas C. "Now, Video Game Players Can Take Show on the Road." *New York Times,* June 5, 1989.

McLuhan, Marshall. *Understanding Media: The Extensions of Man*. Cambridge, MA: MIT Press, 1994.

Menand, Louis. *The Metaphysical Club: A Story of Ideas in America*. New York: Farrar, Straus and Giroux, 2001.

Merabet, Lotfi B., and Alvaro Pascual-Leonoe. "Neural Reorganization Following Sensory Loss: The Opportunity of Change." *Nature Reviews Neuroscience* 11 (January 2010): 45.

Merleau-Ponty, Maurice. *Phenomenology of Perception*. Translated by Colin Smith. London: Routledge Classics, 2003.

Merleau-Ponty, Maurice. *Sense and Non-sense*. Translated by Hubert L. Dreyfus and Patricia Allen Dreyfus. Chicago: Northwestern University Press, 1964.

Metz, Christian. "The Fiction Film and Its Spectator: A Metapsychological Study." Translated by Alfred Guzzetti. *New Literary History* 8, no. 1 (1976): 75–105.

Metz, Christian. *Film Language: A Semiotics of the Cinema*. Translated by Michael Taylor. Oxford: Oxford University Press, 1974.

Metz, Christian. "The Imaginary Signifier [Excerpts]." In *Narrative, Apparatus, Ideology*, edited by Philip Rosen, 244–278. New York: Columbia University Press, 1986.

Midway's Pac-Man: Parts and Operating Manual. Franklin Park, IL: Midway Manufacturing Company, 1980.

Moisse, Katie. "UC Berkeley Scientists 'See' Movies in the Mind." *ABC News*, September 22, 2011. Accessed December 14, 2015. http://abcnews.go.com/Health/MindMoodNews/scientists-youtube-videos-mind/story?id=14573442#.T5G9ve3dOnA.

Münsterberg, Hugo. *Grundzüge der psychologie*. Leipzig: Verlag von Johann Ambrosius Barth, 1900.

Münsterberg, Hugo. "The Photoplay: A Psychological Study." In *Hugo Münsterberg on Film*, edited by Alan Langdale, 43–162. New York: Routledge, 2002.

Münsterberg, Hugo. "Why We Go to the Movies." In *Hugo Münsterberg on Film*, edited by Allan Langdale, 171–182. New York: Routledge, 2002.

Nintendo Co., Ltd. "Consolidated Sales Transition by Region." Accessed June 1, 2015. http://www.nintendo.co.jp.

Nishimoto, Shinji, An T. Vu, Thomas Naserlaris, Yuval Benjamani, Bin Yu, and Jack L. Gallant. "Reconstructing Visual Experiences from Brain Activity Evoked by Natural Movies." *Current Biology* 21, no. 19 (September 22, 2011): 1641–1646.

Noë, Alva. *Action in Perception*. Cambridge, MA: MIT Press, 2004.

Noë, Alva. *Out of Our Heads*. New York: Hill and Wang, 2009.

Noë, Alva. *Varieties of Presence*. Cambridge, MA: Harvard University Press, 2012.

Oeler, Karla. *A Grammar of Murder*. Chicago: University of Chicago Press, 2009.

Parisi, David. "A Counterrevolution in the Hands: The Console Controller as Ergonomic Branding Mechanism." *Journal of Games Criticism* 2, no. 1 (2015).

Parker, Geoffrey G., Marshall W. Van Alstyne, and Sangeet Paul Choudary. *The Age of the Platform*. New York: Norton, 2016.

Pascal, Blaise. *Thoughts*. Translated by W. F. Trotter. New York: P.F. Collier, 1910.

Penley, Constance. *The Future of an Illusion*. Minneapolis: University of Minnesota Press, 1989.

Perez, Gilberto. *The Material Ghost*. Baltimore: Johns Hopkins University Press, 1998.

Plantinga, Carl. *Moving Viewers*. Berkeley: University of California Press, 2009.

"Platform." In *The Barnhart Concise Dictionary of Etymology*, edited by Robert K. Barnhart. New York: H.W. Wilson, 1995: 575.

Plato. *Phaedo*. Translated by David Gallop. Oxford: Clarendon Press, 1988.

Plato. *Theaetetus*. Translated by John Henry McDowell. Oxford: Clarendon Press, 1996.

Polyani, Michael. *The Tacit Dimension*. Chicago: University of Chicago Press, 2009.

Price, Brian. *Neither God nor Master: Robert Bresson and Radical Politics*. Minneapolis: University of Minnesota Press, 2011.

"Retroinspection: Game & Watch." *Retro Gamer* 55 (2008): 44–51.

Richmond, Scott. *Cinema's Bodily Illusions: Flying, Floating, and Hallucinating*. Minneapolis: University of Minnesota Press, 2016.

Rockwell, W. Teed. *Neither Brain nor Ghost: A Nondualist Alternative to the Mind-Brain Identity Theory*. Cambridge, MA: MIT Press, 2005.

Rodowick, D.N. *Reading the Figural, or, Philosophy after the New Media*. Durham: Duke University Press, 2001.

Ryan, Jeff. *Super Mario*. London: Portfolio, 2012.

Salen, Katie, and Eric Zimmerman. *Rules of Play*. Cambridge, MA: MIT Press, 2004.

Saunders, George. *Lincoln in the Bardo*. New York: Random House, 2017.

Schrödinger, Erwin. *What Is Life? The Physical Aspect of the Living Cell*. Cambridge: Cambridge University Press, 1992.

Seng, Phillip. "Dewey and Movies: A Missed Opportunity?" Conference paper, Annual Meeting of the Society for the Advancement of American Philosophy, 2007. Accessed August 1, 2017. http://www.philosophy.uncc.edu/mleldrid/SAAP/USC/TP32.html.

Shaviro, Steven. *The Universe of Things: On Speculative Realism*. Minneapolis: University of Minnesota Press, 2014.

Sheets-Johnstone, Maxine. *The Primacy of Movement*. Philadelphia: John Benjamins, 2011.

Simon, Bart. "Wii Are Out of Control: Bodies, Game Screens, and the Production of Gestural Excess." *Loading* 3, no. 4 (2009): 12.

Skorka-Brown, Jessica, et al. "Playing Tetris Decreases Drug and Other World Cravings in Real-World Settings." *Addictive Behaviors* 51 (2015): 165–170.

Smil, Vaclav. *Creating the Twentieth Century*. Oxford: Oxford University Press, 2005.

Sobchack, Vivian. "The Active Eye" (Revisited): Toward a Phenomenology of Cinematic Movement." *Studia Phaenomenolgica* 16 (2016): 63–90.

Sobchack, Vivian. *The Address of the Eye: A Phenomenology of Film Experience*. Princeton: Princeton University Press, 1992.

Sobchack, Vivian. *Carnal Thoughts*. Berkeley: University of California Press, 2004.

Solnit, Rebecca. *River of Shadows*. New York: Penguin, 2004.

Sontag, Susan. *Against Interpretation*. New York: Picador, 1966.

Spivey, Michael. *The Continuity of Mind*. Oxford: Oxford University Press, 2006.

Steinberg, Marc. "A Genesis of the Platform Concept: i-mode and Platform Theory in Japan." *Asiascape: Digital Asia* 4 (2017): 184–208.

Stickgold, Robert, et al. "Replaying the Game: Hypnagogic Images in Normals and Amnesics." *Science* 290, no. 5490 (October 13, 2000): 350–353.

Sutter, John D., and Doug Gross. "Apple Unveils the 'Magical' iPad." *CNN.com*, January 28, 2010. Accessed June 6, 2017. http://www.cnn.com/2010/TECH/01/27/apple.tablet.

Thompson, Kristin. *Breaking the Glass Armor*. Princeton: Princeton University Press, 1988.

Vertov, Dziga. *Kino-Eye: The Writings of Dziga Vertov*, ed. Annette Michelson, trans. Kevin O'Brien. Berkeley: University of California Press, 1984.

Vitruvius. *The Ten Books on Architecture*. Translated by Morris Hickey Morgan. Cambridge, MA: Harvard University Press, 1914.

von Rezzori, Gregor. *An Ermine in Czernopol*. Translated by Phillip Boehm. New York: NYRB Classics, 2012.

Vygotsky, Lev. *Mind in Society*. Cambridge, MA: Harvard University Press, 1978.

Vygotsky, Lev. *The Psychology of Art*. Cambridge, MA: MIT Press, 1971.

Waddington, David I. "Dewey and Video Games: From Education through Occupations to Education through Simulations." *Educational Theory* 65, no. 1 (2015): 1–20.

Wade, Nicholas J., and Benjamin W. Tatler. *The Moving Tablet of the Eye*. Oxford: Oxford University Press, 2004.

White, Mimi. "Reconsidering Television Program Flows, or Whose Flow Is It Anyway?" *Electronic Journal of Communication / La Revue Electronique de Communication* 5, nos. 2–3 (July 1995). Accessed June 15, 2017. http://www.cios.org/EJCPUBLIC/005/2/00527.html.

Whitehead, Alfred North. *Adventures of Ideas*. Cambridge: Cambridge University Press, 1961.

Whitehead, Alfred North. *Process and Reality*. New York: Free Press, 1978.

Williams, Raymond. *Television: Technology and Cultural Form*. London: Routledge, 2003.

Yokoi, Gunpei, and Makino Takefumi. *Gunpei Yokoi Game House*. Tokyo: ASCII Media Works, 1997.

Yong, Ed. *I Contain Multitudes: The Microbes within Us and a Grander View of Life*. New York: HarperCollins, 2016.

INDEX

Hayles, N. Katherine, 11
Heidegger, Martin, 67, 158, 172–173
Hepworth, Cecil, 49, 50*f*, 56
high-definition multimedia interface
    (HDMI), 127
Hobbes, Thomas, 81–82
Hofstadter, Douglas, 111, 126, 135, 147, 173
A Hole Is to Dig (Krauss and Sendak),
    101, 101*f*
Hollywood filmmaking, 52
Home Pong (Atari), 164
Hookway, Branden, 124, 128, 129–130,
    131, 132, 133, 147
How It Feels to Be Run Over (film), 49–50,
    50*f*, 53–57, 69, 70, 84, 142
Hsiao-kang (character in *What Time Is
    It There?*), 103–106, 126, 143, 144,
    145, 146
humanities, necessity of, 14, 176
Hume, David, 33
Hutto, Daniel D., 78, 85

in, of Dewey, 23, 26, 146
incompleteness, of Game Boy, 168
incorporation, according to Calleja, 155
industrial continuity, 156
Inside Out (film), 23, 43–45, 47
Intel 8080 microprocessor, 161
The Intelligence of a Machine
    (Epstein), 8–9
interaction
    use of term, 13
    use of term according to Dewey and
        Bentley, 27, 79, 132
interactive media, 12, 70, 74, 79, 154
interchangeable read-only memory
    (ROM) cartridges, 156
interface effect, 125, 128
interfaces
    active interface, 124
    defined, 127
    division by, 126–128
    expanded interface, 125, 128–130,
        131, 147
    extending concept of media interface
        along transactional lines, 117

framing function of according to
    Hansen, 35
graphical user interface (GUI), 123,
    125, 127
high-definition multimedia interface
    (HDMI), 127
as level of analysis, 106, 109*f*
passive interface, 124, 124*f*, 126–127
role of, 95
use of term, 75, 123, 124
intra-action, 17, 125, 132, 146, 171
intraface
    contemporary intraface, 146–148
    defined, 125
    encounters at, 123–148
    Galloway's use of term, 17, 125
    grief as intolerable intraface, 134–135
    use of term, 125, 131, 132
    worldly intraface, 130–134
introjective vision, 39–40
iPad, 101
iPhone, 97
It Follows (film), 56–57

James, William, 7, 12, 74, 86, 90
Johnson, Mark, 24, 28, 30, 32, 37–38,
    52, 175
Jolas, Eugene, 80, 81, 84
Jones, Steven E., 116, 119, 155
Juul, Jesper, 62, 66, 67, 68, 166

Kang-sheng, Lee, 105
Kant, Immanuel, 73, 86
Katamari Damacy (video game),
    173–175, 174*f*
Keaton, Buster, 130
Kiarostami, Abbas, 68
Kirsh, David, 77, 78, 79, 140
Kittler, Friedrich, 127
Klevjer, Rune, 155
knowing
    and being, according to Bresson, 111
    as exploratory action rather than as
        absorptive containment, 39
    as form of practical, strategic, skill-based
        action, 78